Career Directions

**A Special Edition
of
Johnson & Wales University**

DONNA J. YENA

*Director of University Planning
Johnson & Wales University*

IRWIN

Homewood, IL 60430

Career Directions: *Special Edition*

Copyright © 1987 by P.A.R. Incorporated

Text and Cover Design by *Stephen Eichhorn Design, Cranston, RI*
Typesetting by *Northeast Typography Inc., Pawtucket, RI*
Book Manufacture by *Murray Printing Company, Westford, MA*
Cover Printing by *E.A. Johnson Company, East Providence, RI*

Carol A. Long, *Senior Editor*

ISBN 0-89702-054-5

2 3 4 5 6 D 6 5 4 3 2 1

Table of Contents
Career Directions: Special Edition

Table of Contents
Career Directions at Johnson & Wales University

Preface

The key to success is knowing how to manage your own career. *CAREER DIRECTIONS* is a course at work. It is a guide for managing your career throughout your lifetime.

An essential part of your career education is learning what to do with that education. *CAREER DIRECTIONS* gives you the "how-to's" for putting your education to work. You will identify your career goals, focus on your course-work, create strategies for obtaining jobs, and develop lifelong career planning skills that will enable you to make successful career moves as you progress through the many phases of your working life. The techniques presented in this text have proven to be 98% successful. The information is based on input from industry representatives nationwide.

Student development counselors can often provide you with direction and offer the resources needed for you to make satisfying career choices, but there are two things student development counselors cannot do for you: *decide what you want* or *go on an interview for you.* **You make it happen!**

As you chart your course to success, you will find the challenges of your career exciting and varied. The plans you create today will allow you to meet those challenges and enjoy the success they bring.

The World of Work in the 1990's

TOMORROW'S CAREERS

QUALIFICATIONS FOR TOMORROW'S CAREERS

Technical Skills	+	High Energy Level
		Positive Attitude
		Flexibility
		Bright
		Hard-Working
		Willing to Learn

"Although technical skills are important, they must be balanced with interpersonal skills." *Patricia Aburdene, co-author with John Naisbitt of Re-Inventing The Corporation*. Business leaders report that students with solid basic skills and positive attitudes are more likely to find and keep jobs than students with vocational skills alone.

New technology has allowed us to access information in greater volume than ever before. The Information Age is here. New technology has allowed us more leisure time increasing the amount of time we spend dining out, traveling and generally using various sources of entertainment. Our life styles are changing and the way we communicate with each other is changing. These and many more changes in the way we live are shaping the world in which we work and the skills with which we need to compete.

THE CHANGING WORKPLACE

Service Industries

Service-producing industries are projected to account for about nine out of ten new jobs through 1995. Employment in service industries is expected to increase 30% from 23.4 million to 31.2 million. The customer is at the center of all service industries.

DIFFERENT TYPES OF SERVICE INDUSTRIES

	Financial Services	*Legal Services*
Retail		*Travel*
Hospitality		*Food Service*
Insurance		*Drafting*
Education	**CUSTOMER**	*Consulting*
Electronics		*Marketing*
Recreation		*Health Care*
Sales	*Computer Services*	

The success of the service industries depends on good customer relations. Your ability to work well with people will be important throughout your entire career. "People skills are more of an asset than I realized at the time I graduated." *Darlene Angle, Class of '83. Tech Service Representative, National Starch & Chemical, Berkeley, Cal.*

Competition

Competition for jobs will remain high. Tomorrow's jobs will be many in number, but quality career opportunities will remain difficult to fill without strong qualifications and a knowledge of how to market them. Competitive skills, a clear goal, and a careful plan must be developed for achievement in your chosen field.

Your ability to market your skills will be important throughout your entire career. "In one typical year, the Bank of Boston conducted 1,200 interviews to hire 50 new recruits."

The Changing Workforce

A changing workforce will require an ability to interact with people at all age levels, with a variety of backgrounds different than yours. The number of adult students training for work in today's school is at a record high.

GROWN-UP BOOMERS

As the enrollment of students in the traditional 18-to-22-year-old age group attending college dwindles, the number of adults over age 25 enrolling in college on a full or part-time basis is on the rise. In fact, by the 1990's older students may be just as numerous as the "typical" college student.

The number of older students attending college has been creeping up for many years, from 2.5 million in 1972 to 4.7 million in 1985. By 1991, government officials estimate, there will be 5.8 million people over the age of 25 in full- or part-time college programs. This may be good news for colleges and schools that expanded programs during the 1960's and 1970's and now, as a result of changing demographics, face an acute shortage of traditional students. Some adults returning to school are men seeking training to enhance midlife career changes, but women comprise two-thirds of the college population over the age of 34. Unlike their younger counterparts, the majority of these older adults attending college go part time, often working full time or part time as well. Following are Department of Education figures showing the increase in the number of adults enrolled in college according to the population in each age group and the percentage increases.

Adults Enrolled in Post Secondary Colleges and Schools

Ages	1972	1985	% Rise
25-29	1,229,000	1,884,000	53
30-34	531,000	1,180,000	122
35 and over	783,000	1,661,000	112

Source: National Center for Education Statistics

The number of professional females continues to grow, requiring an understanding of how men and women's different perspectives can work better together on-the-job. Your ability to see others' points of view will be important throughout your entire career.

The "new management team" involves closer working relationships between management and support staff. There are no longer sharp differences in the importance of different jobs, but rather, recognition that each person performs a critical function for the organization. Such support positions as Data Entry Operators and Secretaries have grown in responsibility and taken on a new

The New Management Team

significance in the management of information and services within companies. Managers work more directly with support staff than ever before in setting and achieving company goals. Managers and support staff work together to create the "New Management Team."

THE NEW MANAGEMENT TEAM

Management   +   Support Staff
Accountants, Computer Specialists, Reservationists, Sales Representative, Distributors, Cooks, Night Auditors, Front Desk Clerks, Secretaries

With an increasing number of professionals seeking top-management jobs, there is a decline of qualified support personnel in organizations throughout the country. That's where many jobs will be. Businesses are recognizing the importance of support personnel that are committed to quality, customer service and teamwork. To be successful, it is no longer necessary to "climb to the top," but rather to become the best at whatever you do to keep the day to day operations of the business thriving. Your ability to work with a team will be important throughout your entire career.

Learning To Learn

Patricia Auburdene, co-author with John Naisbitt of *Re-Inventing The Corporation*, talks about "TLC". Auburdene says, "TLC is our shorthand for learning how to **think,** learning how to **learn,** and learning how to **create.** We think of these as the new basic skills of the Information Society."

Believe it or not, the one thing that may not remain constant is the need for the skills you are learning now. With further advances in technology and in the way we live, new equipment and procedures will require new skills periodically. You may need to retrain several times during your career.

As technical skills for new jobs change, your abilities to work well with people, to market your skills, to see others' points of view and to work with a team will always remain important as you progress throughout your career.

Your success will always depend on the right combination of technical skills and people skills. Both will remain important parts of your "package" of qualifications. Learning how to put together the best package you can is the art of managing your own career. **Get ready — The world of work is changing.**

Managing Your Career

LIFELONG CAREER PLANNING

Self-assessment is the first step to managing your career.

Successful careers are the result of the right combination of personal and professional goals. Knowing who you are will help you decide what you want to do. Self-assessment begins with a look at your *V I P S*.

> **V***alues*
> **I***nterests*
> **P***ersonality*
> **S***kills*

Our values affect most of the choices we make everyday. Values are not right or wrong. What is an acceptable choice for one person may be unacceptable for **you** becauses of your value system.

One way to clarify what values are most important to you is to ask yourself, "What are the top five priorities in my life?" The career you choose should be compatible with your top priorities. List your top five priorities in order of their importance to you:

Example	**Your Priorities**
1. *Family*	1. _____
2. *Financial Reward*	2. _____
3. *Position*	3. _____
4. *Personal Relationships*	4. _____
5. *Where You Live*	5. _____

The way you spend your free time tells much about your interests. Potential employers frequently ask candidates how they occupy their free time because the answer tells the employer a lot about the candidate's motivation and likes and dislikes that may be relevant to the job. For example, if you spend some of your free time as an officer in a club or organization, you may demonstrate leadership qualities. List five interests that you have that you pursue most frequently:

Example		**Your Interests**	
1. *Volunteer Work*		1. _____	
2. *Sports Activities*		2. _____	
3. *Reading*		3. _____	
4. *Membership in a Club*		4. _____	
5. *Taking Lessons to Learn a New Skill*		5. _____	

Your personality can be your biggest asset as you prepare for a career in the service industries. Your personality is the sum total of the way you act and react to everyday events.

You have your own unique personality. Certain types of personalities are better suited for certain careers, For example, if you are pursuing a career in retailing, you will need a high energy level and an outgoing personality. In contrast, if you are pursuing a career in Court Reporting, you may be quieter by nature and able to work at a set pace for a long period of time. Both careers offer excellent opportunities, but both careers require distinctively different personalities.

No matter what career you pursue, your ability to relate to other people is extremely important. Take the computer operator's job. Traditionally, you may think that this position only requires strong technical skills. But the computer operator's job cannot be performed successfully unless he or she can effectively speak to clients about their particular problems or needs. The computer operator should be skilled in communicating with clients so that the person requesting the service feels that their needs are being understood and properly addressed.

The degree to which you will interact with other people will vary with the type of job. Within every career field, jobs range from high people orientation to high task orientation, but in every job in every career field, you will need to relate to other people in order to do your job well.

MARKETING

High People Orientation	High Task Orientation
↓	↓
Sales Representative	Research Analyst

Developing an effective personality is critical to your success. List five positive personality traits that you have:

Example	**Positive Personality Traits I Possess**
1. *Dependable*	1. _____
2. *Teamworker*	2. _____
3. *Positive Attitude*	3. _____
4. *Hard-worker*	4. _____
5. *Sense of Humor*	5. _____

List five personality traits you wish to develop:

Example	**Personality Traits I Desire**
1. *Confidence*	1. _____
2. *Listening Skills*	2. _____
3. *Patience*	3. _____
4. *Leadership*	4. _____
5. *Ability to Take Criticism*	5. _____

You can develop your personality. If there are traits you would really like to strengthen, then start now. For example, the personality traits that are favored in the Hospitality Industry are:

- *Flexibility*
- *Enthusiasm*
- *Drive*
- *Positive Attitude*
- *Good Communication Skills*
- *High Energy Level*

Write a plan for developing each personality trait that you desire. Follow this example:

	Trait	**Plan**
Example	*Confidence*	*I will offer my opinions in class even when they are different from others'.*

1. _____   1. _____

_____

_____

2. _____   2. _____

_____

_____

3. _____   3. _____

_____

_____

4. _____   4. _____

_____

_____

5. _____   5. _____

_____

_____

Skills are something we can all develop. Skills can be either abstract or concrete. For example:

Concrete Skills   **Abstract Skills**
Typing 55 wpm   *Ability to plan*
Shorthand 120 speed   *Ability to organize*
Computer skills   *Ability to develop*

Write down all the skills that you have right now — concrete and abstract.

_____

_____

_____

_____

_____

Next, list the concrete and abstract skills from above that you would like to develop or ones you'd like to have.

_____

_____

_____

_____

_____

Write a plan for developing the concrete and abstract skills you'd like to improve or obtain.

	Skill	**Plan**
Example	*Shorthand*	*Practicing on my own; asking my employer if I can use shorthand more on the job.*

1. _____   1. _____

2. _____   2. _____

3. _____   3. _____

4. _____   4. _____

5. _____   5. _____

Successful self-assessment results in recognizing **both** your major strengths and weaknesses. With this awareness you can develop a plan for working on needed areas and express that plan to an employer during a job interview. Through this process you can honestly turn what may sound like a negative trait into a positive response.

For example: *An employer asks what your major strengths and weaknesses are.*

Your thoughts are: *"I am an excellent typist, but my shorthand is only 60 wpm."*

Your response should be: *"I am an excellent typist. I am working at bringing my shorthand speed up by practicing on my own (or by taking an extra class, or by asking my boss to let me use it more on the job I have now). I like shorthand and realize it is an important skill. I am confident that my speed will improve with practice."*

Your ability to express your weaknesses in a positive way to an employer can mean the difference between the job you really want versus the job that you may settle for. Being comfortable with your weaknesses as well as your strengths comes as a result of having a plan for improving them. With this plan, you gain control over the areas you need to improve, rather than letting those areas control you.

Awareness of your values, interests, personality, skills and knowledge of how to make your major strengths and weaknesses work for you is the goal of self-assessment. Choose a career that is compatible with your own individuality and you will be successful.

Goal Setting

You achieve success through the goals you set and achieve. Careers move in a positive direction because of effective goal setting. You have already begun personal goal setting by listing the skills, traits, and strengths and weaknesses that you want to develop. It is time to concentrate on your career goals. Before setting more goals, you should be aware of the basic characteristics of a goal.

A goal should be **conceivable...**
Can you picture the goal in your own mind?

A goal should be **believable...**
Do you really believe it can happen?

A goal should be **desirable...**
> *Do you really want it?*

A goal should be **achievable...**
> *Is your goal realistic?*

A goal should be **measurable...**
> *Can you set time frames for accomplishing your goals?*

Let's look at a number of areas in which you will set goals throughout your career. You will set goals involving:

- *Your Skills*
- *Your Salary*
- *Your Position*
- *Your Responsibilities*
- *The Quality of Your Work Performance*
- *Your Department*
- *The People You May Lead*
- *Furthering Your Education*

You will certainly set goals to obtain a series of jobs that will help you achieve your major career objective. When you review the next section of this book, "Career Paths," you will be able to come up with a major career goal or professional objective. Before you do that, let's see if you know your career goals. Read and **think** about the following questions.

1. Can you list the job (title) that is your first choice in your chosen field? .... second choice .... third choice?
2. Can you identify the top five companies you want to work for?
3. Can you list, in order of priority, your first three choices of geographic area in which you would like to live/work?
4. Can you list the skills that are important to the position you want?
5. Can you describe what you would be doing everyday, once you got the job you want?
6. Do you know what you want to be doing ten years from now?
7. Do you know how to get there?
8. Do you know the basic salary ranges for your chosen field and is it compatible with the lifestyle you plan?

At this point, you probably have an idea of the answers to these questions but how sure are you of any of these areas? In order to successfully manage your career, you need to be able to answer each one of these questions confidently. You will be able to do so after reviewing the information in the "Career Paths" section of this book.

Why are goals important? Goals provide you with the **motivation** to produce top performance on a daily basis, because goals provide you with **direction**. It is much easier to get excited about what you are doing if you see the end results.

Goals make you a better **decision-maker** because when you have a clear goal, opportunities either fit into the accomplishment of that goal or they do not. You may decide against what at first appears to be a fantastic opportunity because you realize it will not help you achieve your ultimate goal.

The art of successfully managing your career is to constantly set new goals. As you achieve what appeared to be a difficult goal, you gain confidence in your ability to set your sights higher. This process of constantly setting new goals is the way people move successfully through their careers.

Long-term goals give you a focus on the "big picture." If you know that you want to be Vice President of Marketing some day, that may be considered your long-term goal. Your short-term goals will be the steps you need to take to get that position. Based on your knowledge of what the requirements are for becoming a Vice President of Marketing, you can set short-term goals in personal areas as well as in professional areas to build your qualifications. Another way to look at short-term goals is as a positive, planned progression of experiences that leads to your ultimate, long-term goal.

Another important aspect about goals is that you do not have to keep setting goals that will move you "up" the career ladder. Your long-term goal to be a secretary may remain your goal for the entire span of your career. Your short-term goals would then be to update your skills regularly, learn more efficient procedures, expand your responsibilities and improve the quality of your performance. The point is that goal setting is not just for people who want to move "up" the career ladder, but rather, for everyone who seeks challenge, reward, and personal satisfaction from a job well done.

Job vs. Career

What does work mean to you? By definition, "work is labor — an expenditure of physical energy." By past experience, "work" to humans was something we did to earn money to support ourselves. "Work" has also been defined as a place. To hold a job and to work meant to be at a specific place for specific time periods on specific days because it was required. We therefore lived our lives with "work" as something we did for someone else in some other place. The work to be done each day was clear, easily measured and unchanging because the expectation was that the "job" itself would not change. The job, not the person holding it, was important.

The growth of the *Information Age* has changed this perspective dramatically. Personnel officers are becoming human resource managers as corporations focus on people as key contributors in a struggle for quality, excellence and innovation. As a result, the workplace has been identified as people centered. With 80% of the people at work today, working with their minds as opposed to manual skills, corporations have become extremely dependent on their human resources for competition and advancement. The difference between a successful company and one that looses its competitive edge relates directly to the quality of its people. **Corporations are only as successful as the people who work in them!**

Quality performance and true excellence occurs only when every individual in the process is committed to it. You will also find that because of these factors, you will determine your own job satisfaction to a large degree. To count only on an employer to ensure your job satisfaction will result in disappointment. In the *Information Age*, your personal, professional and material rewards will come from your ability to learn and excel at what you are doing. You are very much in control of what happens to you at work.

Different Perspectives

The phrase "job versus career" is used over and over again while people struggle to define the real differences. Rather than looking at the differences, consider how they really complement one another. "A career does not limit one's reach. Work tends to be more of an enjoyment because we're satisfying goals that we've set for ourselves. We have a master plan, a life plan, and our current employment is a phase in that." *Edith Jones, "Do You Know the Difference Between a Job and a Career?", The Black Collegian, Sept/Oct 1986.*

Since there may be many phases of your career, you may hold many jobs throughout your career. At some point, you will probably stop needing to change jobs and will continue in a key position for a long period of time. It may even be the final job you hold. But the growth you experience in that same job for an extended period of time is also a significant phase in your career.

The difference between a job and a career is not how many jobs you have but rather the meaning that your job(s) have for you. To remain in one job for 10 years can be just as successful a career direction as holding a number of jobs. The real determining factors concerning careers are:

1. Your attitude and commitment about what you do goes beyond the tasks you perform every day.
2. Your ability to determine what you want and plan on how to get it as opposed to taking what you can get.
3. Rewards include, but also go beyond, financial rewards.
4. Rewards are characterized by growth and change both in you and in the challenges they provide for you.

5. Rewards provide a certain degree of psychological and emotional satisfaction.

6. Rewards are the result of a planned sequence of related jobs.

Richard Bolles, in *What Color is Your Parachute* defines a job as "a flexible combination of tasks — which can be arranged in a number of different tantalizing ways." Bolles defines career as "a flexible combination of **skills** — which can be arranged and rearranged in a number of different tantalizing ways."

Obviously if you want to manage your career throughout your lifetime, you will want to pay attention to developing the flexible combination of **skills** that can be applied to a wide variety of situations. This will create job security for you and the confidence that you really are in control of your career.

A major difference between a job and a career is one's attitude. It is possible for two people to perform the same task, have the same title and similar educational backgrounds and have a very different outlook on their work.

If your job is only what you do to pay the bills, it can quickly become routine drudgery. You may develop the attitude that life begins at 5 o'clock or whatever time the job ends. You will probably be less willing to look beyond the tasks you need to perform and there may be less enthusiasm for performing them. In a job that is not part of a career direction, there may be no striving for the promotion or planning for the future.

If you see your job in the context of larger career goals, your motivation is different. You see it as a challenge, as an opportunity to gain new skills that will help you in the future. You see a next step. You have goals to achieve. You will probably see the job as part of a life-long learning process. In "Career Paths" you will see the many jobs that comprise the career you choose. You will notice that the jobs are all somewhat related; they just vary in degree of responsibility. You may stop at any point along the path and derive satisfaction or you may want to continue along the path to become a member of senior management. *Remember, a career is not determined by where you stop or how far you continue, but rather the attitude with which you perform the job you have at any point in time.*

Career Phases

As you follow along your particular "Career Path" you will notice changes in the nature of the jobs you may hold. Throughout any career, there are three phases that are characterized by different types of jobs.

In the **entry-level phase** of your career you will probably be more of a generalist, being trained in and exposed to a wide variety of company procedures. The purpose of the broad scope of entry level jobs is to acquaint you with a broad picture of your job and its fit in the company. This first phase may last anywhere from six months to several years.

The **second phase** of your career will be characterized by jobs that are more specialized. You can expect to spend many years in mid-management and/or specialist jobs. It is in the second phase of your career that you may make the most job changes as you move through a variety of specializations. In each "Career Path" you will notice that the widest variety of jobs exists in the second phase.

It is important to note that many successful careers revolve around staying in mid-management and specialist jobs. These jobs play a very significant role in the company because senior management relies so heavily on the expertise and specific knowledge of people in those jobs. A significantly rewarding career can result in maintaining jobs within this area due to the tremendous impact they have on the company and the challenge and variety they can offer the individuals.

The **third phase** of your career is management which moves you back to a more generalist position. If you choose to pursue your career into management at some point you will find yourself relying on the specialists because your focus will have to cover many broad areas on a day to day basis.

Thus there are many ways of looking at jobs and careers. The most important point to remember is that you manage your career by the jobs you choose and the attitude with which you perform them. **You** determine those jobs, what you want and take responsibility for getting there. "People are divided into three groups: those who make things happen; those who watch things happen; and those who wonder what happened." *John W. Newbern.*

Employer Expectations

Employers expect certain attributes in candidates who have had some level of professional training. Their fulfilled expectations result in successful employees.

In his book, *Does Your Resume Wear Blue Jeans?*, C. Edwards says that employers prefer candidates who exhibit:

An Ability to Communicate	Ability to Handle Stress
Intelligence	Goal Achievement
Self-Confidence	Competitiveness
Willingness to Accept Responsibility	Vocational Skills
	Direction
Initiative	Job Motivation
Leadership	Organization
Energy Level	Attention to Detail
Imagination	Analysis
Interpersonal Skills	Decision-Making
Self-Knowledge	Career Ambition
Ability to Handle Conflict	Persuasiveness

Do you spend as much time developing these attributes as you do your technical skills? When you review your "Career Path" section, you will see which of these are most important to the career you wish to pursue.

1. Employers expect students to have a positive attitude.
2. Employers expect students to know how their skills can benefit the company.
3. Employers expect students to know their career direction.
4. Employers expect students to tell them why they're interested in working for their particular company.
5. Employers expect students to be enthusiastic about their careers.
6. Employers expect students to have realistic expectations.

It is important to realize that very often an employer will accept a candidate with weaker skills or grades over another just because the candidate seems to be the "right type" for the job. Usually the "right type" is someone who is bright, energetic, willing to learn and willing to work hard.

If you really want to understand employer expectations, read the classified ads. Read the qualifications sought for a wide variety of careers in and out of your own chosen field. List all of the common attributes that appear in the ads. Do you see many similarities, much repetition? This is a good indication to you that regardless of differing technical skill requirements, there are certain qualities employers expect candidates to demonstrate. These qualities are important to the employer because they are, to a large measure, predictors of success.

What Employers Look For

Decent Grades "For many employers, a high grade point average, particularly in your major area of study, is the way to distinguish yourself as a candidate today."

"Recruiters who visit campuses with heavy interviewing schedules often use the grade point average criterion as a way of screening out less desirable job candidates."

"Good grades indicate that the applicant is motivated and goal oriented. The person who has earned high grades throughout college is particularly impressive."

Communication/Interpersonal Skills The ability to communicate effectively with others and get along with a variety of different types of personalities are two of the most desirable qualities in job candidates. Whether your job involves working in a library or a lab or brings you face to face with the public, your ability to express your thoughts will affect your success. Everyone who works has to communicate verbally and in writing on a daily basis. If you cannot make yourself understood, you will find it difficult to do your job, and others will find you difficult to work with. Your willingness to accept individual differences and work with people whom you may not otherwise choose to associate with is necessary to becoming a team player.

The way a job candidate interacts with an interviewer tells a lot about how strong their communication and interpersonal skills are. Failure to make eye contact when talking to a recruiter, for example, suggests insecurity or lack of self-confidence. Work at becoming an active rather than a passive listener so that you can follow-up someone else's conversation with a relevant statement or question. Finally, think before you speak.

Enthusiasm Your interest in a company and a particular job can be a deciding factor in your getting hired. It's not enough just to have the right qualifications; an employer needs to know that you are willing to give 100% to your job. One of the best ways to communicate enthusiasm is to learn as much about a company before the interview. "I'm amazed by the number of applicants who walk into interviews knowing very little about what the companies do," *says Donald Dinsel, Manager of Special Staffing at E.I. du Pont de Nemours & Co., Inc.*

You can also communicate enthusiasm by your attitude and behavior during the interview. Listening to what the interviewer is saying and asking thoughtful follow-up questions is one way to do that. Maintaining eye contact and smiling at appropriate moments are good non-verbal signs of interest. "I am very impressed with your company and hope I have the opportunity to make a contribution to it." Avoid exaggerating your enthusiasm.

Flexibility In a rapidly changing high-tech world, employers need to know that the people they hire can expand and change as their companies do. "Applicants who are receptive to new ideas and concepts are highly valued by employers." "A company's growth and future development are dependent on employees who are able to see beyond the moment and who are willing to take risks."

Flexibility also involves a personal willingness to consider career goals different from the ones you had as a graduate. According to many recruiters, flexibility is an easy trait to spot. Job candidates who mention work or academic experiences in which they did assignments in an unconventional but successful way are thought to be adaptable. So are people who have put themselves in unfamiliar situations and learned new procedures and ways of working. People who are flexible also have a wide range of interests; they are open to new people, situations and ideas.

Leadership Even when they interview job candidates for entry-level positions, most employers look for evidence of leadership qualities. That is because successful companies need self-starters who are not afraid to take responsibility for doing the best job possible. "Graduates who know to take initiative stand out from the crowd," *says Robert Hopkins, Director of Placement Service at the University of Pittsburg.* "They're especially valued by innovative and high-tech companies who want to hire people they can put to work quickly with minimum training."

You may not be asked the direct question, "Do you have leadership qualities?", but you should be prepared to bring up instances where you were able to organize or lead a group of people to take responsibility in an emergency situation. If you have held a part-time or summer job, think back to those times when you had to take responsibility beyond what was expected. Don't hesitate to bring up those instances when you took over for your boss, made a decision on your employer's behalf or suggested a more efficient way of doing a certain office procedure. They all factor into an employer's judgment about your potential as an employee.

Problem Solving Ability It's a quality highly prized by employers because much of the success of their business depends on the resourcefulness of their employees. So naturally, interviewers try to evaluate whether you possess problem solving ability before they hire you.

High Energy Level An employer needs to know that you are willing to give 100% to your job. Employers want to know that you are committed to devoting the prime hours of your day to the job.

Maturity Maturity essentially means knowing how to handle yourself in a business situation. Employers do not want to hire recent graduates who do not know how to behave in front of clients, co-workers and bosses. Misplaced humorous remarks, giggling at inappropriate moments or being indiscreet about company information are telltale signs of immaturity.

To a large extent, interviewers will make an assessment as to how mature they believe you are by the way you conduct yourself during the job interview. Having the courage to address the person across from you in a normal fashion will make you seem more adult.

Depending on the field in which you are applying for a job and the style of the company itself, different combinations of the above qualities will be more or less important. In the final analysis, your ability to come up with examples of those traits that matter most to a particular interviewer is what counts. "The more specific you are in your examples, the better," says Dinsel. "Just citing an incident is not as effective as giving detailed information explaining what you did, how you did it and what its effect was." If you are prepared to talk about your personal qualities in this way, you can be sure that employers will listen and be impressed. *Bob Weinstein "What Employers Look for" Business Week. Careers Special Edition.*

Negative Factors which most often lead to Job Rejection

1. Poor scholastic record — low grades without reasonable explanation — low level of accomplishment.
2. Inadequate personality — poor attitude — lack of poise — lack of self-confidence — timid, hesitant approach — too introverted.
3. Lack of goals/objectives — poorly motivated — does not know interests — indecision — poor planning.
4. Lack of enthusiasm — lack of drive — not sufficiently aggressive — little evidence of initiative.
5. Lack of interest in our type of business — lack of interest in our company — not interested in the type of job we have to offer.
6. Inability to express him or herself — poor speech — inability to sell him or herself.
7. Unrealistic salary demands — more interested in salary than in opportunity — unrealistic expectations — over emphasis on management positions — unwilling to start at the bottom.

8. Poor personal appearance — lack of neatness — careless dress.
9. Lack of maturity — no evidence of leadership potential.
10. Lack of extracurricular activities — inadequate reasons for not participating in activities — no accomplishment in activities.
11. Failure to get information about our company — lack of preparation for the interview — did not read the literature.
12. Objects to travel — geographical preference — unwilling to relocate.
13. Excessive interest in security and benefits — "What can you do for me?"
14. Inadequate preparation for type of work — inappropriate background.

Source: *The Endicott Report, 1965: Copyright, Northwestern University*

The Sales Process

It has already been well established that knowing yourself and being able to communicate effectively is important to your success. Once you have your own sense of direction and have determined what you want, you need to know how to get it. To successfully compete in tomorrow's workplace you need to be **convincing**. Knowing yourself and your goals is the first step, but communicating them effectively to the people that count is the key to successfully managing your career.

The person with the hardest job of convincing is the salesperson. The sales process is really the process you will go through on a job interview. Before learning the many specific interviewing techniques that exist, you will want to consider the sales process as an approach to obtaining the jobs you want.

*The Universal Hiring Rule: Any employer will hire any applicant as long as he or she is **convinced** that the applicant will bring in more value than it costs to hire that person.*

In the employment process, think of the **employer as the customer** and **you as the product.** You have a certain set of skills and attributes to bring to the employer. The employer offers an opportunity for you to use those skills and attributes.

Why are some people with similar skills and attributes hired and others not if their qualifications meet those needed for the job? The difference lies in the candidates ability to sell themselves. There is a difference between marketing and sales. Both are important in the employment process. *Marketing* involves surveying the market, both employers and potential employers, and assessing their needs and wants.

Sales means convincing! Sales is the formal process of exchanging what you have for what someone else has. In the employment process your skills are exchanged for a job. Both you and the employer benefit if it is the right match. If it's not, it's not beneficial to either one of you. So beyond having effective sales ability, you need to be sure you want the job you are going after and that the employer really needs you. Identifying customer needs is one of the keys to effective salesmanship. Let's take a look at why people buy and compare it to why an employer might hire you.

Why People Buy	**Employer Interests**
1. *To satisfy a need*	1. *To fill a job opening*
2. *Cost effectiveness*	2. *Increase profitability*
3. *Comfort and convenience*	3. *Employees' professional preparation and ability to "fit in"*

It costs a company money to hire you. It costs the company money if you don't work out in the job. High company recruiting costs result in competitive candidate selection.

The Bank of Boston recently estimated that it costs $80,000 before new managers get through their training program. Ten thousand dollars is spent on recruiting, $50,000 is spent on training and $20,000 is spent on relocating and travel expenses. The costly hiring process makes companies highly selective. In one typical year, 1,800 students were interviewed and 50 hired. The Bank of Boston "cut down" to 1,200 interviews to hire 50 people. The average recruiting cost per new recruit is $1,600. Whether a company visits your school to interview you or runs ads in the newspaper, it costs money to hire someone new.

You stand a good chance of competing for a job if you have the skills to do the job, if you are sure that you want the job before taking it so that replacement costs won't sky-rocket for the company, and if you can reinforce the employer's feelings that you've been professionally trained.

Let's look at the first criteria — the skills to do the job. You need to be able to **convince** an employer that you have excellent skills for the job. *Remember,* the *Product Is You* and product knowledge is essential to a successful sale. To be convincing you need to feel comfortable bragging about yourself a little.

Many students are reluctant to talk about their strengths in front of each other. One of the most effective ways to rehearse presenting your skills is through the use of a **Jist Card*. The *Jist Card* is a 3″ × 5″ blank index card highlighting your skills. Following are two examples.

Freda Melton   Phone: (609) 274-1046
                                                                           691-5229

Position Desired: Clerical

Skills: Over three years experience in clerical field. Can answer
              phone, screen calls, take messages, greet public, and do
              filing. Can operate electronic typewriter, copier, calculator,
              and other general office machines.
              Love a challenge.

Prompt, Reliable, Adaptive.

Clara Newman   Phone: (414) 752-1861

Position Desired: General Office

Skills: 12 months experience in clerical field. Efficient full-charge
              bookkeeper. Knowledgeable of current office practices.
              Accurately type 55-60 wpm. Can file alphabetically and
              numerically. Can operate basic office equipment. Enjoy
              greeting customers.

MATURE   WELL-ORGANIZED   RESPONSIBLE   DEPENDABLE

The *Jist Card* is just a helpful reminder to you of your strengths which you should have in front of you when speaking to an employer over the phone or when filling out a job application. Learning to use the *Jist Card* requires telephone conversations with potential employers. You may use the card to confidently conduct an informational interview over the phone or apply directly for a position that you know is available. Using this method as a means of reaching employers by phone is one way of convincing the employer that you are a good candidate. Look at the *Jist Card* as a form of telemarketing and compare the advantages and disadvantages.

*From The Workbook by Michael Farr

Advantages

1. *Saves money*
2. *Saves time*
3. *More results in less time*

Disadvantages

1. *Can't see employers expressions, body language, etc.*
2. *Employers can't see you*

Rules for Using the Jist Card

1. Be enthusiastic — be up
2. Be prepared — know yourself — be organized
3. Establish a rapport (be genuine)
4. Ask questions — **listen** — learn employers needs
5. Sell **benefits**, not features
6. Accomplish something

Eighty percent of all learning is visual while only 11% is auditory. An employer must be able to **visualize** your value to his or her organization. It is essential that you **create a word picture** of your skills, abilities and past accomplishments and that you link these to the employer's needs.

Proof By Example
*Help the employer **visualize** what you can do for them. Here's how:*

*Excerpted from Career Development Seminars, Robert Morris College

1. Present three concrete examples of a skill you wish to present to a potential employer.
   one at a time   most extraordinary
2. Qualify examples by describing circumstances.
   who   what   when   where   why   how
3. Quantify examples with measurable data.
   numbers, percentages, frequency, volume, years, months, weeks, etc.
4. Specify results. . . . What happened?
   data   specific outcomes
5. Link and Think: How will each statement help the employer visualize:
   increased profits
   decreased turnover
   improved productivity
   improved worker morale
   less personal frustration
   solution to problems

Shocking Statistics

Why People Stay Unemployed

40% present poor personal appearance
42% frictional unemployment
80% cannot describe their own job skills
85% do not look hard enough
90% cannot answer problem questions

- Between 1980 and 1990, 15 million graduates with professional training will enter the labor force and two to three million will be unable to find jobs that fit their abilities and expectations, according to the Bureau of Labor Statistics.
- Only 20% of our population are happy with their jobs, the rest are underemployed.
- 20-30 million Americans suffer extended unemployment each year.
- Only 5% of all job seekers have had any job search training.
- In 1984, the unemployment rate among 20-24 year olds with 1 to 3 years of high school was 26.7%
- The rate for those with 4 years of high school was less than half that, 13%.
- The unemployment rates for those with 1-3 years of professional training or college and 4 or more years of college were only 7.8 and 4.9% respectively.
- The disadvantages that less educated workers suffer when seeking jobs is clearly shown.
- The connection between higher unemployment rates and low levels of education shows the importance of education in a job market that increasingly requires more formal training.
- At least 1 million new openings exist in the national job market each month!

The message is clear. Job opportunities are plentiful. Many people do not qualify for jobs because of inadequate education, lack of motivation, lack of direction and lack of effective job search skills.

There is a difference between getting a job and managing a career. Managing your career is a lifelong career planning process. Getting a job is an immediate satisfaction of the need to work. The effects of having no career strategy include unemployment, underemployment, aimless job hopping, and general unhappiness. Unhappiness leads to low morale, absenteeism, and boredom on the job.

When you develop a personal career strategy, you are future oriented. With a career strategy, you can master lifelong career planning skills and plan your personal development. *With direction, you put yourself in control!*

PERSONAL DEVELOPMENT

Personal development starts with your commitment to be better. Your **commitment** is the key ingredient to your own personal development because ultimately, you are the only one in control of it. After you've studied the major growth areas that affect your career, only you can make the decision **to do** something in each area. Personal development involves the inner you and the outer you. Both aspects of yourself relate to the world in which you live. How well you manage your own growth will be a factor to your success. Personal development, like managing your career, is an on-going process. Personal development involves establishing and maintaining good relationships. It is taking control of your time, social skills, communication skills, appearance and attitude to make them all work **for** you. You set certain goals for yourself in previous exercises. In addition to your technical skills, your personal development is critical to the achievement of those goals. Your personal development as it relates to your career involves:

- *Human Relation Skills*
- *Qualities of Success*
- *Communication Skills*
- *Time & Stress Management*
- *Grooming and Dress*
- *Business Etiquette*

Human Relations Skills

Begin with yourself. Do you basically like the person you are? If you do, it will show. If you are happy with the direction your life is taking, it will be easier to be positive with others. If you are confident about yourself, it will be easier to be positive with others. You have to like yourself before you can like other people. When you like who you are and what you do, you are enthusiastic and have a high energy level. People like to be around enthusiastic people. Think enough about yourself to care about how you look and feel and how others perceive you. Your own happiness is the first step to good human relations skills.

Your Relationship With Your Boss

Your relationship with your boss can enhance your personal development as well as your professional growth. You have the ability to create a positive and productive working relationship with your boss. The following should help you out:

- *Loyalty* sets the stage for trust. You can be loyal to your boss and to yourself even when you don't both agree by being upfront and discussing the issue honestly with him or her only.
- Don't talk negatively about your boss or the company you work for to other people.
- Don't waste your boss's time.
- Be aware of your boss's priorities.
- Help your boss get promoted. It may help you in the same way.
- Incorporate the boss's point of view in your decision-making. Try to see his or her point of view, and you may make better decisions.
- Take criticism from your boss as a learning experience. Criticism should not be interpreted as a threat. It should be seen as a desirable challenge.
- Admit your mistakes.
- Ask for feedback.
- Don't ever upstage your boss.
- Avoid bad news early or late in the day or week.
- No surprises — keep your boss informed.

Remember you are part of the management team regardless of what position you hold. Your relationship with your boss should be mutually beneficial. You should foster an environment of cooperation so that you help each other achieve personal and company goals. Being a team player with your boss makes both of your jobs more productive and meaningful.

Your Relationship With Your Associates

When you are at the top of your graduating class, you are used to being number one. You've earned the job you have now but something is different. You've been hired along with a lot of other "number one's" and suddenly, the skills and talents that once put you on top, now put you in competition. Yes, there are other people who are smarter, who can do it better, and who will challenge you. Learning to work with others and respect their opinions, talents, and contributions to your organization can be a difficult adjustment. Perhaps one of the hardest things you will face in your career is having to work with people you really don't like. Learn to separate your personal feelings and preferences about people and situations from professional life. The person you dislike the most might be an important link in your team. Tomorrow's jobs require the ability to get things done with other people. You will actually be measured on team efforts as well as your individual accomplishments. You will be treated the way you treat other people. The following should help you out:

- Be a teamplayer.
- Build working relationships with those at your level and in other departments.
- Realize the power of praise. Compliment people for a job well done.
- Say "Thank You."
- Listen to what other people have to say.
- Respect other people the way you want them to respect you.
- Be objective; if there is a problem ask yourself what's wrong, am I part of the problem, what can I do about it.
- Deal with pressure. Control your temper and emotions and remain level headed when the going gets rough. You may say or do something you'll be sorry about.
- Look at competition as an opportunity to do the best job you can. Above all, play fair as you compete to reach whatever goal you have set for yourself.
- Demonstrate common sense.
- Demonstrate a genuine interest in other people. Show that you are sensitive to their individual needs.
- Be courteous.
- Cooperate. Work is more difficult when the climate is tense. Cooperation builds spirit and is often more productive than individual effort.
- Be humble. If you are humble you will still receive the credit you deserve. Don't be caught up in always having to win, to have the best idea or to be number one. You have a long career ahead of you and if these are goals, you will be disappointed many times.

Your Role As A Leader

If you are in the position to lead a team, then your human relation skills will determine your success. People want to be led, not managed. You manage projects, things and your time. You lead people.

Leadership can be developed if you know its essential ingredients and have a real desire to lead. The strong desire is important because leadership requires much time, energy, commitment and skill and if you really don't want the responsibility you will give up easily. If you really don't want a leadership role, don't accept it. You won't do yourself justice, nor will it be fair to the people looking for the leadership. If you do think the leadership challenge is for you, here are some qualities of a good leader that you should master:

Leadership Qualities

- Vision
- Self-Starter
- Positive Attitude
- Intelligence
- Character
- Integrity
- Courage
- Risk-Taking
- Energy Level
- Enthusiasm
- Ability to Motivate Others
- Ability to Plan and Organize

Leaders create an atmosphere in which others can grow and enhance their abilities. Guidelines for effective leadership focus on putting the people in your responsibility area first.

1. Recognize the power of people in your area.
2. Empower commitment and loyalty by example.
3. Recognize individual accomplishments as well as team efforts.
4. Combine monetary rewards with other benefits such as free time, a new opportunity or additional authority.

Qualities Of Success

Successful people have their own definition of success. They don't get where they want with other people's dreams. They create their own. In fact, for many people today, success means carving out their own niche. Finding something that they have to do and doing it well. Personal fulfillment might be your overriding goal. Enjoyment may be another goal. Most successful people talk about having fun with what they do. As you attempt to define your own success, don't limit yourself to measure up to the corporate ladder, but rather broaden your idea to something you can really feel in your gut! When you feel the drive for something that strongly, you must want it badly enough to really go after it. Personalize success.

Goals

Successful people have goals. Each one of their small successes helps to build bigger successes in the future. Successful people make the most of their intelligence. They have and use common sense. They are willing to explore new avenues of information. Some of the most interesting are those individuals who read extensively, listen well and absorb all the facts they can from around them.

Positive Attitude

Successful people are positive. They have ways of dealing with disappointments and setbacks so that they don't become obstacles to their goal. By being positive, successful people attract people to themselves. Along with a positive attitude is the ability to trust yourself. Successful people believe in themselves and in other people and act on that belief. Successful people accept failure as part of the course. Failure only happens when you are not able to cash in on the experience you have had.

Enthusiasm

Successful attitudes are also built on enthusiasm. Enthusiasm comes from within and has a strong affect on other people. Enthusiasm gets and keeps people interested in what you are doing and saying. It attracts attention. People like to be around enthusiastic people. Companies want enthusiastic employees who are eager to make contributions to the company and do so in a positive way. Whether you are a secretary in a small company, a chef in a restaurant that you own and operate, or the vice president of a large corporation, the degree of enthusiasm you have for your work will make you stand out. A fantastic idea can be rejected for another idea that was delivered more enthusiastically. Enthusiasm lends credibility to what you do and results in your own satisfaction.

Motivation

Motivation is an incentive or inducement to act. Motivation is the result of having a goal. Motivation goes hand in hand with enthusiasm. If you are motivated to do something you can be enthusiastic about it. Motivation makes you productive. Motivation comes from within and is reinforced by others. Motivation allows you to work well independently. If you are motivated, you have a healthy interest in yourself. It has been said that the person who is motivated and possesses successful attitudes is unbeatable. Take the career path you are choosing to follow and ask yourself, "How motivated am I to make my career happen?" Think about the goals you have set for yourself, how motivated are you to achieve them? Successful careers and successful lives are based on motivation. Motivation goes hand in hand with a high energy level and a love for what you do.

When you feel enthusiastic, motivated and positive inside, it shows on the outside. Your appearance portrays your success attitude. What does **your** appearance demonstrate?

- Self-Confidence
- Direction
- Sensitivity
- Know How
- Professionalism
- Attitude
- Self-Respect
- Organization
- Individuality
- Motivation

None of these will come through unless they come from within. Successful people become that way largely because of these personal qualities and how they have applied them to opportunities in their lives. Success doesn't just happen, **you** create it. These qualities of success are not something someone else can give you unless you feel them yourself.

Pride in a job well done is success. The personal satisfaction is the key. It doesn't matter if your career choice is to be a data entry operator, an accountant, a food and beverage manager; it is not just the level of achievement that defines success. Success is an attitude. To be the best at what you do, to care about quality commitment and efficiency is to have a successful career, not just a routine job. By simply making a commitment to be the best that you can be you have made a commitment to be successful.

With these perspectives on success, it is time for you to really think about what it means to you. **Your** definition of success will affect the choices you make throughout your career. How then do **you** define success?

Success And You

The **YOU** in this question is the key to the answer. Success can be defined by:

1. *Status of Position* _____

2. *Respect of Associates* _____

3. *Financial Success/Status* _____

4. _____

5. _____

6. _____

The answer(s) depend on your values, your goals, your energy level and your personality, both personally and professionally.

Changing Perspectives On Success

Talk to any successful person and ask them what their definition of success was when they first started their careers. Some responses would include:

Bigger is better	*Control*
Financial reward	*Power*
Accumulation of significant wealth	*Status*
Maximizing personal potential	

Then ask if that definition of success has changed over the years. In almost all cases, the answer will be yes. When asked about their **definitions of success**, people very well established in their careers give varied responses:

Balance in life
Enjoyment of work
Making a meaningful contribution
Doing what you want to do to the best of your ability
Maximizing personal potential

Attitudes about success change throughout your lifetime. These changing attitudes will be an important factor to consider as you continue the process of managing your career throughout your lifetime. Changing values affect attitudes about success. Both your age and the society in which you live affect your values. In his book, *Taking Chances*, Dale Dauten highlights changing values with regard to the definition of success.

Past Symbols	**Present Symbols**	**Future Symbols**
Fame	*Unlisted phone numbers*	*Free time anytime*
Being in Who's Who	*Swiss bank accounts*	*Recognition as a creative person*
Five-figure salary	*Connections with celebrities*	*Oneness in work and play*
College training	*Deskless office*	*Rewarded less by money than*
Splendid house	*Second and third house*	*by honor and affectioon*
Executive position	*Owning a rare foreign car*	*Major societal commitments*
New car every year	*Being a vice president*	*Easy laughter,*
Membership in the club	*Being published*	*unembarrassed tears*
	Frequent and unpredictable	*Wide-ranging interests and*
	World travel	*activities*
		Philosophical independence
		Loving and in touch with self

As you progress through your career, changes in your personal life and in the world around you will have an impact on your goals. In the "Information Age", the emphasis on human resources will bring new approaches to reward systems in the workplace. The traditional meaning of the words reward, recognition and compensation will change to meet the new values of the worker in the 1990's. The values of tomorrow's workers, which include you, are changing the workforce as we've known it in the past. For these reasons, lifelong career planning will involve periodic review of your definition of success and your strategies for achieving it.

Communication Skills

- As much as 85% of your day may be spent in some form of communication — most of it speaking and listening to others, according to a survey of business people conducted at Arizona State University's College of Business Administration.
- The typical working American gives about a dozen "speeches" a year: oral presentations to staff, clients, community groups, labor unions and professional associations.
- You spend two to four times as much time talking on the telephone as you do using any other technology, including computers and word processors. If you are an executive, you spend about fourteen percent of your day on the phone.
- **Communication skills rate second only to job knowledge** as important factors in a business person's success, according to one study of five hundred executives.

*The First Four Minutes

It takes only two to four minutes to make a positive or negative first impression. You never get a second chance to make a good first impression. You succeed or fail by the impressions you create. First impressions are made of the things people notice about you during those crucial first minutes. The four key questions that define a successful communicator are:

1. What Do I **Look** Like?
2. What Do I **Sound** Like?
3. What Do I **Say**?
4. How Well Do I **Listen**?

Knowing what kind of communicator you are is critical to success for communication is what we people — especially business people — do most. During your first few minutes of interaction with others, their attention span is at its greatest and their power of retention at its highest: their eye and ear focus is on you and their brains receive what they see and hear.

I. **FIRST** people tend to focus on what they can **SEE**. The specific order by which others process information about you is:

1. *color of skin*
2. *gender*
3. *age*
4. *appearance*
5. *facial expression*
6. *eye contact*
7. *movement*
8. *personal space*
9. *touch*

What you look like constitutes more than half the total message. Fifty-five percent of your meaning is conveyed by facial expressions and body language alone.

II. People focus on what they can **HEAR**.

    1. *rate of speech*   **3.** *tone*
    2. *pitch*   **4.** *articulation*

Your voice, not including your actual words, may transmit as much as 38% of your meaning in face to face conversations.

III. What do I **LOOK** like?

Depending on the background and experience of the perceiver, significance may be given to a "part" of you that has little to do with your skills or expertise. Your handshake, for example, or how quickly you speak may be noticed rather than your qualifications or your verbal message.

IV. What do I **SOUND** like?

Your voice tells a lot about your personality, attitude and anxiety level. Supervisors' voices can affect employee performance. Knowing what you sound like can have a big payoff in formal situations, such as job interviews, press conferences, oral presentations, or questioning witnesses. You can learn to recognize signs of tension and stress in your own voice and in the voices of others, as well as use one of several vocal characteristics, such as rate or loudness to energize an audience, client or jury.

V. What do I **SAY**?

Verbal skills should support and balance the nonverbal and vocal messages already conveyed. **What** you say is reflected by **how** you say it. Balance between language and delivery is critical in making first impressions. In interpersonal communications, there must be an ongoing and perceived consistency between what you say and how you say it. Trust, and ultimately, success are built on such consistency.

VI. How well do I **LISTEN**?

Listening is the final component in making positive first impressions. It is the other half of the communication process. Consider the importance of the listening process; the higher you go in your profession, the more of your working day is spent listening to others. Listening is a skill that can be learned and practiced. It can make you a more powerful communicator.

First Impression, Best Impression, "The First Four Minutes" Janet G. Elsea, Simon & Schuster Inc., New York, N.Y., 1984.

Test Yourself — Are You A Good Listener?

1. Are you attentive?
2. Do you maintain eye contact?
3. Do you ever start speaking before another person has finished speaking?
4. Are you tuned in to the other person's facial expression, gestures, body language and tone of voice?

Action Plan

Whatever you decide needs to be done to make you **LOOK** or **SOUND** better, **DO IT NOW!**

Check off what you need to do:

_____ Exercise

_____ Lose weight

_____ Buy a new wardrobe

_____ Sit up straight

_____ Practice facial expressions in the mirror

_____ Smile

_____ Walk with more confidence

_____ Make more direct eye contact

_____ Hear yourself as others do

_____ Listen to your voice samples

_____ Practice out loud and listen to your progress

_____ Change your language (choice of words, organization and support of your ideas)

Strategies

1. *Do it yourself.*
2. *Hire an expert.*
3. *Work with a group.*

Feeling harried, hurried and unappreciated? You might be experiencing the effects of too much stress. Stress is a physical, psychological or performance-related reaction to internal or external events. Try a few of these techniques to ward off stress and increase your productivity:

Time & Stress Management

1. Build resistance by regular sleep, a moderate exercise plan, healthy eating habits, and by participating in outdoor work activities.
2. Try to find a 10-20 minute period for total body relaxation. Tense each set of muscles for a short period — then relax them. With practice anyone can induce a state of relaxation through muscle control.
3. Talk over problems with persons who are peers on the job. Social support reduces stress.
4. Set clear goals and work toward them at as even a pace as possible; deal with one item at a time.
5. Develop a benevolent sense of humor.
6. If morning is your high energy time, tackle jobs that cause you the most stress then.
7. Attack problems — not people *(including yourself)*.
8. Remember, it's not necessarily **what** happens to you, but how you **interpret** events.

From "Harness Your Stress," Carolyn Gold, Training Manager, The Sheraton Corporation.

R. Alec Mackenzie writes in *The Time Trap*, "Nothing is easier than being busy, and nothing more difficult than being effective." Do you know someone who is constantly busy, has a lot of different activities going on at once, and never seems to get anyone of them done?

Sometimes you are never really sure what that person has done, but they emanate an air of urgency and importance. You may view that person as an extremely competent person, but don't until you have had a chance to see exactly what was accomplished.

To be able to see a task through from start to finish is time management. To be able to see an **important** task through on time, and with **quality** results is **good** time management. The amount of time spent doing something tells nothing about the quality of the results or the person's ability.

Time management is defined informally as **becoming more efficient at doing things that are important.** In this case, "efficient" refers to quality and productivity, while "important" refers to what really needs to be done. Look over the following list of activities for the month of May:

May

At School	On The Job
1. *Term paper*	**1.** *Your performance review*
2. *Final exams*	**2.** *Proposal deadline*
3. *Counseling session*	**3.** *Monthly statements*
4. *Spring weekend*	**4.** *Train a temporary*
5. *Oral report*	**5.** *Attend a company function*

Either of these scenarios may be familiar to you. If both of them are, chances are you have already had a lot of experience with time management. Read each list carefully. Think about how you would accomplish these activities successfully. List a few of the decisions you need to make.

1. _____

2. _____

3. _____

4. _____

5. _____

If it was April 1st, what actions would you take knowing your schedule in May?

1. _____

2. _____

3. _____

4. _____

5. _____

Did these decisions come easy to you? For many people, there isn't even a decision process but rather a "do whatever comes next" approach. That approach may have even worked for you up to now, but what will happen when:

1. Another important project is given to you that **must** get done
2. You get sick the second week of May
3. Your car breaks down

Will you still meet your deadlines efficiently?

Here Are Some Ways To Develop Time Management Skills

1. First and most important, believe that you are in control!
2. Learn to say "No" graciously.
3. Delegate appropriately. Don't give the very important work to someone else, yet don't be afraid to ask for help.
4. Handle interruptions; don't let them handle you.
5. Prioritize.

    You prioritize by *evaluating and asking:*

    a. How critical the work is
    b. How long will it take from start to finish
    c. What you need to do to get it done
    d. Whom you need to deal with

    When you are asked to do something, very often the person asking may have no idea about your present involvement. If it's your boss asking you to do something, you will probably assume you should do it right away. But maybe it can wait. There is nothing wrong with explaining to your boss that you have several important things going on right now. Express to him or her your concern with his or her needs and simply ask, "How critical is this in relation to *(name another top priority you are already working on)?*" So many times in your eagerness to please, you may spend time working on something that can really wait awhile. You don't know unless you ask. You will also want to check with the people with whom you need to work to be sure they will be around when you need them. If the secretary in the office is scheduled for vacation, be sure you know what needs to be done before she leaves.

6. Set some *timetable* to measure how you are doing.
7. If the job seems overwhelming, break it down into more easily manageable steps. Don't avoid it. But remember that people who work 16 hours a day when there is enough work to warrant it, are not doing themselves a favor. Proper rest, nutrition and exercise are especially important during busy times.
8. Have alternatives for how you will spend your time if you have to put something aside for awhile to wait for someone or something.
9. Build in some free time. During very busy times, it is important to take care of your physical and mental health. The quality of your work is easily affected by burnout.
10. Have fun, don't take yourself seriously. Instead of becoming consumed with getting things done, enjoy each accomplishment along the way. Take time to pat yourself on the back for a job well done. Look at the challenge in whatever you are doing. When you do, you will feel the reward will bring you more satisfaction.

Grooming & Dress

Professional appearance is a statement of confidence. People will be more apt to listen to you if you look like you take your job seriously. Professional appearance starts with a combination of good grooming and proper dress. When you look professional, you feel better about yourself and your behavior on the job is affected positively. Professional appearance should be as individual as you are. Above all, you should be yourself. Your professional look should be attractive and easy to take care of. You have to find a style that fits your own personality. There are some basic points of which you should be aware.

1. Rules for proper dress and appearance vary from company to company.
2. Rules for proper dress vary according to the type of work being done.

   For example: What will be appropriate dress for someone working in a "hands-on" job in the electronics industry will be much different than what will be appropriate for an accountant in a CPA firm. One style is casual and one is formal. Both are properly suited to the workplace.

3. Regardless of these variations, you should always dress formally for a first interview. As you discover the style of the company or employer, then decide on what will be appropriate dress on a day to day basis.
4. Regardless of how casual or formal the work environment is, good grooming is **always** a must.

Good grooming includes looking and feeling good. Grooming involves basic hygiene, proper exercise and diet and regular sleep and relaxation patterns. It is both a reflection of how you feel about yourself and it is a measure of how other people will perceive you. It is also essential to good health.

In addition to good everyday hygiene, you should pay attention to your hair and skin and makeup. So many times students spend a lot of money on expensive outfits for interviews but keep the same haircut, wear too much or too little makeup and do not end up with a total look. You need to look at yourself from head to toe to evaluate your appearance. Start with your haircut. Stay away from extremely trendy cuts, but do look stylish and clean. Be clean shaven. Wear light makeup that accentuates your features, not changes your looks. Be sure your outfit coordinates and that it is both clean and neatly pressed. Stay away from extremely trendy outfits or clothes that do not suit your personality. Shoes also make or break your total look. Be sure they are polished and looking new. Spike heels, boat shoes or sneakers are inappropriate for professional offices. Now, a final test, look in a full length mirror and ask yourself, "Would *you* hire the person you see?"

Part of good grooming and looking good is staying healthy. You will look and feel brighter, more alert and more energetic if you are healthy. Diet and exercise are often neglected by students. Due to constantly changing work and course schedules, there is often no set routine for the student. Do the best you can to follow these basic guidelines.

Exercise

Exercise every day, even if only for a few minutes. Exercise not only keeps you looking fit, but more important, keeps you feeling and thinking well. Routine exercise, no matter how basic, reduces stress, tiredness and low motivation! Walking is the most beneficial, safe, no cost, moderate form of exercise. You do not need to join a fancy health club to stay in shape. Check with your doctor before getting involved in any rigorous exercise programs.

Tips For Effective And Healthy Dieting

1. Eat when you are hungry, but only enough to satisfy that hunger.
2. Remember that excess eating occurs mostly on weekends, on holidays, and on nights when you are at home with nothing to do.
3. Increase your activity to burn more calories.
4. Give up sweets totally for three to six months. You will, as a result, lose much of your desire for them. In time, a piece of cake or candy will not seem as enticing as before.
5. If you want to lose less than ten or twelve pounds, instead of counting calories, put yourself on a sensible eating regimen and eliminate bread (other than whole wheat or dark break), butter, cake and cookies, candy, chocolate, cream, fried foods, fatty meats, gravy, ice cream, jams and jellies, noodles, nuts, oil, potatoes, pastry, pudding, creamy or thick soups, spaghetti, and sugar.
6. Salt makes body tissues hold more water, and that water may add a pound or two to your weight. While you are dieting, cut down on your salt intake.
7. As long as all essential food elements are included in your diet, or added to it by supplemental vitamins, and you are healthy to start with, your good health will remain throughout your dieting program.
8. Alcoholic beverages and mixers are high in calories. Save your calories for more nutritious foods.
9. If you want to lose only a few pounds, eat half of your usual foods. If you usually have a sandwich and a glass of milk, eat half a sandwich and drink half a glass of milk instead.
10. Eat some sort of breakfast, even if you normally don't. If you can't eat that early in the morning, have a boiled egg or a piece of fruit later in the morning.
11. Consider this: You can eliminate nearly 500 calories a day just by NOT consuming one doughnut (135 calories), one hamburger (150 calories), one eight ounce soda (105 calories), and two pats of butter (100 calories).

Moderation

Healthy dieting and exercise are based on MODERATION and consistency. If you try to overdo either one at a point time, the effects won't be long lasting and the effect on your health can be damaging.

Dress

Dressing for business doesn't mean wearing a corporate uniform. So much has been written about successful dressing, that if everyone did everything that's been written, everyone would look alike and probably feel very uncomfortable.

Follow These Basic Guidelines

1. *Be Yourself!* The way you dress should be compatible with your entire lifestyle and your own personality. Your lifestyle includes your work environment. Since preferences vary, **avoid** extremes.
2. *Dressing Up!* The cocktail dress you wear to your spring weekend dance is not the kind of "formal dressing" that is appropriate for an interview or in the workplace. Many times you spend a lot of money on a dress for a special occasion and categorize it as one of your "good outfits." So it is only natural, when a special day is coming at work, to automatically think it is appropriate to wear your "good clothes." In most cases, this is a mistake. Remember — there's a difference between "dressing up" and professional dressing.
3. *Think About It All!* Professional dressing doesn't always begin in the workplace at 9:00 a.m. and end in the workplace at 5:00 p.m. There will be many occasions when you will still need to be conscious of the image you portray by the way you dress.
4. *Looking Good Doesn't Have To Cost!* In fact, think about how many times you have complimented someone on something they were wearing, that looked terrific on them, only to have them tell you they bought it at their favorite "off-price" or discount store.

"Off-The-Job" Situations

Casual Events: Cookouts, sporting events and business vacations are examples of some opportunities you may have to socialize with your colleagues away from the workplace. Choose nice, casual clothing so that you look comfortable and ready to take part yet not sloppy. Someone unexpected may show up or the group you are with may want to stop at a restaurant or some other public place and if you are not appropriately dressed, you may feel embarrassed or not want to participate.

Formal Events: Dinner meetings, most conferences, fundraisers, and charity dinners, and award ceremonies are examples of more formal occasions where formal, more conservative attire is required.

Social Events: Christmas parties, retirement parties, and going away parties provide an opportunity for you to have fun while celebrating some special occasion. Dress for these events is usually somewhere inbetween very casual and very formal.

The degree of flexibility in these situations varies according to the company for which you work. You will know what's right once you are part of the company. If you are a new employee, it would be best to ask around and find out what usually is appropriate. This will avoid you the embarrassment of being dressed inappropriately.

What's important is not how much you spend or where you buy your clothes but how well you select clothes that can be matched together and are easy to care for. If you are on a budget and yet need to buy a lot of clothes, have a game plan.

As a student, you should have at least one complete professional outfit other than a uniform that you may be required to wear everyday on the job. There are times when it works in your favor to dress professionally when you don't really have to. For example, if it's not already a requirement at your school, you should dress professionally at Career Fairs, part-time jobs whether on or off campus, at Guest Speakers' Programs and at least once when you visit your school's placement office.

When you dress properly for your school's placement office, you'll have the opportunity to ask about how you are presenting yourself and what improvements, if any, could be made. You'll also make a more favorable impression on the person who will be assisting you in finding a job. Usually a placement officer has the first opportunity to talk with an employer about you. It can't hurt to really do something to be remembered positively. The more confident a placement officer is about you, the easier it is for that person to help you.

If your school has a Cooperative Education, Internship, or On-Campus Interviewing program it will be necessary for you to dress professionally in order to participate. When uniforms are required for work or the classroom, treat them as you would any other good clothing you would buy. Keep them clean, pressed, and "new looking" at all times. Uniforms should not be an excuse "not to have to worry about dressing for work everyday".

Once you start your full-time job, you will need items in the following categories.

Women	**Men**
Suits	*Suits*
Blazers	*Blazers*
Blouses	*Shirts*
Sweaters	*Sweaters*
Skirts	*Ties*
Dresses	*Vests*
Pants	*Slacks*
Coats	*Coats*
Shoes	*Shoes*
Boots	*Boots*
Handbags	*Hats*
Belts	*Belts*
Scarves	*Scarves*
Gloves	*Gloves*

You may not need all of the above items on the job. For instance, a man's vest as the third part of a three-piece suit may not be the standard of dress in a company. Rather, a two-piece suit may be sufficient. Your guide to proper business dress should be your fellow employees. Using the Basic Wardrobe Chart that follows and the attire of your colleagues once you are on the job, assess your present clothing inventory and those items you need to purchase. Then, each week or two, purchase one item in the "Need" column until you have a "Working Wardrobe" appropriate for your job.

Basic Wardrobe Chart

Women	Have	Need	Approx. Cost
Suits			
Blazers			
Blouses			
Sweaters			
Skirts			
Dresses			
Pants			
Coats			
Shoes			
Boots			
Handbags			
Belts			
Scarves			
Gloves			
TOTAL:			

Basic Wardrobe Chart

Men	Have	Need	Approx. Cost
Suits			
Blazers			
Shirts			
Sweaters			
Vests			
Slacks			
Pants			
Coats			
Shoes			
Boots			
Hats			
Belts			
Scarves			
Gloves			
TOTAL:			

Grooming + Dress + Personal Style = Your Professional Image

Your personal style includes your personality, the way you talk, the way you walk and the personal touch you give to everything you do. Has anyone ever told you regarding something you wanted to buy, "That's you"? It could be anything from a fun item to a piece of clothing or a certain brand of necessity item. Don't stop at the way you dress when trying to develop your professional image. Your personal style should be made evident by the way you keep your workspace or living space as well as how you look. Following are items that are associated with your professional image:

Luggage: Discard outdated and worn bags you have and invest in some good luggage.

Briefcase: Regardless of the position you hold, using a briefcase is the best way to transport your paperwork to and from the office. Briefcases are not limited to executives; they are a useful and efficient way to keep important information organized.

Leather Bound Notebook: These are for holding or attending meetings, keeping daily "to do" lists, or attending conferences and workshops. They look better than a notepad or looseleaf paper and provide a convenient way to keep papers together.

Calendars: Keep one on your desk, one at home, and one in your pocket or handbag. There will be many times when you will be asked if you are available when you are not in your work area and it is very frustrating not to be able to check your schedule immediately. Keeping one at home that records your business schedule is extremely helpful when starting a new week or day.

Watch: Wear a watch so you can be on time.

Personalized Stationery: Two types of personalized stationery may suit your needs. You may find one that you want to use for personal correspondence and a different one for business. In either case, your correspondence is more personalized when you use it.

Subscriptions to Trade Journals: Useful information about current trends in your career field is found regularly in trade journals. Make a habit of reading at least one regularly.

These are just a few examples of items that indirectly add to your professional image. These items also make up a terrific gift list for graduation, holiday giving, birthdays or the start of your first job.

Etiquette means knowing how to move through sometimes awkward situations with ease and grace. Business etiquette has become an essential ingredient to success in today's service industries. With today's emphasis on people in organizations, the art of successful interaction is dependent upon your ability to handle yourself professionally in many different situations.

Your ability to do the right thing at the right time or to say the right thing at the right time is not only important on the job interview, but is especially important once you are on the job. Business etiquette spans the whole company from the secretary to the president. Secretaries now have broader responsibilities that require an awareness of proper protocol.

Many meetings between executives occur at luncheons, breakfasts and dinners, as well as in the boardroom. Salespeople are constantly creating an image for their company with clients. There is no doubt, that no matter what your role will be in the organization in which you choose to work, that you will play a major role in portraying the company's image. In fact, people really are the company image!

In every daily business contact you have, you will be in the powerful position of creating a positive or a negative response from others. Those others will be your superiors, subordinates, associates and most important, your customers. How all of these people see you is critical to your own career success. Remember, you have the power to elicit the response you want from them by exercising basic business etiquette. The following are guidelines for you to follow that will enhance your social skills on the job.

Business Etiquette

*"Manners Make Your Image"

Twelve fatal business faults:

1. Assuming that all your business associates prefer to be addressed by their first names
2. Sending out sloppy-looking business letters
3. Mistreating business associates' secretaries
4. Chewing gum
5. Lack of business manners on the telephone
6. Inconsiderate about keeping business appointments
7. Failure to plan properly for business travel
8. Smoking in the wrong place
9. Inviting a business associate to lunch and then not paying the total bill
10. Talking strictly about business at a business/social gathering
11. Inviting your boss or other supervisors out socially before they have offered an invitation to you
12. Not writing thank-you notes

Copyright © 1981 George Shinn, "Leadership Development"

Important Conversational Aptitudes

A good conversationalist:

1. Is well-informed and talks on a broad range of subjects
2. Shows interest in what other people do for a living
3. Does not have tunnel vision but keeps abreast of the major news in the world
4. Is able to make a fast subject switch
5. Adjusts to the person with whom he or she is talking
6. Makes statements based on knowledge and experience, not just conjecture
7. Looks a person straight in the eye when talking to him or her
8. Avoids correcting another's grammar or pronunciation in public
9. Shows genuine interest in good news about colleagues
10. Doesn't interrupt
11. Knows how to question a stranger in a friendly rather than prying way
12. Accepts compliments gracefully
13. Knows how to pay compliments gracefully
14. Knows when and how to talk about nonbusiness subjects
15. Doesn't overdose on their own interests in their conversation
16. Doesn't burst someone else's balloon
17. Addresses everyone within the group, not just one or two people
18. Knows how to make a shy person feel part of the group
19. Is aware of when he or she may have begun to bore their audience
20. Steps in to fill an embarrassing void in the conversation
21. Is diplomatic when he or she has a lot of work to do on a trip and is seated next to a person who insists on talking

From: Letita Baldrige's, "Complete Guide to Executive Manners"

Subjects To Avoid In Conversation

- *Your health*
- *Other people's health*
- *Controversial subjects when you don't know where people stand*
- *How much things cost*
- *Personal misfortunes*
- *Trite and overdone subjects*
- *Stories in questionable taste*
- *Gossip that is harmful*

Proper Meeting Behavior

1. Arrive on time.
2. Introduce yourself.
3. Do not take a seat until someone motions you to a particular place.
4. If the meeting is delayed, turn to someone and begin an informal conversation.
5. Arrive prepared for the meeting.
6. Rehearse your remarks well if you are to do a presentation.
7. Sit straight.
8. Pay attention, even when topics don't relate directly to you; don't shift to converse with others when the topic shifts.
9. Avoid interrupting.
10. Don't monopolize the time.
11. Ask for clarification if you don't understand.
12. Be positive and tactful when disagreeing.
13. Use "we" instead of "I" when talking to the group; "we" signifies being part of the group.
14. Think before you speak.
15. Don't smoke in a room where it is not permitted.
16. Pour soft drinks into a cup; never drink from a can at a business meeting.
17. Say "Thank You" quietly and leave at the end of the meeting or when the chairperson indicates you should leave.
18. After the meeting, congratulate anyone who performed exceptionally well in his or her presentation.

Executive Telephone Manners

Management should be aware of employee's telephone manners and the attitudes that are being projected to the general public.

Secretaries and other key staff members contribute in a major way to the successful management of the company through their professional manner on the telephone.

Telephone Skills For Secretaries

1. The telephone should be answered at once, on the first ring is best.
2. No one should ever be left on hold for more than one minute. The first call always has priority.
3. An efficient secretary may help an executive return calls by keeping a neat list and:
    a. asking the executive if she can place the return call for him/her.
    b. asking the executive if she can get the party on the line when the executive has free time.
4. Personal telephone calls are a distraction to the smooth running of an office. Not only do they detract from concentration, but they also detract from the professional image of the office.
5. Screening calls is important but can be a problem if not conducted in a professional manner.
6. The act of transferring an important call to the right executive requires tact and thorough knowledge of the organization, of the different divisions' duties and responsibilities and of the names of key people who will handle the call properly.
7. The person who takes messages for others efficiently and pleasantly is an asset to any organization. The minute the phone rings, you are assuming the responsibility of handling that call properly, even if it is directed to someone who is not there.

The Art Of Taking A Good Message

- *Name of the caller (correctly spelled)*
- *Telephone number, and extension (include area code if needed)*
- *Name of caller's company*
- *Date and hour of the call*
- *Your name or initials*
- *A request to call back immediately, if the call was urgent*
- *The* **message***!*

Career Paths

INTRODUCTION

> *"Today, 105,748,000 Americans will go to work.*
> *Do you know what they will do when they get there?*
> *Career Paths, Bob Adams, Inc.*

Career Path Objectives
- You will become aware of the many career choices available to you
- You will learn how to choose a career area
- You will map out a plan in order to make successful career moves

If there was ever a time to do the work that you really love, to do the kind of work that you are really attracted to, it's now. Your career training enables you to choose a variety of traditional career paths. It also opens doors to many of the new and exciting career paths emerging in the workplace.

Take some time to think about any and every career direction that exists for you. When you do this, you will feel more confident about the decisions you make because you will know that you have considered all of your options. In this age of change, it will be necessary for you to consider new options periodically. Learning to be flexible now will be helpful as your world of work changes.

> "Think about what you want to do and what job it applies to. Be open to different possibilities." *Leslie Loftus, Class of '84, Project Analyst for Hallmark Cards, Kansas City, MO*

You have already made your first step in choosing a career area by deciding on your major or program. Unfortunately, many times, students do not have access to all the information they need to decide how to best apply their professional training in the workplace. Focusing in on your career means selecting an area within your field that interests you the most.

For example, if you are a Retailing major, you may choose to become involved in management, buying, distribution, visual merchandising or sales within the retail field. As a Business Administration/ Management student, you may put your professional training to work in banking, insurance, finance, personnel, retailing, advertising, production or distribution. Your first step then is to look at career areas directly related to your major or program.

Don't stop there. Your talents can go to work in many other areas as well. For example, if you are pursuing professional training in Accounting, you may first look into private and public accounting firms, but you should also consider accounting work in a retail firm or a hotel as a possibility. If you are pursuing a degree in Secretarial Sciences, you may consider secretarial work in any type of business or industry that is of interest to you. You may also want to explore jobs that allow you upward mobility into management or sales.

Most important to choosing your career area is really understanding the jobs in each area. Without a clear understanding of what a job involves, you cannot really know if it's what you want, nor can you convince a potential employer that you are right for that job. Job titles don't tell us what we need to know. They are only a start. Everyday, people perform in the jobs that we think we want someday. What the job really consists of or how we would spend our time every day while on-the-job, is often something we're not familiar with. Then how can we be sure this is what we really want to do? One way to find out is to become familiar with job descriptions. Once employed in the workplace, you'll then be likely to say, "There's more to this job than you think there is."

This next section entitled, "Career Paths" presents you with over 500 job titles representing fourteen different career areas. The actual job descriptions for each job title can be found in the back of this book in the *Index of Job Descriptions*.

HOW TO USE "CAREER PATHS"

Fashion and Retail Management
Career Overview ❸

❷ Level	Career Areas ❶ → *Management*	*Buying*	❹ *Distribution*	*Sales*
Entry (*$$$$*)	Job Titles	Job Titles	Job Titles	Job Titles
Mid-Management/Specialists (*$$$$*)	Job Titles	Job Titles	Job Titles	Job Titles
Management (*$$$$*)	Job Titles	Job Titles	Job Titles	Job Titles
❻ →	*Recommended Pre-Professional Part-Time/Summer Experience*			

❶ **Consider** the different career areas available in the field as presented in the overview.

❷ **Review** the entry, mid-management/specialists and management positions and their related salary ranges.

❸ **Focus** on the area/s in which you have the most interest.

❹ Look down that column of job titles and ask yourself what each one represents. You may wish to ask yourself, "What does a Merchandise Analyst do every day?"

❺ Review the corresponding job description in the Index of Job Descriptions located at the back of this book if you are unclear about the responsibilities of a particular job title. This Index also opens up a whole variety of jobs available to you about which you may have had no previous knowledge.

❻ Look at the Recommended Pre-Professional Part-Time/Summer Experience for your career area to gain insight into the kinds of part-time work employers see as valuable in order to obtain an entry level professional position.

"Start working in a field you like part-time while you are in school." Bryan Haas, Class of '82, Manager of Belk's Department Store, West Jefferson, NC

After each career overview the following information is presented:

- *Experience Needed*
- *Salaries*
- *Qualifications*
- *Where The Jobs Are*
- *Trade Publications*
- *Professional Associations*

Some points to remember:

1. The *Job Titles* listed in each area are the basic job titles used most often however there may be two, three or more different job titles representing the same job. The ones chosen here are the most popular today.
2. In *Where The Jobs Are*, the most common areas and the areas in which entry level jobs are most available are listed. For each area, there may be many more possible employers depending on your level of experience and future trends in business.
3. *Salaries* vary with geographic location. The salaries listed are those averages for 1991. For each year after, you may estimate at least a 6-8% increase.
4. Under *Qualifications* you will find the most common and necessary traits to be successful in tomorrow's jobs!

Those common qualifications often include:

- *Positive attitude*
- *Enthusiasm*
- *Effective written and verbal skills*
- *Well-groomed appearance*
- *Teamworker*
- *High-energy level*
- *Flexibility*
- *Ability to learn*
- *Bright*
- *Technical skills*

5. Because a successful career includes keeping up-to-date on current trends in your field and adapting to those trends, it is important to be aware of the basic *Trade Publications and Professional Associations* appropriate for your career.
6. It should become obvious by studying the Career Paths outlined here that each career area is made up of **a planned sequence of related jobs.**

"Career Paths" is your beginning to understanding your own career options. **Don't stop there!** After you have obtained your first job, you will need to refer to this information periodically to decide on your next move. By understanding the jobs in the Mid-Management/Specialists and Management segment of your career, you can create a clear vision of where you are going and how long it might take to get there.

ACCOUNTING

Level	Public Accounting	Private/Mgt. Accounting	Government
1 Entry *($18,000-$23,000)*	Staff Accountant Junior Accountant	Junior Accountant	Revenue Officer
2 Mid-Management/ Specialists *($22,000-$37,000)*	Accountant Senior Accountant	Accountant Senior Accountant General Accountant Chief Internal Auditor Department Manager Tax Accountant Cost Accountant	Accountant Internal Auditor
3 Management *($30,000-$60,000+)*	Manager Partner	Vice-President Treasurer Controller Chief Financial Officer	Chief Internal Auditor

Recommended Pre-Professional Part-time/Summer Work Experience
Inventory Clerk, Data Entry Clerk, Accounts Payable/Receivable Clerk, General Office Clerk, Proofreader, Teller, Cashier, CRT Clerk, File Clerk, Salesclerk, Accounting Clerk

Public Accounting

Level	Job Title	Experience Needed
Entry	Staff or Junior Accountant	Professional Training
2	Accountant	1-3 years
2	Senior Accountant	3-4 years
3	Manager	5-7 years
3	Partner	8+ years

Salaries in Public Accounting

Entry	$18,000 to $21,000	medium-size firm
	$20,000 to $23,000	large firm
2	$22,000 to $26,000	medium-size firm
	$24,000 to $27,500	large firm
2	$27,000 to $35,000	medium-size firm
	$28,000 to $37,000	large firm
3	$37,000 to $46,000	medium-size firm
	$40,000 to $60,000	large firm

Salaries vary with the size of the firm and are higher for 2 or 4-year college graduates, CPA's and those with graduate degrees.

Qualifications

Personal: Good communication and concentration skills. Accuracy and attention to detail. Flexibility. Objectivity. Ability to judge and make decisions. Reliability.

Professional: Writing and communication skills. Exceptional mathematical ability. Commitment to professional standards. Ability to work independently.

Where The Jobs Are
CPA Firms
Public accounting is divided into two tiers: the ''Big Six,'' and other national, regional, and local practices.

"The Big Six"
Arthur Andersen & Company, Chicago, IL
Coopers & Lybrand, New York, NY
DeLoitte & Touche, New York, NY

Ernst & Young, Cleveland, OH
KPMG Peat Marwick
Price Waterhouse & Company, New York, NY
These companies have branches throughout the country.

Private Management Accounting

Level	Job Title	Experience Needed
Entry	Junior Accountant	Professional Training
2	Accountant	1-3 years
2	Senior Accountant	3-4 years
2	General Accountant	4-8 years
	Department Manager	4-8 years
	Chief Internal Auditor	4-8 years
3	Vice President	15 + years
	Treasurer	15 + years
	Controller	15 + years
	Chief Financial Officer	15 + years

Salaries in Private/Management Accounting

Level	Salary	Firm
Entry	$20,000 to $22,000	medium-size firm
	$20,000 to $23,000	large-size firm
2	$23,000 to $29,000	medium-size firm
	$26,000 to $31,000	medium-large-size firm
	$28,000 to $33,000	large-size firm
3	$30,000 to $36,000	medium-size firm
	$36,000 to $56,000	large-size firm

Salaries vary with the size of the firm and are higher for 2- or 4-year college graduates, CPA's, those with graduate degrees, and accountants whose jobs require extensive travel.

Qualifications

Personal: Reliability. Ability to work independently. Flexibility. Discipline.

Professional: Understanding of business and the marketplace. Willingness to increase knowledge of practical accounting techniques.

Where The Jobs Are
Private Corporations
Consulting

Government

Level	Job Title	Experience Needed
Entry	Revenue Officer	Professional Training
2	Accountant	1-3 years
2	Internal Auditor	1-3 years
3	Chief Internal Auditor	3-5 years
3	Chief Accountant	5-7 years

The goal of the accounting department of a typical government agency is to function within the budgetary constraints mandated by legislative action. The IRS is the largest employer of accountants in the U.S.

Salaries in Government
Positions are comparable to salaries in private industry and much of the work performed is the same. Salary rates are based on varying grade levels.

Qualifications

Personal: Reliability. Ability to work independently. Flexibility. Discipline.

Professional: Knowledge of standard accounting procedures; ability to design accounting techniques; interest in publishing work in professional journals.

Where The Jobs Are
Department of Agriculture
Department of Defense Audit Agencies
Department of Energy
Department of Health & Human Services
Department of the Air Force
Department of the Navy
Department of the Army
General Accounting Office
Treasury Department
(includes the Internal Revenue Service)

Special Certifications

C.M.A. *(Certificate in Management Accounting)*

The C.M.A. exam is sponsored by the National Association of Accountants and tests decision-making capability and knowledge of business law, finance and organization.

C.I.A. *(Certificate in Internal Auditing)*

The C.I.A. exam is sponsored by the Institute of Internal Auditors and tests the theory and practice of internal auditing. Both exams are open to graduating seniors, but work experience is required for certification. Multiple certification is permissible and encouraged.

C.P.A. *(Certificate in Public Accounting)*

The advantages of holding the C.P.A. are many as it serves as tangible proof of your skill and your commitment to the profession. Public accounting firms, particularly the largest, often expect their accountants to receive certification as quickly as state law allows. Beyond the entry level, the C.P.A. is often a requirement for advancement. Information on how to prepare for the C.P.A. exam as well as test dates is available through C.P.A. Review Courses.

Trade Publications

CPA Journal (monthly), New York Society of Certified Public Accountants, 600 Third Avenue, New York, NY 10016

Government Accountant's Journal (quarterly), Association of Government Accountants, 727 South 23rd Street, Arlington, VA 22202

Journal of Accountancy (monthly), American Institute of Certified Public Accountants, 1211 Avenue of the Americas, New York, NY 10036

Management Accounting (monthly), Warren, Gorham, and Lamont, Inc., 210 South Street, Boston, MA 02111

The Practical Accountant (monthly), Warren, Gorham, and Lambert, Inc., 210 South Street, Boston, MA 02111

The Wall Street Journal (daily), 23 Cortland Street, New York, NY 10007

Professional Associations

American Institute of Certified Public Accountants
1211 Avenue of the Americas
New York, NY 10036

American Society of Women Accountants
35 East Wacker Drive
Chicago, IL 60601

Association of Government Accountants
727 South 23rd Street
Arlington, VA 22202

Institute of Internal Auditors
249 Maitland Avenue
Altamonte Springs, FL 32701

National Association of Accountants
919 Third Avenue
New York, NY 10022

BUSINESS ADMINISTRATION

Level	Banking	Insurance	Finance	Personnel
1 Entry *($18,000-$25,000)* *Management Trainee*	Bank Officer Trainee Systems Trainee	Adjuster Trainee Claims Examiner Underwriter Trainee Actuarial Trainee Beginning Agent	Registered Representative	Employment Recruiter Interviewer Personnel Assistant Job Analyst
2 Mid-Management/ Specialists *($20,000-$38,000)*	Assistant Loan Officer Loan Officer Department Mgr. Supervisor Systems Analyst Systems Consultant Senior Systems Consultant Branch Mgr. Loan Mgr.	Assistant Underwriter Underwriter Specialist Senior Underwriter Assistant Actuary Actuary Senior Claims Adjuster	Investment Banker Trader Purchasing Agent Research Analyst Trust Officer Financial Analyst Portfolio Mgr. Credit Mgr.	College Recruiter Training Mgr. Employment Mgr. Corporate Recruiter Personnel Mgr. Wage & Salary Administrator Benefits Coordinator Labor Relations Specialist Plant Safety Specialist EEO Coordinator
3 Management *($35,000-$76,000)*	Manager Division Mgr. Vice President President	Underwriting/ Supervisor Office Mgr. Chief Actuary Agent Regional VP Vice President	Treasurer/Controller Vice President President	Director of Human Resources Vice President of Human Resources

Level	Retailing	Advertising	Production	Distribution
1 Entry *($18,000-$25,000)* *Management Trainee*	Department Mgr. Store Mgr. Trainee Buyer Trainee	Junior Copywriter Media Buyer Project Coordinator Account Executive Trainee	Expeditor Assistant Buyer Assistant Purchasing Agent Production Planner Assistant Quality Assurance Mgr.	*See Careers in Fashion &* *Retail Management*
2 Mid-Management/ Specialists *($20,000-$38,000)*	Assistant Store Mgr. Sales Representative Display Coordinator Distribution Coordinator Merchandise Analyst Assistant Buyer	Copywriter Senior Copywriter Media Planner Media Department Head Project Director Research Account Director Associate Research Director Account Executive Senior Account Executive	Purchasing Agent Purchasing Mgr. Traffic Mgr. Inventory Mgr. Quality Assurance Mgr. Buyer	
3 Management *($35,000-$76,000 +)*	Merchandise Mgr. Buyer Store Mgr. Operations Mgr. VP/Operations Sales Mgr.	Accounts Supervisor/Mgr. Department Mgr. Copy Chief Creative Director Director of Media Advertising Research Director	Plant Mgr. Materials Mgr. Manufacturing Mgr. Regional Mgr. Operations Research Analyst VP/Production	

Recommended Pre-Professional Part-time/Summer Work Experience
Salesclerk, Cashier, Messenger, Data Entry Clerk, General Office Clerk, Inventory Clerk, File Clerk, Accounting Clerk, Receptionist, Teller, Typist, CRT Clerk, Proofreader, Waitperson, Shipper/Receiver.

Banking

Level	Job Title	Experience Needed
Entry	Bank Officer Trainee	Professional Training
Entry	Systems Trainee	Professional Training
2	Assistant Loan Officer	1-2 years
2	Supervisor	1-2 years
2	Systems Analyst	2 years
2	Systems Consultant	3 years
2	Department Manager	3-5 years
2	Loan Officer	3-5 years
2	Branch Manager	3-5 years
2	Senior Systems Consultant	5 years
2	Loan Manager	5-6 years
3	Division Manager	6 + years
3	Manager	6 + years
3	Vice President	8-10 years
3	President	10 + years

Salaries in Banking

Entry	$18,000 to $25,000
2	$22,000 to $31,000
2	$29,000 to $35,000
3	$35,000 to $50,000
3	$50,000 +

Salaries are higher for those with 2- or 4-year college degrees.

Qualifications

Personal: Strong analytical skills. Strong negotiation skills. Strong interpersonal skills. Ability to work under pressure. Ability to work with figures.

Professional: Familiarity with business applications of software and hardware. Ability to analyze financial statements and do creative financial planning. Good business judgement.

Where The Jobs Are

Credit Lending	Operations
Trusts	Systems

Insurance

Level	Job Title	Experience Needed
Entry	Adjuster Trainee	Professional Training
Entry	Claims Examiner	Professional Training
Entry	Underwriter Trainee	Professional Training
Entry	Actuarial Trainee	Professional Training
Entry	*Sales Trainee	Professional Training
2	Assistant Underwriter	1-2 years
2	Assistant Actuary	1-2 years
2	Underwriter Specialist	2-4 years
2	Agent	2-4 years
2	Actuary	3-5 years
2	Senior Underwriter	3-5 years
2	Senior Claims Examiner	4-6 years
3	Underwriting Supervisor	6 + years
3	Office Manager	5 + years
3	Chief Actuary	6 + years
3	Regional Director	5 + years
3	Vice President	8 + years

Salaries in Insurance
(See Salaries in Banking)

*New sales workers earn about $2,000 a month during the first six months of training. Most sales workers are paid on commission. The size of the commission depends on the type and amount of insurance sold. Insurance sales workers generally pay their own automobile and travel expenses. Independent sales workers must also pay office rent, clerical salaries, and other operating expenses out of their own earnings.

Salaries are higher for those with 2- and 4-year college degrees.

Qualifications

Personal: Enthusiasm. Self-motivation. Attention to detail. Good analytical skills. Excellent communication skills. Good quantitative skills. Confidence.

Professional: Accurate thinking and writing skills. Ability to write concisely. Aptitude for computers. Ability to supervise.

Where The Jobs Are
Home Offices/Headquarters
Branch Offices
Independent Agencies
Private Corporations
Real Estate

Finance

Level	Job Title	Experience Needed
Entry	*Registered Representative	Professional Training
Entry	Manager Trainee	Professional Training
2	Trader	1-2 years
2	Financial Analyst	2-3 years
2	Research Analyst	3-5 years
2	Investment Banker	3-5 years
2	Purchasing Agent	3-5 years
2	Portfolio Manager	5-6 years
2	Credit Manager	5-6 years
2	Trust Officer	6-8 years
3	Treasurer/Controller	6 + years
3	Vice President	8-12 years
3	President	12-15 years

Salaries in Finance
(See Salaries in Banking)

*Trainees are usually paid a salary until they meet licensing and registration requirements. During training, salesworkers earn from $900-$1,200 a month. After licensing, earnings depend on commission from sales of stocks, bonds, life insurance or other securities.

Salaries are higher for those with 2 or 4-year college degrees.

Qualifications

Personal: Interest in economic trends. Ability to handle frequent rejection. Ability to work independently. Good grooming. Good communication skills.

Professional: State licensing and successful completion of exams prepared by securities exchanges or NASD (National Association of Securities Dealers, Inc.)

Where The Jobs Are
Financial Institutions
Banks
Private Corporations
Consulting Firms
Government
Securities Exchanges

Personnel

Level	Job Title	Experience Needed
Entry	Interviewer	Professional Training
Entry	Employment Recruiter	Professional Training
Entry	Personnel Assistant	Professional Training
Entry	Job Analyst	Professional Training
2	College Recruiter	1-3 years
2	Training Manager	2-4 years
2	Corporate Recruiter	3-5 years
2	Benefits Coordinator	1-3 years
2	Plant Safety Specialist	3-5 years
2	Equal Employment Opportunity Coordinator	1-3 years
2	Labor Relations Specialist	4-6 years
2	Wage & Salary Administrator	4-6 years
2	Employment Manager	4-6 years
2	Personnel Manager	5-7 years
3	Personnel Director	5-7 years
3	Vice President of Human Resources	7-10 years

Salaries in Personnel

Entry	$18,000 to $23,000
2	$23,000 to $33,000
2	$28,000 to $38,000
3	$33,000 to $55,000
3	$55,000 to $76,000 +

Salaries are higher for those with 2- and 4-year college degrees.

Qualifications

Personal: Excellent communication skills, listening skills especially important. Ability to speak and write effectively. Ability to work under pressure.

Professional: Fair-mindedness. Good decision-making skills. Ability to enforce policies.

Where The Jobs Are
Private Corporations
Education
Government Agencies
Consulting Firms
Independent Businesses

Retailing

(See Careers in Fashion & Retail Management)

Advertising

Level	Job Title	Experience Needed
Entry	Assistant Media Planner	Professional Training
Entry	Junior Copywriter	Professional Training
Entry	Project Director	Professional Training
Entry	Account Executive Trainee	Professional Training
2	Copywriter	1-3 years
2	Account Executive	1-3 years
2	Research Account Executive	1-3 years
2	Media Planner	3-5 years
2	Associate Research Director	3-8 years
2	Senior Account Executive	5-8 years
2	Associate Media Director	5-7 years
2	Research Director	7-10 years
2	Senior Copywriter	7-10 years
2	Media Director of Planning	7-10 years
3	Accounts Supervisor/Manager	10-13 years
3	Department Manager	10 + years
3	Copy Chief	10 + years
3	Creative Director	10 + years
3	Director of Media Advertising	10 + years
3	Research Director	10 + years

Salaries in Advertising

Level	Salary
Entry	$18,000 to $22,000
2	$20,000 to $24,000
2	$24,000 to $26,000
2	$26,000 to $30,000
2	$30,000 to $33,000
2	$33,000 to $38,000
3	$38,000 to $41,000
3	$41,000 to $47,000
3	$47,000 to $62,000
3	$62,000 to $75,000 +

Salaries are higher for those with 2 or 4-year college degrees.

Qualifications

Personal: Strong interpersonal skills. Ability to work with a team. Problem-solving mentality.

Professional: Good writing skills, knowledge of the media. Sales ability. Negotiation skills.

Where The Jobs Are
Advertising Agencies
Media
Private Corporations
Consulting
Freelancing

Production

Level	Job Title	Experience Needed
Entry	Expeditor	Professional Training
Entry	Assistant Buyer	Professional Training
Entry	Assistant Purchasing Agent	Professional Training
Entry	Production Planner	Professional Training
Entry	Assistant Quality Assurance Manager	Professional Training
2	Purchasing Agent	1-3 years
2	Purchasing Manager	3-5 years
2	Traffic Manager	2-4 years
2	Inventory Manager	2-4 years
2	Quality Assurance Manager	3-5 years
2	Buyer	4-6 years
3	Plant Manager	5-6 years
3	Materials Manager	5-6 years
3	Manufacturing Manager	5-6 years
3	Regional Manager	6-8 years
3	Operations Research Analyst	6-8 years
3	Vice President/Production	7-10 years

Qualifications

Personal: Good organizational skills. Aptitude for figures. Ability to plan and make quick decisions. Flexibility.

Professional: Ability to interpret computer data. Ability to supervise and think ahead.

Where The Jobs Are
Manufacturing
Distribution
Private Corporations

Salaries in Production
(See Salaries in Banking)

Distribution

(See Careers in Fashion & Retail Management)

Trade Publications

Advertising Age (weekly), Crain Communications, Inc., 740 North Rush Street, Chicago, IL 60611

Adweek (weekly), Adweek Publications, 820 Second Avenue, New York, NY 10017 (regional editions for East, Southeast, West, Southwest, and Midwest)

ABA Banking Journal (monthly), 345 Hudson Street, New York, NY 10014

American Banker (daily), One State Street Plaza, New York, NY 10014

The Banker's Magazine (bimonthly), Warren, Gorham, and Lamont, Inc., 210 South Streeet, Boston, MA 02111

Bank News (monthly), 912 Baltimore Avenue, Kansas, MO 64105

Professional Associations

The Advertising Council
825 Third Avenue
New York, NY 10022

Advertising Research Foundation Information Center
3 East 54th Street
New York, NY 10022

American Advertising Federation
1400 K Street, N.W.
Suite 1000
Washington, DC 20005

American Association of Advertising Agencies
200 Park Avenue
New York, NY 10017

Association of National Advertisers
155 East 44th Street
New York, NY 10017

American Bankers Association
1120 Connecticut Avenue, N.W.
Washington, DC 20036

Consumer Bankers Association
1725 K Street, N.W.
Washington, DC 20006

National Association of Bank Women
111 East Wacker Drive
Chicago, IL 60601

United States League of Savings Association
111 East Wacker Drive
Chicago, IL 60601

American Management Association
135 West 50th Street
New York, NY 10020

COMPUTER SYSTEMS

Level	Programming	Operations	Marketing/Sales	Support Services
1 Entry *($18,000-$25,000)*	Programmer Trainee Programmer Analyst	Tape Librarian Data Entry Supervisor Computer Operator	Sales Representative	Instructor Product Support Representative Service Representative
2 Mid-Management/ Specialists *($21,000-$34,000)*	Senior Programmer Senior Analyst	Supervisor/Systems Operators Peripheral Systems Operator MIS Supervisor Systems Analyst	Account Representative	Training Mgr. Documentation Specialist District Mgr.
3 Management *($30,000-$75,000+)* *MIS Director*	Lead Programmer Lead Analyst Mgr. of Programming	Operations Mgr. EDP Auditor Mgr./Systems Analysis	Account Supervisor VP/Account Services	Consultant Regional Mgr. Vice President President

Recommended Pre-Professional Part-time/Summer Work Experience
CRT Clerk, Typist, Data Entry Clerk, Coder, Salesclerk, File Clerk, Cashier, General Office Clerk

Programming

Level	Job Title	Experience Needed
Entry	Programmer Trainee	Professional Training
Entry	Programmer Analyst	Professional Training
2	Senior Programmer	1-3 years
2	Senior Analyst	1-3 years
3	Lead Programmer	3-5 years
3	Lead Analyst	3-5 years
3	Manager of Programming	3-5 years
3	MIS Director	6-8 years

Salaries in Programming

Entry	$18,000 to $22,000
Entry	$20,000 to $24,000
2	$22,000 to $28,000
2	$28,000 to $34,000
3	$34,000 to $40,000

Salaries are higher for those with 2 or 4-year college degrees.

Qualifications

Personal: Patience. Persistence. Ability to work with extreme accuracy. Ability to work under pressure and with deadlines. Good written and verbal communication skills.

Professional: Ability to think logically. Capable of doing highly analytical work. Problem-solving ability. Decision-making skills. Teamworker.

Where The Jobs Are
Manufacturing Firms
Data Processing Service Organizations
Government
Banks
Insurance
Education

Operations

Level	Job Title	Experience Needed
Entry	Tape Librarian	Professional Training
Entry	Data Entry Supervisor	Professional Training
Entry	Computer Operator	Professional Training
2	Systems Operators Supervisor	1-2 years
2	Peripheral Equipment Operator	1-2 years
2	Systems Analyst	2-4 years
2	MIS Supervisor	2-4 years
3	Operations Manager	3-6 years
3	EDP Auditor	3-6 years
3	Manager of Systems Analysis	6-8 years
3	MIS Director	6-10 years

Salaries in Operations
(See Salaries in Programming)

Qualifications

Personal: Patience. Persistence. Ability to work under pressure. Flexibility. Good communication skills. Detail oriented. Manual dexterity. Interest in learning new procedures.

Professional: Ability to make quick decisions and supervise others. Analytical skills essential. Teamworker.

Where The Jobs Are
Manufacturing
Data Processing Service Organizations
Government
Banks
Insurance
Education

Marketing/Sales

Level	Job Title	Experience Needed
Entry	Sales Representative	Professional Training
2	Account Representative	1-3 years
3	Account Supervisor	3-6 years
3	Vice President/Account Services	6-10 years

Salaries in Marketing/Sales

Level	Salary
Entry	$19,000 to $24,000
2	$24,000 to $26,000
3	$26,000 to $34,000
3	$34,000 to $54,000
3	$54,000 to $75,000 +

Salaries are higher for those with 2 or 4-year college degrees.

Qualifications

Personal: Excellent verbal communication skills. Confidence. Enthusiasm. Well-groomed. Ability to work independently. Self-motivated. Flexibility.

Professional: Product knowledge. Perception of customer needs. Willingness to learn.

Where The Jobs Are
Computer Service Organizations
Consulting
Computer Manufacturers
Government

Support Services

Level	Job Title	Experience Needed
Entry	Product Support Representative	Professional Training
Entry	Service Representative	Professional Training
2	Training Manager	2-4 years
2	Documentation Specialist	1-2 years
2	District Manager	3-5 years
2	Academic Department Head	3-5 years
3	Consultant	5 + years
3	Regional Manager	5-8 years
3	Vice President	8-10 years
3	President	8-10 + years

Salaries in Support Services

Level	Salary
Entry	$19,000 to $25,000
2	$21,000 to $26,000
2	$24,000 to $30,000
3	$30,000 to $35,000
3	$35,000 to $55,000 +

Salaries are higher for those with 2 or 4-year college degrees.

Qualifications

Personal: Excellent communication skills. Self-motivated. Well-groomed. Patience. Ability to work independently. Confidence.

Professional: Product knowledge. Perception of customer needs. Teamworker. Ability to make decisions.

Where The Jobs Are
Computer Service Organizations
Computer Manufacturers
Consulting
Education
Banks
Insurance
Manufacturing

Trade Publications

Byte (monthly), 70 Main Street, Peterborough, NH 03458

Computer Decisions (monthly), 50 Essex Street, Rochelle Park, NJ 07662

Computer Design (monthly), 11 Goldsmith Street, Littleton, MA 01460

Computer Times, P.O. Box 13918, Philadelphia, PA 19101

Computer and Electrical Engineering (quarterly), Pergamon Press, Maxwell House, Fairview Park, Elmsford, NY 10523

Computer and People (bimonthly), Berkley Enterprises, Inc., 815 Washingbton Street, Newtonville, MA 02160

Computerworld (weekly), CW Communications, Inc., Box 880, 375 Cochituate Road, Framingham, MA 01701

Datamation (monthly), Technical Publishing Company, 666 Fifth Avenue, New York, NY 10103

Data Processor, IBM Corporation, 1133 Westchester Avenue, White Plains, NY 10604

Information Systems News (bimonthly), 333 East Shore Road, Manhasset, NY 11030

Software News (monthly), 5 Kane Industrial Drive, Hudson, MA 01749

Professional Associations

American Foundation of Information Processing Societies
1815 North Lynn Street
Suite 800
Arlington, VA 22209

American Society for Information Science
1010 Sixteenth Street, N.W.
Washington, DC 20036

Association for Computational Linguistics
c/o Dr. D. E. Walker
SRI International
Menlo Park, CA 94025

Association for Computer Programmers and Analysts
294 Main Street
East Greenwich, RI 02818

Association for Systems Management
24587 Bagley Road
Cleveland, OH 44138

Microcomputer Software Association
1300 North 17th Street, No. 300
Arlington, VA 22209

Women in Data Processing
P .O. Box 8117
San Diego, CA 92102

COURT REPORTING & RELATED CAREERS

Level	Court Reporting	Hearing Reporting	Legislative Reporting	Conference Reporting	Freelance Reporting
1 Entry *($16,000-$23,000)*	Court Reporter	Hearing Reporter	Legislative Reporter	Conference Reporter	Freelance Reporting
2 Mid-Management/ Specialists *($23,000-$42,000)*	*See Paralegal Careers*				
3 Management *($42,000-$60,000)*					

Recommended Pre-Professional Part-time/Summer Work Experience
Typist, CRT Clerk, General Office Clerk, Messenger, File Clerk, Court Clerk, Coder, Research Assistant, Law Clerk

Court Reporting & Related Careers

Level	Job Title	Experience Needed
Entry	Court Reporter	Professional Training
Entry	Hearing Reporter	Professional Training
Entry	Legislative Reporter	Professional Training
Entry	Conference Reporter	Professional Training
Entry	Freelance Reporter	Professional Training
2	Paralegal	2-4 years *(With further education)*
2	Legal Assistant	2-4 years
2	Legal Technician	2-4 years
2	Paralegal Instructor	2-4 years
2	Proofreader	2-4 years
2	Marketing Representative	2-4 years
2	Sales Representative	2-4 years
2	Paralegal Supervisor	4-6 years
2	Senior Legal Assistant	4-6 years
2	Research Assistant	5-8 years
2	Information Specialist	5-8 years
2	Litigation Paralegal	5-8 years
2	Placement Director	5-8 years
2	Editor	5-8 years
2	Systems Programmer	5-8 years
3	Law Office Administrator	8-10 years
3	Lawyer	8-10 years *(With further education)*
3	Law Office Administrator	8-10 years
3	Law Library Manager	8-10 years
3	Program Director	8-10 years
3	Consultant/Advisor	8-10 years
3	Marketing Analyst	8-10 years

Salaries in Court Reporting & Related Careers

Entry	$16,000 to $20,000
Entry	$18,000 to $23,000
2	$23,000 to $28,000
2	$28,000 to $34,000
2	$34,000 to $42,000
3	$42,000 to $60,000 +

Qualifications

Personal: Strong concentration. Physical stamina. Manual dexterity. Detail oriented. Professional appearance. Ability to work under pressure.

Professional: Accurate thinking and spelling. Transcription skills. Familiarity with legal terminology. Excellent written and verbal communication skills. Positive attitude. High energy level.

Where The Jobs Are

Courts	Conventions
Legal Firms/Departments	Sales
Freelancing	Stockholders' Meetings
Business & Industry	
(meetings & conferences)	

Trade Publications

American Bar Association Journal, 750 N. Lake Shore Drive, Chicago, IL 60611

National Shorthand Reporters Association, 118 Park Street, Southeast, Vienna, VA 22180

Professional Associations

National Shorthand Reporters Association
118 Park Street, Southeast
Vienna, VA 22180

DATA ENTRY

Level	Operations
1 Entry *($14,000-$17,000)*	Data Entry Operator Keypunch Operator Tape Librarian
2 Mid-Management/ Specialists *($17,000-$22,000)*	Computer Operator Peripheral Equipment Operator Supervisor of Data Entry Services
3	

(SEE Careers in Computer Systems: Programming, Operations, Marketing/Sales, and Support Services.

Recommended Pre-Professional Part-time/Summer Work Experience
Keypunch Operator, CRT Clerk, Typist, General Office Clerk, Word Processing Operator

Operations

Level	Job Title	Experience Needed
Entry	Data Entry Operator	Professional Training
Entry	Tape Librarian	Professionial Training
2	Computer Operator	2-4 years
2	Peripheral Equipment Operator	2-4 years
2	Supervisor of Data Entry Services	4-6 years

Salaries in Data Entry

Entry	$14,000 to $17,000
2	$17,000 to $22,000
3	*(See Salaries in Computer Systems)*

Qualifications

Personal: Attention to detail. Good attention span. Ability to do repetitive work. Ability to work under close supervision. Patience. Manual dexterity.

Professional: Positive attitude. Enthusiasm. Teamworker. Ability to make decisions. Problem-solving skills. Excellent communications skills.

Where The Jobs Are
Insurance Companies
Research Organizations
Education
Hospitals
Government
Computer Service Organizations
Banks

Trade Publication
(See Careers in Computer Systems)

Professional Associations
(See Careers in Computer Systems)

DENTAL ASSISTANT

Level	Private Practices, Hospitals, Health Maintenance Organizations	Education	Marketing/Sales
1 Entry *($14,000-$19,000)*	Dental Assistant	Instructor	Sales Representative
2 Mid-Management/ Specialists *($19,000-$23,000)*	Clinical Dental Assistant Administrative Dental Assistant Dental Hygienist *(With further education)* Claims Examiner Claims Representative Research Assistant	Academic Department Head	Sales Manager
3 Management *($23,000-$32,000+)*	Office Mgr. Research Analyst Dentist *(With further education)*	School Director Administrator/Education	Director of Marketing & Sales

Recommended Pre-Professional Part-time/Summer Work Experience
Receptionist, File Clerk, Typist, CRT Clerk, Sales, Accounting Clerk

Private Practices, Hospitals, Health Maintenance Organizations

Level	Job Title	Experience Needed
Entry	Dental Assistant	Professional Training
2	Clinical Dental Assistant	1-2 years
2	Administrative Dental Assistant	1-2 years
2	Dental Hygienist	*Further education*
2	Medical Claims Examiner	1-2 years
2	Medical Claims Representative	1-2 years
2	Research Assistant	2-4 years
3	Office Manager	4-6 years
3	Research Analyst	4-6 years
3	Dentist	*Further education*

Salaries in Private Practices, Hospitals, Health Maintenance Organizations

Level	Salary
Entry	$14,000 to $19,000
2	$17,000 to $21,000
2	$21,000 to $23,000
3	$23,000 to $26,000
3	$26,000 to $32,000+

Salaries are higher for those with 2 or 4-year college degrees.

Qualifications

Personal: Patience. Concentration. Good grooming and hygiene. Manual dexterity. Congenial personality. Ability to work with people who may be under stress.

Professional: Knowledge of medical terminology. Ability to learn on-the-job. Familiarity with billing procedures and health plans.

Where The Jobs Are
Private Practices
Hospitals
Health Maintenance Organizations
State & Local Public Health Departments
Government *(hospitals and dental clinics of the U.S. Public Health Service and the Veterans Administration)*

Education

Level	Job Title	Experience Needed
Entry	Instructor	Professional Training and/or College Degree
2	Academic Department Head	4-5 years
3	School Director	8-10 + years
3	Administrator/Education	6-8 years

Salaries in Education
(See Salaries in Teacher Education)

Qualifications

Personal: Patience. Good communication skills. Ability to manage.

Professional: Awareness of policies and laws in the Health Care field. Planning and organizational skills. Ability to work with budgets.

Where The Jobs Are
Dental Schools
Hospital Dental Departments

Sales/Marketing

Level	Job Title	Experience Needed
Entry	Sales Representative	Professional Training
2	Sales Manager	3-5 years
3	Director of Marketing/Sales	5 + years

Salaries in Sales/Marketing
(See Salaries in Careers in Marketing)

Qualifications

Personal: Positive attitude. Good communication skills. Ability to work independently. Self-motivated. Tolerance for rejection. Confidence.

Professional: Product knowledge. Perception of customer needs. Familiarity with medical terminology.

Where The Jobs Are
Medical Suppliers
Dental Suppliers

Trade Publications

The Dental Assistant, American Dental Assistants Association, Suite 1130, 666 N. Lake Shore Drive, Chicago, IL 60611

Dental Assisting, P.O. Box 7573, Waco, TX 76714

Dental Products, Readers Service Center, P.O. Box 2610, Clinton, Iowa 52735

Dental Management, 7500 Old Oak Blvd., Cleveland, OH 44130

Dental Economics, P.O. Box 3408, Tulsa, OK 74101

The Journal of Dental Education, American Association of Dental Schools, 1625 Massachusetts Ave., NW, Washington, DC 20036

Dental Abstracts, American Dental Association, 211 East Chicago Avenue, Chicago, IL 60611

Professional Associations

American Dental Assistants Association
Suite 1130
666 N. Lake Shore Dr.
Chicago, IL 60611

National Association of Dental Assistants
3837 Plaza Drive
Fairfax, VA 22030

Commission on Dental Accreditation
American Dental Association
211 E. Chicago Ave.
Suite 1814
Chicago, IL 60611

Dental Assisting National Board, Inc.
666 North Lake Shore Dr.
Suite 1136
Chicago, IL 60611

DRAFTING

Level	Operations	Support Services	Education
1 Entry *($19,000-$24,000)*	Junior Drafter	Junior Drafter	Instructor
2 Mid-Management/ Specialists *($24,000-$29,000)*	Senior Drafter	Junior Consultant	Academic Department Head
3 Management *With Further Education* *($29,000-$50,000+)*	Engineer Designer Architect	Senior Consultant	Program Director School Director

Recommended Pre-Professional Part-time/Summer Work Experience
CRT Clerk, Data Entry Operator, Runner for Architectural, Engineering or Construction Firm

Operations

Level	Job Title	Experience Needed
Entry	Junior Drafter	Professional Training
2	Senior Drafter	4-6 years
3	Engineer	*With further education*
3	Designer	*With further education*
3	Architect	*With further education*

Salaries in Operations

Level	Salary
Entry	$19,000 to $24,000
2	$24,000 to $29,000
3	$29,000 to $50,000+

Salaries are higher for those with 2 or 4-year college degrees.

Qualifications

Personal: Good eyesight. Manual dexterity. Attention to detail. Patience. Ability to work independently. Accuracy. Neatness. Excellent communication skills. Ability to work under pressure.

Professional: Ability to do free-hand drawings of three-dimensional objects. Artistic ability. Ability to conceptualize. Ability to meet deadlines. Teamworker.

Where The Jobs Are
Engineering and Architectural Firms
Durable Goods and Manufacturing Industries
(machinery, electrical equipment, and fabricated metals)
Construction
Transportation
Communications
Utilities Industries

Support Services

Level	Job Title	Experience Needed
Entry	Junior Drafter	Professional Training
2	Senior Drafter	4-6 years
2	Junior Consultant	6-8 years
3	Senior Consultant	8-10 years

Salaries in Support Services
(See Salaries in Operations)

Qualifications

Personal: Positive attitude. Enthusiasm. High energy level. Excellent communication skills. Professional appearance.

Professional: Technical knowledge. Perception of customers' needs. Teamworker. Ability to work independently. Strong marketing and sales skills.

Where The Jobs Are
(See "Where the Jobs Are" in Operations)

Education

Level	Job Title	Experience Needed
Entry	Instructor	Professional Training and/or College Degree
2	Academic Department Head	4-6 years
3	Program Director	6-8 years
3	School Director	8-10 years

Salaries in Education
(See Salaries in Teacher Education)

Qualifications

Personal: Positive attitude. Enthusiasm. High energy level. Excellent communication skills. Listening skills. Flexibility. Ability to work under pressure.

Professional: Ability to organize and plan. Technical knowledge. Managerial skills. Ability to work with budgets. Teamworker.

Where The Jobs Are
Technical Schools
Vocational Schools
Drafting Departments

Trade Publications

Design and Drafting News, American Institute for Design and Drafting, 966 Hungerford Drive, Suite 10-B, Rockville, MD 20854

Professional Associations

American Institute for Design and Drafting
966 Hungerford Drive
Suite 10-B
Rockville, MD 20854

American Institute of Technical Illustrators Association
2513 Forest Leaf Parkway
Suite 906
Ballwin, MO 63011

Coordinating Council for Computers in Construction
1221 Avenue of the Americas
New York, NY 10020

National Association of Trade and Technical Schools
2021 K Street, N.W.
Washington, DC 20006

ELECTRONICS

Level	Repair	Research	Support Services	Production	Education

1
Entry
($19,000-$24,000)
	Electronics
	  Technician
		Electronics
		  Technician
			Sales/Field
			  Representative
			Customer Service
			  Representative
				Electronics
				  Technician
					Instructor

2
Mid-Management/
Specialists
($22,000-$28,000)
	Robotics Technician
	Broadcast Technician
	Engineering Technician
	Communications/
	  Equipment Technician
	Computer Technician
	Digital Technician
	Office Machine Repairer
	Commercial/Industrial
	  Technician
	Medical Technician
	Health Technician
	Service Technician
		Design Technician
		Research Technician
			Production Technician
			Instructor
			Sales/Service Mgr.
			Training Supervisor
				Production Technician	Academic
					  Department Head

3
Management
($28,000-$40,000 +)
	Electronics Engineer
	  (With further education)
		Director of Research
		  & Development
			Consultant
			Administrator
			Director of Marketing
			  & Sales
				Production Mgr.	Program Director
					School Director

Recommended Pre-Professional Part-time/Summer Work Experience
Assistant Technician, Repair Person, CRT Clerk, Computer Operator, Data Entry Operator

Repair

Level	Job Title	Experience Needed
Entry	Electronics Technician	Professional Training
2	Robotics Technician	1-3 years
2	Broadcast Technician	1-3 years
2	Engineering Technician	1-3 years
2	Communications Equipment Technician	1-3 years
2	Medical Technician	1-3 years
2	Health Technician	1-3 years
2	Service Technician	1-3 years
3	Electronics Engineer	*With further education*

Salaries in Repair

Entry	$19,000 to $22,000
2	$22,000 to $25,000
2	$25,000 to $28,000
3	$28,000 to $35,000
3	$35,000 to $40,000 +

Salaries are higher for those with 2 or 4-year college degrees.

Qualifications

Personal: Ability to do detailed work. Ability to work independently. Accuracy. Manual dexterity. Good communication skills.

Professional: Aptitude for mathematics and science. Aptitude for technical work. Creative talent. Perception of customers' needs. Problem-solving ability. Teamworker.

Where The Jobs Are

Defense Contractors	Computer Service
Private Corporations	Organizations
Government	Research Organizations
Education	Radio & TV Stations
Broadcasting	

Research

Level	Job Title	Experience Needed
Entry	Electronics Technician	Professional Training
2	Design Technician	3-5 years
2	Research Technician	3-5 years
3	Director of Research & Development	6-10 years *With further education*

Salaries in Research

Level	Salary
Entry	$19,000 to $24,000
2	$22,000 to $25,000
2	$25,000 to $28,000
3	$28,000 to $35,000
3	$35,000 to $40,000 +

Salaries are higher for those with 2 or 4-year college degrees.

Qualifications

Personal: Ability to do detailed work. Ability to work independently. Accuracy. Good communication skills. Resourcefulness. Flexibility. Analytical skills.

Professional: Aptitude for mathematics and science. Aptitude for technical work. Ability to interpret and predict. Familiarity with computer. Problem-solving ability. Teamworker. Ability to conceptualize.

Where The Jobs Are
Defense Contracts
Private Corporations
Government
Education

Support Services

Level	Job Title	Experience Needed
Entry	Sales/Field Representative	Professional Training
Entry	Customer Service Representative	Professional Training
2	Instructor	1-3 years
2	Sales/Service Manager	2-5 years
2	Training Supervisor	2-5 years
3	Consultant	5-7 years
3	Administrator/Educator	6-8 years
3	Director of Marketing & Sales	7-10 years *With further education*

Salaries in Support Services
(See Salaries in Careers in Marketing and Teacher Education)

Qualifications

Personal: Positive attitude. Enthusiasm. Good communication skills. Well-groomed appearance. Self-motivated. Ability to work independently. Confidence. Tolerance for rejection.

Professional: Product knowledge. Perception of customers' needs. Effective marketing and sales skills.

Where The Jobs Are
Defense Contractors
Private Corporations
Government
Education
Manufacturers of Electronic Equipment

Production

Level	Job Title	Experience Needed
Entry	Electronics Technician	Professional Training
2	Production Technician	2-4 years
3	Production Manager	5-7 years

Salaries in Production
(See Salaries in Electronics Repair)

Qualifications

Personal: Accuracy. Good communication skills. Manual dexterity. Ability to do detailed work. Positive attitude. Enthusiasm. Ability to work under pressure.

Professional: Ability to plan, organize, coordinate and supervise. Concern for quality. Teamworker. Knowledge of safety procedures. Aptitude for figures, finances, inventories and quotas.

Where The Jobs Are
Manufacturing

Education

Level	Job Title	Experience Needed
Entry	Instructor	Professional Training and/or College Degree
2	Academic Department Head	4-6 years
3	Program Director	6-8 years
3	School Director	8-10 years

Salaries in Education
(See Salaries in Teacher Education)

Qualifications

Personal: Positive attitude. Enthusiasm. High energy level. Excellent communication skills. Listening skills. Flexibility. Ability to work under pressure.

Professional: Ability to organize and plan. Technical knowledge. Managerial skills. Ability to work with budgets. Teamworker.

Where The Jobs Are
Technical Schools
Vocational Schools
Electronic Departments

Trade Publications

EDN, Cahners Publishing Company, Cahner Building, 275 Washington Street, Newton, MA 02158

Electri·onics, Lake Publishing Corp., Box 159, 17730 West Peterson Road, Libertyville, IL 60048

Electronics, McGraw-Hill Publications, 1221 Avenue of the Americas, New York, NY 10020

Professional Associations

International Society of Certified Electronic Technicians
2708 W. Berry
Suite 3
Fort Worth, TX 76109

Jets Inc.
345 East 47th Street
New York, NY 10017

FASHION & RETAIL MANAGEMENT

Level	Management	Buying	Distribution	Visual Merchandising & Design	Sales
1 Entry *($15,000-$24,000)*	Mgr. Trainee Department Mgr. Assistant Store Mgr. Customer Service Representative	Buyer Trainee	Merchandise Planner	Window Trimmer Display Coordinator	Sales Representative

2
Mid-Management/
Specialists
($19,000-$30,000)
	Assistant Store Mgr.
	Area Mgr.
	Group Mgr.
	Divisional Mgr.
	Personnel Assistant
	Training Specialist
	Credit Mgr.
		Junior Buyer
		Merchandise Analyst
		Fashion Coordinator
			Administrative/Analyst
			  Planner
			MIS Specialist
			Coordinator of
			  Scheduling
			Traffic Manager
			Production Coordinator
			Inventory Coordinator
			Transportation
			  Specialist
				Display Director
				Freelancer
				Fashion Writer
				Design Assistant
				(With further education)
				Fashion Display
				  Specialist
					Sales Mgr.
					District Sales Mgr.

3
Management
($25,000-$70,000 +)
	Store Mgr.
	Personnel Mgr.
	Operations Mgr.
	Director of Training
	Director of Human
	  Resources
	VP/Human Resources
	VP/Operations
		Buyer
		Merchandise Mgr.
		VP/Merchandising
			MIS Director
			Transportation Mgr.
			Administrative Mgr.
			Inventory Control Mgr.
			Distribution Mgr.
			Warehousing/
			  Operations Mgr.
			VP/Operations
				Consultant
				Fashion Designer
				(With further education)
					Regional Sales Mgr.
					VP/Sales
					VP/Manufacturing

Recommended Pre-Professional Part-time/Summer Work Experience
Sales, Shipping/Receiving, Cashier, Waitperson, Inventory Clerk, Posting Clerk, Data Entry Clerk, CRT Clerk, Telephone Sales, Demonstrators, General Office Clerk

Management

Level	Job Title	Experience Needed
Entry	Manager Trainee	Professional Training
Entry	Department Manager	Professional Training
Entry	Assistant Store Manager	Professional Training
Entry	Customer Service Representative	Professional Training
2	*Assistant Store Manager	1-3 years
2	Area Manager	1-3 years
2	Group Manager	2-4 years
2	Divisional Manager	3-5 years
2	Personnel Assistant	3-5 years
2	Training Specialist	3-5 years
2	Credit Manager	5-6 years
3	Personnel Manager	6-8 years
3	Operations Manager	1-10 years
3	*Store Manager	3-8 years
3	Director of Training	5-7 years
3	Director of Human Resources	7-9 years
3	Vice President/Operations	9 + years
3	Vice President/ Human Resources	9 + years

(Varies greatly depending on size and type of retail operation)

Salaries in Management

Level	Salary
Entry	$16,000 to $24,000
2	$19,000 to $30,000
3	$30,000 to $45,000 +

Salaries are higher for those with 2- & 4-year college degrees and vary greatly with the size and type of retail operation.

Qualifications

Personal: Enthusiasm. Positive attitude. Ability to learn quickly. Flexibility. Willingness to work weekends, nights and holidays. Willingness to relocate helpful. Diplomacy.

Professional: Demonstrated leadership ability. Aptitude for dealing with figures, finances, inventories and quotas. Teamworker.

Where The Jobs Are
Department Stores
Specialty Stores
Bookstores
Grocery/Supermarkets
Boutiques
Computer Sales Centers
Government Surplus Organizations

Buying

Level	Job Title	Experience Needed
Entry	Buyer Trainee	Professional Training
2	Junior Buyer	1-3 years
2	Merchandise Analyst	3-5 years
2	Fashion Coordinator	1-3 years
3	Buyer	5-7 years
3	Merchandise Manager	5-7 years
3	Vice President of Merchandising	7-10 years

Salaries in Buying

Level	Salary
Entry	$16,000 to $22,000
2	$20,000 to $25,000
2	$22,000 to $29,000
3	$25,000 to $60,000
3	$35,000 to $70,000 +

Salaries are higher for those with 2 or 4-year college degrees and vary greatly depending on the size and type of retail operation.

Qualifications

Personal: Ability to make quick decisions. Ability to work at a fast pace. Ability to conceptualize. Good written and verbal communication. Creativity. Risk-taker. Negotiation skills. Willingness to travel extensively.

Professional: Product knowledge. Aptitude for dealing with figures, finances, inventories and quotas. Marketing and sales skills.

Where The Jobs Are
Department Stores
Specialty Stores Buying Offices
Resident Buying Offices

Distribution

Level	Job Title	Experience Needed
Entry	Merchandise Planner	Professional Training
2	Inventory Coordinator	1-2 years
2	Production Coordinator	1-2 years
2	Traffic Manager	2-4 years
2	Transportation Specialist	2-4 years
2	Administrative/Analyst Planner	3-5 years
2	Coordinator of Scheduling	3-5 years
2	MIS Specialist	3-5 years
3	Distribution Manager	4-6 years
3	Transportation Manager	4-6 years
3	Administrative Manager	4-6 years
3	Inventory Control Manager	4-6 years
3	Warehousing/Operations Manager	4-6 years
3	MIS Director	6-10 years
3	Vice President/Operations	6-10 years

Salaries in Distribution

Level	Salary
Entry	$17,000 to $22,000
2	$20,000 to $25,000
2	$25,000 to $30,000
2	$28,000 to $32,000
3	$32,000 to $36,000
3	$36,000 to $40,000
3	$40,000 to $50,000+

Salaries are higher for those with 2 or 4-year college degrees.

Qualifications

Personal: Ability to write and speak effectively. Patience. Listening skills. Ability to get along with people. Attention to detail. Organizational skills. Initiative. Good decision-making skills.

Professional: Familiarity with computers. Ability to plan and supervise. Aptitude for figures, finances, inventories and quotas.

Where The Jobs Are
Distribution Centers
Manufacturing Firms
Carriers
Public Warehouses
Material Handling Equipment Manufacturers
   and Dealers
Consulting Firms
Education
Print Media
Communications
Government
Computer Service Organizations

Visual Merchandising & Design

Level	Job Title	Experience Needed
Entry	Window Trimmer	Professional Training
Entry	Display Coordinator	Professional Training
2	Fashion Display Specialist	1-3 years
2	Display Director	3-5 years
2	Freelancer	2-5 years
2	Fashion Writer	2-5 years
2	Design Assistant	*With further education*
3	Consultant	5-7 years
3	Fashion Designer	*With further education*

Salaries in Visual Merchandising

Level	Salary
Entry	$15,000 to $19,000
Entry	$19,000 to $23,000
2	$20,000 to $25,000
2	$25,000 to $30,000
3	$30,000 to $35,000
3	$35,000 to $50,000
3	$50,000 to $65,000+

Salaries are higher for those with 2 or 4-year college degrees.

Qualifications

Personal: Ability to conceptualize. High energy level. Ability to make quick decisions. Ability to work under pressure.

Professional: Ability to work with budget restrictions. Willingness to travel. Willingness to work long hours including nights, weekends and holidays. Familiarity with current trends and events.

Where The Jobs Are
Manufacturers' Showrooms	Magazines
Design Houses	Consulting
Retail Stores	Apparel
Advertising Agencies	Manufacturers

Sales

Level	Job Title	Experience Needed
Entry	Sales Representative	Professional Training
2	Sales Manager	2-5 years
2	District Sales Manager	4-6 years
3	Regional Sales Manager	5-8 years
3	Vice President of Sales	7-10 years

Salaries in Sales
(See Salaries in Marketing Careers)

Qualifications

Personal: Positive attitude. Enthusiasm. High energy level. Ability to take rejection. Ability to work independently. Self-motivated. Negotiation skills. Confidence. Excellent communication skills. Tolerance for rejection.

Professional: Product knowledge. Perception of customer needs. Willingness to learn. Diplomacy. Good grooming.

Where The Jobs Are
Clothing Manufacturers
Design Houses
Apparel Manufacturers
Resident Buying Offices
Computer Manufacturers

Trade Publications

Advertising Age (weekly), Crain Communications, 740 North Rush Street, Chicago, IL 60611

Journal of Retailing (quarterly), New York University, 202 Tisch Building, New York, NY 10003

Stores Magazine (monthly), National Retail Merchants Association, 100 West 31st Street, New York, NY 10001

Women's Wear Daily (daily), Fairchild Publications, Inc., 7 East 12th Street, New York, NY 10003

Professional Associations

American Marketing Association
250 South Wacker Drive
Chicago, IL 60606

American Retail Federation
1616 H. Street, N.W.
Washington, D.C. 20006

Association of General Merchandise Chains
1625 I Street, N.W.
Washington, D.C. 20006

National Retail Merchants Association
100 West 31st Street
New York, NY 10001

MARKETING

Level	Sales/Management	Market Research	Telemarketing	Retailing

1
Entry
($17,000-$23,000)
	Sales Representative
	Customer Service
	  Representative
		Coder-Editor
		Junior Analyst
		Associate Analyst
			Telemarketing
			  Representative
			Junior Account
			  Executive
				Buyer Trainee
				Sales Representative

2
Mid-Management/
Specialists
($21,000-$50,000)
	Sales Supervisor
	Branch Sales Mgr.
	District Sales Mgr.
	Regional Sales Mgr.
	Central Region
	  Sales Mgr.
	Advertising Mgr.
		Analyst
		Senior Analyst
		Research Mgr.
		Product Mgr.
			Telemarketing Trainer
			Account Executive
			Telemarketing
			  Communicator
			Script Writer
			Supervisor
			Telemarketing
			  Center Mgr.
				Assistant Buyer
				Sales Mgr.
				Buyer
				Merchandise Mgr.

3 Management *($35,000-$65,000 +)*	National Sales Mgr. VP/Marketing & Sales President	Market Research Director Vice President President	Executive Administrator	Executive

Recommended Pre-Professional Part-time/Summer Work Experience
Sales, Telemarketing, General Office, Demonstrator, Messenger, Research Clerk, Coder, Data Entry Clerk, CRT Clerk, Waitperson

Sales/Management

Level	Job Title	Experience Needed
Entry	Sales Representative	Professional Training
Entry	Customer Service Representative	Professional Training
2	Sales Supervisor	1-2 years
2	Branch Sales Manager	2-4 years
2	District Sales Manager	3-5 years
2	Regional Sales Manager	5 + years
2	Central Region Sales Manager	6-8 years
2	Advertising Manager	6-8 years
3	National Sales Manager	7-9 years
3	Vice President/Marketing & Sales	7-9 years
3	President	8-10 years

Salaries in Sales/Management

Entry	$17,000 to $23,000
2	$23,000 to $35,000
2	$35,000 to $50,000
3	$50,000 to $65,000
3	$65,000 +

Salaries are higher for those with 2 or 4-year college degrees.

Qualifications

Personal: Positive attitude. Enthusiasm. Flexibility. High energy level. Good listening skills. Ability to speak and write effectively. Tolerance for rejection. Initiative. Self-motivation. Resourcefulness. Goal orientation.

Professional: Logic. Product knowledge. Perception of customer needs. Time management skills. Commitment. Good grooming. Professional social skills.

Where The Jobs Are

Private Industry	Computer Services
Advertising	Publishing Houses
Insurance	Equipment Suppliers
Financial Services	Product Manufacturers
Retailing	

Market Research

Level	Job Title	Experience Needed
Entry	Coder-Editor	Professional Training
Entry	Junior Analyst	Professional Training
Entry	Associate Analyst	Professional Training
2	Analyst	2-4 years
2	Senior Analyst	4-6 years
2	Research Manager	4-6 years
2	Product Manager	6-8 years
3	Market Research Director	7-9 years
3	Vice President	7-9 years
3	President	10 years +

Salaries in Market Research

Level	Salary
Entry	$17,000 to $23,000
2	$21,000 to $25,000
2	$23,000 to $27,000
2	$26,000 to $32,000
2	$32,000 to $40,000 +
3	$35,000 to $40,000
3	$40,000 to $50,000 +

Salaries are higher for those with 2 or 4-year college degrees.

Qualifications

Personal: Detail oriented. Good communication skills. Good organizational skills. Initiative. Patience. Resourcefulness. Ability to handle confidential information.

Professional: Familiarity with computers. Aptitude for figures. Analytical thinking. Problem-solving. Ability to conceptualize. Ability to evaluate and predict.

Where The Jobs Are
Private Industry
Government

Telemarketing

Level	Job Title	Experience Needed
Entry	Telemarketing Representative	Professional Training
Entry	Junior Account Executive	Professional Training
2	Telemarketing Trainer	2-4 years
2	Account Executive	2-4 years
2	Telemarketing Communicator	2-4 years
2	Script Writer	2-4 years
2	Supervisor	5-7 years
2	Telemarketing Center Manager	5-7 years
3	Executive/Administrator	7-10 years

Salaries in Telemarketing

Level	Salary
Entry	$17,000 to $22,000
2	$22,000 to $35,000
2	$35,000 to $50,000
3	$50,000 +

Salaries are higher for those with 2 or 4-year college degrees.

Qualifications

Personal: Positive attitude. Good listening skills. Enthusiasm. Goal orientation. Self motivation. Tolerance for rejection.

Professional: Product knowledge. Perception of customers' needs.

Where The Jobs Are
Private Industry
Education
Government
Telemarketing
Consulting
Advertising Agencies
Computer Service Organizations
Publishing Houses

Retailing

(See Careers in Fashion & Retail Management)

Trade Publications

Telemarketing Magazine, 17 Park Street, Norwalk, CT 06854

Teleprofessional Magazine, Box 123, Del Mar, CA 92014

Telemarketing Insiders Report, 470 Main Street, Suite 108, Keyport, NJ 07735

Professional Associations

Telemarketing Recruiters, Inc.
114 East 32nd Street
New York, NY 10016

Telemarketing Council
Direct Marketing Association
6 East 43rd Street
New York, NY 10017

American Telemarketing Association
104 Wilmot Street
Deerfield, IL 60615

MEDICAL ASSISTANT

Level	Private Practices, Hospitals, Health Maintenance Organizations	Education	Medical Suppliers
1 Entry *($16,000-$23,000)*	Medical Assistant	Instructor	Sales Representative
2 Mid-Management/ Specialists *($23,000-$28,000)*	Claims Examiner Claims Representative Research Assistant Clinical Medical Assistant Administrative Medical Office Assistant	Department Head Medical Librarian	Sales Manager

3
Management
($28,000-$35,000+)
	Medical Records
	   Administrator
	Office Mgr.
	Nurse
	(With further education)
	Research Analyst
	Doctor
	(With further education)
		School Director
		Administrator/Education
			Director of Marketing
			   & Sales

Recommended Pre-Professional Part-time/Summer Work Experience
Office Clerk, Receptionist, General Office Clerk, Lab Assistant, Nurse's Aid, Volunteer

Private Practices, Hospitals, Health Maintenance Organizations

Level	Job Title	Experience Needed
Entry	Medical Assistant	Professional Training
2	Claims Examiner	1-3 years
2	Claims Representative	2-5 years
2	Clinical Medical Assistant	1-3 years
2	Administrative Medical Office Assistant	3-5 years
3	Medical Records Administrator	5-7 years
3	Nurse	*With further education*
3	Research Analyst	7-10 years
3	Doctor	*With further education*

Salaries in Private Practices, Hospitals, Health Maintenance Organizations

Entry	$16,000 to $23,000
2	$23,000 to $25,000
2	$25,000 to $28,000
3	$28,000 to $31,000
3	$31,000 to $35,000 +

Salaries are higher for those with 2 or 4-year college degrees.

Qualifications

Personal: Listening skills. Courtesy. Neat, well-groomed appearance. Patience.

Professional: Ability to train on-the-job. Confidentiality. Computer and word processing skills. Good organizational and management skills.

Where The Jobs Are
Physicians' Group Practice
Physician's Independent Practice
Clinics
Freestanding Emergency Centers
Hospitals
Nursing Homes
Health Care Centers
Rehabilitation Centers
Health Maintenance Organizations

Education

Level	Job Title	Experience Needed
Entry	Instructor	Professional Training and/or College Degree
2	Academic Department Head	4-5 years
2	Medical Librarian	4-5 years
3	School Director	8-10 + years
3	Administrator/Education	6-8 years

Salaries in Education
(See Salaries in Teacher Education)

Qualifications

Personal: Patience. Good communication skills. Ability to manage.

Professional: Awareness of policies and laws in the health care field. Planning and organizational skills. Ability to work with budgets.

Where The Jobs Are
Career Schools
Hospitals
Medical Assistant Departments

Medical Suppliers

Level	Job Title	Experience Needed
Entry	Sales Representative	Professional Training
2	Sales Manager	3-6 years
3	Director of Marketing & Sales	7-10 years years *(May need further education)*

Salaries with Medical Suppliers
(See Salaries in Careers in Marketing)

Qualifications

Personal: Positive attitude. Good communication skills. Ability to work independently. Self-motivated. Tolerance for rejection. Confidence.

Professional: Product knowledge. Perception of customer needs. Familiarity with medical terminology.

Where The Jobs Are
Medical Supply Companies
Pharmaceutical Houses

Trade Publication

Professional Medical Assistant, American Association of Medical Assistants, 20 North Wacker Drive, Chicago, IL 60606

Professional Associations

The American Association of Medical Assistants
20 North Wacker Drive
Suite 1575
Chicago, IL 60606

American Medical Technologists
Registered Medical Assistants
710 Higgins Rd.
Park Ridge, IL 60068

PARALEGAL

Level	Private Practices, Community Legal Services, Government Agencies	Corporations	Law Libraries	Education	Legal Publishing Houses	Computer Firms
1 Entry ($19,000-$24,000)	Paralegal Legal Assistant	Paralegal	Legal Technician	Paralegal Instructor	Paralegal	Sales Representative
2 Mid-Management/ Specialists ($24,000-$40,000)	Paralegal Supervisor	Senior Legal Assistant	Research Assistant Information Specialist Litigation Paralegal	Placement Director	Editor	Systems Programmer
3 Management ($40,000-$55,000+)	Law Office Administrator Lawyer (With further education)	Law Office Administrator	Law Library Mgr.	Program Director	Consultant/ Advisor	Marketing Analyst

Recommended Pre-Professional Part-time/Summer Work Experience
General Office Clerk, Messenger, Library Clerk, Research Assistant, Coder, Legal Secretary, Court Reporter, Sales, Telemarketing

Private Practices, Community Legal Services, Government Agencies

Level	Job Title	Experience Needed
Entry	Paralegal	Professional Training
Entry	Legal Assistant	Professional Training
2	Paralegal Supervisor	2-5 years
3	Law Office Administrator	5-7 years
3	Lawyer	With further education

*Salaries in Private Practices, Community Legal Services, Government Agencies

Entry	$19,000 to $24,000 (10-25% for overtime)
2	$24,000 to $34,000
2	$34,000 to $40,000
3	$40,000 to $55,000+

After two years on the job, Paralegal salaries often increase by more than 20%.

Qualifications

Personal: Courtesy. Proven written and verbal communication skills. Interest in current events and history. Detail-oriented. Patience.

Professional: Familiarity with legal terminology. Research and investigative skills. Ethical. Confidentiality. Logic. Teamwork.

Where The Jobs Are
Community Legal Service Projects
Government Agencies
Private Practices

Corporations

Level	Job Title	Experience Needed
Entry	Paralegal	Professional Training
2	Senior Legal Assistant	2-5 years
3	Law Office Administrator	5-8 years

*Salaries in Corporations

(See Salaries in Private Practices, Community Legal Services and Government Agencies)

Qualifications

Personal: Positive attitude. Professional appearance. Enthusiasm. Detail oriented. Proven written and verbal communication skills. Patience.

Professional: Familiarity with legal terminology. Research and investigative skills. Ethical. Confidentiality. Logic. Teamwork.

Where The Jobs Are
Private Corporations
Public Businesses

Law Libraries

Level	Job Title	Experience Needed
Entry	Legal Technician	Professional Training
2	Research Assistant	3-6 years
2	Information Specialist	4-7 years
2	Litigation Paralegal	5-7 years
3	Law Library Manager	7-10 years

Salaries in Law Libraries

(See Salaries in Private Practices, Community Legal Services, Government Agencies)

Qualifications

Personal: Positive attitude. Detail oriented. Patience. Interest in current events and history.

Professional: Familiarity with legal terminology. Research and investigative skills. Ethical. Confidentiality.

Where The Jobs Are
Law Libraries

Education

Level	Job Title	Experience Needed
Entry	Paralegal Instructor	Professional Training
2	Placement Director	3-5 years
3	Program Director	6-10 years

Salaries in Education

(See Salaries in Teacher Education)

Qualifications

Personal: Leadership qualities. Excellent communication skills. High energy level. Positive attitude. Enthusiasm. Patience.

Professional: Ethics. Knowledge of subject matter. Teamworker. Well organized. Willingness to retrain.

Where The Jobs Are
Education
Private Corporations
Consulting

Legal Publishing Houses

Level	Job Title	Experience Needed
Entry	Paralegal	Professional Training
Entry	Proofreader	Professional Training
Entry	Marketing Representative	Professional Training
2	Junior Editor	3-5 years
3	Senior Editor	6-8 years
3	Consultant/Advisor	8-10 years

Salaries in Legal Publishing Houses

Entry	$19,000 to $24,000
Entry	$24,000 to $26,000
2	$26,000 to $30,000
3	$30,000 to $37,000
3	$37,000 to $50,000 +

Qualifications

Personal: Positive attitude. Enthusiasm. Detail oriented. Proven written and verbal communication skills. Initiative. Professional appearance.

Professional: Problem-solving ability. Analytical thinking. Ability to conceptualize. Decision-making skills. Familiarity with legal terminology.

Where The Jobs Are
Legal Publishing Houses

Computer Firms

Level	Job Title	Experience Needed
Entry	Sales Representative	Professional Training
2	Systems Programmer	3-5 years
3	Marketing Analyst	5-8 years

Salaries in Computer Firms

(See Salaries in Computer Systems)

Qualifications

Personal: Excellent verbal communication skills. Confidence. Enthusiasm. Professional appearance. Ability to work independently. Self-motivated. Flexibility.

Professional: Product knowledge. Perception of customer needs. Willingness to learn. Problem-solving skills. Decision-making skills.

Where The Jobs Are
Computer Manufacturers
Computer Sales Firms
Research Organizations
Consulting
Computer Service Organizations

Trade Publications

National Paralegal Reporter, National Federation of Paralegal Associations, P.O. Box 40158, Overland Park, KS 66204

American Association for Paralegal Education Newsletter, American Association for Paralegal Education, P.O. Box 40244, Overland Park, KS 66204

Bulletin of the American Association for Paralegal Education, American Association for Paralegal Education, P.O. Box 40244, Overland Park, KS 66204

International Legal Practitioner, International Bar Association, Two Harewood Place, Hanover Square, London WIR 2HB, England, United Kingdom

Professional Associations

National Association of Paralegal Personnel
Box 8202
Northfield, IL 60093

National Association of Legal Assistants
1420 S. Utica
Tulsa, OK 74104

National Paralegal Association
10 South Pine Street
Doylestown, PA 18901

National Federation of Paralegal Associations
Box 40158
Overland Park, KS 66204

American Bar Association
750 N. Lake Shore Drive
Chicago, IL 60611

Standing Committee on Legal Assistants
American Bar Association
750 North Lake Shore Drive
Chicago, IL 60611

SECRETARIAL SCIENCES

Level	Administration	Information Processing	Specialization
1 Entry *($17,000-$24,000)*	Receptionist Secretary Administrative Secretary Executive Secretary	Word Processor Page Creator Editor Coder Proofreader	Legal Secretary Medical Secretary Technical Secretary School Secretary Membership Secretary Sales Secretary Travel Secretary Social Secretary International Group Secretary Statistical Typist City Mortgage & Real Estate Secretary

2
Mid-Management/
Specialists
($24,000-$29,000)
	Administrative Assistant
	Conference & Meeting
	  Coordinator
	Department Manager
		Information Packager
		Systems Administrator
		Information Broker
		Information Manager
		Coding Clerk Supervisor
			Paralegal
			Legal Assistant
			Personnel Clerk
			Medical Records Technician
			Customer Service
			  Representative

3 Management *($29,000-$40,000 +)*	Executive Assistant Private Secretary Office Manager	Production Planner Financial Analyst Marketing Director Research Analyst *(See Careers in Word Processing)*	Personnel Assistant Sales Assistant Manager Trainee Office Manager *(See Paralegal Careers)*

Recommended Pre-Professional Part-time/Summer Work Experience
Sales, File Clerk, CRT Clerk, Typist, Receptionist, Word Processor, Data Entry Operator, Inventory Clerk, Computer Operator, Library Assistant, General Office Clerk, Messenger

Administration

Level	Job Title	Experience Needed
Entry	Receptionist	Professional Training
Entry	Secretary	Professional Training
Entry	Administrative Secretary	Professional Training
Entry	Executive Secretary	Professional Training
2	Administrative Assistant	1-3 years
2	Conference & Meeting Coordinator	2-4 years
2	Department Manager	3-5 years
3	Executive Assistant	4-6 years
3	Private Secretary	5-7 years
3	Office Manager	5-7 years

Salaries in Administration

Entry	$17,000 to $24,000
2	$24,000 to $29,000
3	$29,000 to $40,000 +

Qualifications

Personal: Positive attitude. Enthusiasm. Detail oriented. Excellent communication skills. Flexibility. Ability to work well under pressure. Self-starter. Dependable.

Professional: Good typing, spelling, and grammar skills. Decision-making skills. Professional appearance. Responsible. Teamworker. Resourcefulness. Ability to work independently.

Where The Jobs Are

Insurance	Medical Offices
Banking	State & Local Government
Hotels	Federal Government
Travel Corporations	Manufacturing
Education	Private Corporations
Law Offices	

Information Processing

Level	Job Title	Experience Needed
Entry	*Word Processor	Professional Training
Entry	Page Creator	Professional Training
Entry	Editor	Professional Training
Entry	Coder	Professional Training
Entry	Proofreader	Professional Training
2	Information Packager	2-4 years
2	Systems Administrator	2-4 years
2	Information Broker	2-4 years
2	Information Manager	3-5 years
2	Coding Clerk Supervisor	3-5 years
3	Production Planner	4-6 years
3	Financial Analyst	5-7 years
3	Marketing Director	7-10 years
3	Research Analyst	7-10 years

See Careers in Word Processing

Salaries in Information Processing

Entry	$17,000 to $22,000
2	$23,000 to $27,000
3	$27,000 to $33,000 +

Qualifications

Personal: Positive attitude. Enthusiasm. Detail oriented. Excellent written communication skills. Ability to work well under pressure. Ability to meet deadlines.

Professional: Proofreading skills, ability to edit texts effectively. Good typing, spelling and grammar. Ability to work independently. Team-worker. Professional appearance.

Where The Jobs Are
Insurance
Banking
Education
Publishing Houses
Advertising Agencies
Media
Law Offices
State & Local Government
Federal Government
Private Corporations

Specialization

Level	Job Title	Experience Needed
Entry	Legal Secretary	Professional Training
Entry	Medical Secretary	Professional Training
Entry	Technical Secretary	Professional Training
Entry	School Secretary	Professional Training
Entry	Membership Secretary	Professional Training
Entry	Sales Secretary	Professional Training
Entry	Travel Secretary	Professional Training
Entry	Social Secretary	Professional Training
Entry	International Group Secretary	Professional Training
Entry	Statistical Typist	Professional Training
Entry	City Mortgage & Real Estate Secretary	Professional Training
2	*Paralegal	3-5 years
2	Legal Assistant	3-5 years
2	Personnel Clerk	3-5 years
2	Medical Records Technician	3-5 years
2	Customer Service Representative	3-5 years
3	Personnel Assistant	5-7 years
3	Sales Assistant	5-7 years
3	Management Trainee	5-7 years
3	Office Manager	6-8 years

*See Paralegal Careers

Salaries in Specialization

Entry	$17,000 to $22,000
2	$22,000 to $27,000
3	$27,000 to $35,000 +

Qualifications

Personal: Positive attitude. Enthusiasm. Excellent verbal & written communication skills. Flexibility. Ability to work well under pressure. Dependable.

Professional: Good typing, spelling and grammatical skills. Decision-making skills. Professional appearance. Teamworker. Resourcefulness. Ability to work independently. Knowledge of specialized terminology.

Where The Jobs Are
Law Offices
Hospitals
Medical Offices
Travel Corporations
Hotels
Real Estate Companies
Insurance
Banking
Education
State & Local Government
Federal Government

TRAVEL TOURISM

Level	Travel Agencies	Corporate Travel	Tourist Bureaus/ Offices	Convention & Visitors' Bureaus
1 Entry *($13,000-$19,000)*	Travel Counselor Reservationist Travel Agent Receptionist	Reservationist Travel Agent Receptionist Travel Counselor	Information Coordinator	Coordinator/Travel Information Center Coordinator of Membership Sales
2 Mid-Management/ Specialists *($19,000-$24,000)*	Incentive Travel Specialist Outside Sales Agent Employment Interviewer	Travel Specialist	Attractions Specialist Research Analyst Surveyor Assistant Marketing Director Interpreter	Destinations Promoter Public Relations Specialist Convention Sales Mgr. Convention Center Mgr. Finance Mgr. Director of Transportation
3 Management *($24,000-$45,000 +)*	Travel Director Travel Agency Manager Personnel Manager Owner/Operator	Travel Director Corporate Travel Mgr.	Director of Marketing & Sales State Travel Director Chief Tourism Officer Deputy Commissioner of Tourism Development Commissioner of Tourism	Executive Director VP/Sales & Marketing

Level	Chambers of Commerce	Department of Economic Development	Education	Tour Operations
1 Entry *($13,000-$19,000)*	Membership Coordinator	Information Coordinator	Instructor	Tour Guide Tour Escort Tourist Information Assistant
2 Mid-Management/ Specialists *($19,000-$24,000)*	Sales Mgr. Research Analyst Program Coordinator	Economic Development Coordinator Demographer Urban Planner Director of Public Safety	Academic Department Head	Tour Operator Director of Escort Services Director of Tour Guides Tour Director
3 Management *($24,000-$45,000 +)*	Executive Director VP/Marketing & Sales	Executive Director	Education Consultant	Mgr. of Tour Operations

Recommended Pre-Professional Part-time/Summer Work Experience
Sales, Receptionist, General Office Clerk, Volunteer, Coder, Telephone Sales, Waitperson, Travel Assistant

TRAVEL TOURISM

Level	Associations	Conference & Meeting Planning	Hotels, Motels & Resorts	Public Relations
1 Entry *($13,000-$19,000)*	Sales Representative Coordinator of Membership Sales	*See Careers in Hotels, Motels & Resorts*	**Resorts** Reservationist Reservations Manager Reception Manager Front Desk Clerk Concierge	Account Representative
2 Mid-Management/ Specialists *($19,000-$24,000)*	Public Relations Specialist Research Analyst Meeting Planner Special Events Coordinator Sales Manager		Meeting Planner Conference Planner Convention Planner Front Office Mgr. Mail & Information Coordinator Special Events Coordinator Conference Service Coordinator	Account Manager Speaker Informer Research & Evaluator Special Events Coordinator Press Coordinator Communications Technician
3 Management *($24,000-$45,000 +)*	Director of Marketing & Sales Executive Director VP/Marketing & Sales		Group Sales Mgr. Convention Sales Mgr.	Account Executive Director of Public Relations VP/Communications

Level	Travel Writing	Airlines/Airports	Car Rental Agencies	Cruiselines
1 Entry *($13,000-$19,000)*	Travel Writer	Reservationist Customer Service Representative Flight Attendant Ticket Agent Sales Representative	Customer Service Agent Rental Sales Representative	Sales Representative Reservationist
2 Mid-Management/ Specialists *($19,000-$24,000)*	Proofreader Coder Freelancer	Airport Operations Agent Passenger Service Agent Ramp Agent Customs Inspector	Station Manager Lead Agent	Activities Coordinator Health Club Director Recreation Director
3 Management *($24,000-$45,000 +)*	Travel Editor	Supervisor of Gate Services Airline Schedule Analyst Airport Manager Airport Security Officer Schedule Planning Manager	City Manager	Cruise Director Director of Sales & Marketing

Recommended Pre-Professional Part-time/Summer Work Experience
Sales, Receptionist, General Office Clerk, Volunteer, Coder, Telephone Sales, Waitperson, Travel Assistant

Travel Agencies

Level	Job Title	Experience Needed
Entry	Travel Counselor	Professional Training
Entry	Reservationist	Professional Training
Entry	Travel Agent	Professional Training
Entry	Receptionist	Professional Training
2	Incentive Travel Specialist	1-2 years
2	Outside Sales Agent	1-2 years
2	Employment Interviewer	2-4 years
3	Travel Director	4-6 years
3	Travel Agency Manager	4-6 years
3	Personnel Manager	4-6 years
3	Owner/Operator	Varies

Salaries in Travel Agencies

Entry	$13,000 to $16,000
Entry	$16,000 to $19,000
2	$19,000 to $22,000
3	$22,000 to $26,000 +

Qualifications

Personal: Positive attitude. High energy level. Enthusiasm. Ability to work with budgets. Negotiation skills. Good communication skills. Effective interpersonal skills. Flexibility. Patience.

Professional: Familiarity with computers. Familiarity with geographic areas and destinations. Strong marketing and sales skills.

Where The Jobs Are
Travel Agencies
Department Stores

Corporate Travel

Level	Job Title	Experience Needed
Entry	Reservationist	Professional Training
Entry	Travel Agent	Professional Training
Entry	Receptionist	Professional Training
Entry	Travel Counselor	Professional Training
2	Travel Specialist	1-3 years
3	Travel Director	3-5 years
3	Corporate Travel Manager	3-5 years

Salaries in Corporate Travel

Entry	$17,000 to $20,000
Entry	$20,000 to $22,000
2	$22,000 to $25,000
2	$25,000 to $28,000
3	$28,000 to $31,000
3	$31,000 to $35,000 +

Qualifications

Personal: Good communication skills. Effective interpersonal skills. Professional appearance. Positive attitude. Enthusiasm. Articulate. Initiative. Flexible.

Professional: Awareness of product knowledge. Strong sales and marketing skills.

Where The Jobs Are
Corporate Travel Firms
Private Industry
Government

Tourist Bureaus/Offices

Level	Job Title	Experience Needed
Entry	Information Coordinator	Professional Training
2	Attractions Specialist	Professional Training
2	Research Analyst	1-3 years
2	Surveyor	1-3 years
2	Asst. Marketing Director	3-5 years
2	Interpreter	3-5 years
3	Director of Marketing & Sales	5-8 years
3	State Travel Dieector	5-8 years
3	Chief Tourism Officer	8-10 years
3	Deputy Commissioner of Tourism Development	8-10 years
3	Commissioner of Tourism	8-10 years

Salaries in Tourist Bureaus/Offices

Level	Salary
Entry	$13,000 to $16,000
2	$16,000 to $19,000
2	$19,000 to $21,000
2	$21,000 to $24,000
3	$24,000 to $27,000
3	$27,000 to $34,000
3	$34,000 to $50,000 +

Qualifications

Personal: Positive attitude. Enthusiasm. Resource-fulness. Ability to communicate well. Effective interpersonal skills. Flexibility. Detail oriented. Well groomed.

Professional: Ability to interpret, predict and organize. Knowledge of area lodging, restaurants, attractions. Strong marketing and sales skills. Familiarity with computers. Attention to national trends. Successful completion of civil service exam.

Where The Jobs Are
Research Division
Promotion Division
Information Division
News Division
Public Affairs Division

Convention & Visitors' Bureau

Level	Job Title	Experience Needed
Entry	Coordinator/Travel Information Center	Professional Training
Entry	Coordinator of Membership Sales	Professional Training
2	Destination Promoter	1-3 years
2	Public Relations Specialist	1-3 years
2	Convention Sales Manager	3-5 years
2	Convention Center Manager	3-5 years
2	Finance Manager	3-5 years
2	Director of Transportation	3-5 years
3	Executive Director	5-7 years
3	Vice President of Sales & Marketing	7-10 years

Salaries in Convention & Visitors' Bureaus
(See Salaries in Travel Tourism — Tourist Bureaus/Offices)

Qualifications

Personal: Positive attitude. Enthusiasm. Accurate writing skills. Detail oriented. Flexibility. Good communication skills. Effective interpersonal skills. Well groomed. Resourcefulness.

Professional: Ability to conceptualize. Strong marketing and sales skills. Good organizational skills. Knowledge of area attractions, services, lodging and restaurants.

Where The Jobs Are
Convention & Visitors' Bureau

Chambers of Commerce

Level	Job Title	Experience Needed
Entry	Membership Coordinator	Professional Training
2	Sales Manager	3-5 years
2	Research Analyst	1-3 years
2	Program Coordinator	1-3 years
3	Executive Director	5-7 years
3	Vice President/Marketing & Sales	7-10 years

Salaries with Chambers of Commerce
(See Careers in Travel Tourism — Tourist Bureau Offices)

Qualifications

Personal: Positive attitude. Enthusiasm. Resourcefulness. Ability to communicate well. Flexibility. Detail oriented. Well groomed.

Professional: Awareness of area businesses. Ability to coordinate and plan. Strong marketing and sales skills.

Where The Jobs Are
Sales
Research
Promotion

Department of Economic Development

Level	Job Title	Experience Needed
Entry	Information Coordinator	Professional Training
2	Economic Development Coordinator	1-3 years
2	Demographer	2-4 years
2	Urban Planner	2-4 years
2	Director of Public Safety	3-5 years
3	Executive Director	5-7 years

Salaries with Departments of Economic Development
(See Salaries in Travel Tourism — Tourist Bureau/Offices)

Qualifications

Personal: Detail oriented. Ability to work independently. Accurate writing skills. Resourcefulness.

Professional: Familiarity with computers. Ability to evaluate, plan, coordinate and interpret data. Awareness of local and national economic trends.

Where The Jobs Are
Promotion
Research

Education

Level	Job Title	Experience Needed
Entry	Instructor	Professional Training and/or College Degree
2	Academic Department Head	4-5 years
3	School Director/ Administrator	6-8 years
3	Education Consultant	8-10 years

Salaries in Education
(See Salaries in Careers in Teacher Education)

Qualifications

Personal: Listening skills. Patience. Enthusiasm. Positive attitude. Detail oriented. Flexibility. High energy level. Good communication skills.

Professional: Familiarity with computers. Broad knowledge of Travel and Tourism industry. Good organizational skills.

Where The Jobs Are
Schools
Consulting Firms
Travel Companies

Tour Operations

Level	Job Title	Experience Needed
Entry	Tour Guide	Professional Training
Entry	Tour Escort	Professional Training
Entry	Tourist Information Assistant	Professional Training
2	Tour Operator	1-2 years
2	Director of Escort Services	3-5 years
2	Director of Tour Guides	3-5 years
2	Tour Director	3-5 years
3	Manager of Tour Operations	5 + years

Salaries in Tour Operations
(See Salaries in Travel Tourism - Travel Agencies)

Qualifications

Personal: High energy level. Enthusiasm. Positive attitude. Effective interpersonal skills.

Professional: Problem solving ability. Leadership skills. Ability to settle complaints and give advice. Background in geography.

Where The Jobs Are
Tour Operators
Attractions
Government
Private Industry

Associations

Level	Job Title	Experience Needed
Entry	Sales Representatives	Professional Training
Entry	Coordinator of Membership Sales	Professional Training
2	Public Relations Specialist	1-3 years
2	Research Analyst	1-3 years
2	Meeting Planner	1-3 years
2	Special Events Coordinator	1-3 years
2	Sales Manager	3-5 years
3	Director of Sales & Marketing	5-7 years
3	Executive Director	5-7 years
3	VP/Marketing & Sales	7-10 years

Salaries with Associations
(See Salaries in Travel Tourism - Tourist Bureaus/Offices)

Qualifications

Personal: Good communication skills. Enthusiasm. Positive attitude. Initiative. Detail oriented. Accurate writing skills.

Professional: Strong marketing and sales skills. Familiarity with computers. Awareness of local and national business interests. Ability to supervise.

Where The Jobs Are
Professional Associations
Chambers of Commerce

Conference & Meeting Planning

(See Careers in Travel Tourism - Hotels, Motels & Resorts)

Where The Jobs Are
Company or Corporate Meeting Planners
Associations *(or similar and usually not-for-profit organizations)*
Independent Meeting Planners

Hotels, Motels & Resorts

Level	Job Title	Experience Needed
Entry	Reservationist	Professional Training
Entry	Reservations Manager	Professional Training
Entry	Reception Manager	Professional Training
Entry	Front Desk Clerk	Professional Training
Entry	Concierge	Professional Training
2	Meeting Planner	1-2 years
2	Conference Planner	1-2 years
2	Convention Planner	1-2 years
2	Front Office Manager	1-2 years
2	Mail & Information Coordinator	1-2 years
2	Special Events Coordinator	3-5 years
2	Conference Service Coordinator	3-5 years
3	Group Sales Manager	5 + years
3	Convention Sales Manager	5 + years

Salaries in Hotels, Motels & Resorts

Entry	$16,000 to $22,000	
2	$22,000 to $25,000	
2	$25,000 to $29,000 +	
3	$29,000 to $33,000	
3	$33,000 to $35,000 +	

Qualifications

Personal: Positive attitude. High energy level. Patience. Confidence. Good grooming. Professional appearance. Flexibility. Excellent interpersonal skills.

Professional: Negotiation skills. Sales and marketing skills. Ability to supervise.

Where The Jobs Are
Hotels
Motels
Resorts

Public Relations

Level	Job Title	Experience Needed
Entry	Account Representative	Professional Training
2	Account Manager	1-3 years
2	Speaker	2-4 years
2	Informer	2-4 years
2	Researcher & Evaluator	2-4 years
2	Special Events Coordinator	2-4 years
2	Press Coordinator	3-6 years
2	Communications Technician	3-6 years
3	Account Executive	6-8 years
3	Director of Public Relations	6-8 years
3	Vice President of Communications	8-10 years

Salaries in Public Relations
(See Salaries in Careers in Marketing - Advertising/Public Relations)

Qualifications

Personal: Exellent written and verbal communication skills. Effective interpersonal skills. Detail oriented. Positive attitude. Enthusiasm. High energy level. Flexibility. Ability to work under pressure.

Professional: Ability to meet deadlines. Strong sales and marketing skills. Ability to supervise.

Where The Jobs Are
Convention & Visitors' Bureaus
Hotels, Motels & Resorts
Civic Centers
Tourist Bureaus/Offices
Chambers of Commerce
Conference & Meeting Planning
Departments of Economic Development

Travel Writing

Level	Job Title	Experience Needed
Entry	Travel Writer	Professional Training
2	Proofreader	1-2 years
2	Coder	1-2 years
2	Freelancer	2-4 years
3	Travel Editor	5-8 years

Salaries in Travel Writing

Salaries can pay well but will vary. Many publications feel that travel is a perk and pay less - even one-third - for travel stories than for other features.

Qualifications

Personal: Excellent writing skills. Detail oriented. High energy level.

Professional: Ability to conceptualize. Knowledge of subject matter. Ability to meet deadlines.

Where The Jobs Are

Travel Journals
Publishing Houses
Magazines
Public Relations Departments
Advertising Agencies
Research Organizations

Airlines/Airports

Level	Job Title	Experience Needed
Entry	Reservationist	Professional Training
Entry	Custom Service Representative	Professional Training
Entry	Flight Attendant	Professional Training
Entry	Ticket Agent	Professional Training
Entry	Sales Representative	Professional Training
2	Airport Operations Agent	1-3 years
2	Passenger Service Agent	1-2 years
2	Ramp Agent	1-2 years
2	Customs Inspector	1-3 years
3	Supervisor of Gate Services	3-5 years
3	Airline Schedule Analyst	3-5 years
3	Airport Manager	5-8 years
3	Airport Security Officer	3-5 years
3	Schedule Planning Manager	5-7 years

Qualifications

Personal: Positive attitude. Enthusiasm. Good communication skills. Effective interpersonal skills. Well groomed. Willingness to work nights, holidays, and weekends. Flexibility.

Professional: Awareness of airline/airport policies and procedures. Familiarity with computers. Supervisory skills. Planning skills.

Where The Jobs Are

Airlines
Airports

Salaries in Airlines/Airports

Level	Salary
Entry	$16,000 to $20,000
2	$20,000 to $23,000
2	$23,000 to $25,000
3	$25,000 to $28,000
3	$28,000 to $32,000
3	$32,000 to $39,000 +

Car Rental Agencies

Level	Job Title	Experience Needed
Entry	Customer Service Agent	Professional Training
Entry	Rental Sales	
	Representative	Professional Training
2	Station Manager	1-3 years
2	Lead Agent	1-3 years
3	City Manager	3-5 years

Salaries with Car Rental Agencies

Entry	$13,000 to $19,000
2	$19,000 to $24,000
3	$24,000 to $35,000
3	$35,000 to $50,000+

Qualifications

Personal: Positive attitude. Enthusiasm. High energy level. Good communication skills. Effective interpersonal skills.

Professional: Ability to work with figures. Negotiation skills. Knowledge of geographic areas helpful. Resourcefulness.

Where The Jobs Are
Car Rental Agencies
Airports
Hotels
Major Shopping Malls

Cruiselines

Level	Job Title	Experience Needed
Entry	Sales Representative	Professional Training
Entry	Reservationist	Professional Training
2	Activities Coordinator	1-3 years
2	Health Club Director	2-4 years
2	Recreation Director	2-4 years
3	Cruise Director	5-8 years
3	Director of Sales	
	& Marketing	7-9 years

*Salaries with Cruiselines

Entry	$13,000 to $19,000
Entry	$19,000 to $21,000
2	$21,000 to $23,000
2	$23,000 to $26,000
3	$26,000 to $37,000+

Most sales positions pay 25% in incentive pay & bonuses

Qualifications

Personal: Positive attitude. High energy level. Enthusiasm. Good communication skills. Effective interpersonal skills. Flexibility.

Professional: Knowledge of safety policies and procedures. Strong marketing and sales skills.

Where The Jobs Are
Cruiselines (on board)
Cruiselines (on land)

Trade Publications

Meeting News, 1515 Broadway, New York, NY 10036

Travel Weekly, One Park Avenue, New York, NY 10016

International Travel News, 2120-28th Street, Sacramento, CA 95818

Travelhost, 8080 N. Central Exp., 14th Floor, Dallas, TX 75206

Courier, National Tour Association, 546 East Main Street, Lexington, KY 40058

Professional Associations

National Tour Association
546 East Main Street
Lexington, KY 40058

Travel Industry Association of America
Suite 600
1899 L. St., NW
Washington, DC 20036

Association of Travel Marketing Executives
804 D. St., NE
Washington, DC 20002

Travel and Tourism Research Association
Box 8066
Foothill Station
Salt Lake City, VT 84108

International Association of Convention & Visitor Bureaus
Box 758
Champaign, IL 61820

American Society of Travel Agents
4400 MacArthur Blvd., NW
Washington, DC 20007

WORD PROCESSING

Level	Corporations	Education	Vendor Companies	Consulting	Employment Agencies
1 Entry *($17,000-$20,000)*	Word Processor Lead Word Processing Operator	Instructor	Sales Representative	Training Specialist	Instructor

2
Mid-Management/
  Specialists
($20,000-$24,000)
	Coordinator/Scheduler
	Records Manager
	Proofreader
	Trainer
		Academic Department
		  Head
			Marketing Support
			  Representative
			Sales Manager
				Consultant	Employment
					Counselor

3
Management
($24,000-$28,000 +)
	Administrative
	  Support Mgr.
	Night Shift Supervisor
	Word Processing
	  Center Mgr.
		Program Director
		Consultant
			Director of Marketing
			  & Sales
			VP/Marketing & Sales
				President/Owner	Owner/Manager

Recommended Pre-Professional Part-time/Summer Work Experience
Data Entry Operator, Clerk Typist, Messenger, Word Processing Operator Trainee, File Clerk, CRT Clerk

Corporations

Level	Job Title	Experience Needed
Entry	Word Processor	Professional Training
Entry	Lead Word Processing Operator	Professional Training
2	Coordinator/Scheduler	1-3 years
2	Records Manager	3-5 years
2	Proofreader	1-3 years
2	Trainer	3-5 years
3	Administrative Support Manager	5-7 years
3	Night Shift Supervisor	4-6 years
3	Word Processing Center Manager	5-7 years

Salaries in Corporations

Entry	$17,000 to $20,000
2	$20,000 to $22,000
2	$22,000 to $24,000
3	$24,000 to $26,000
3	$26,000 to $28,000 +

Qualifications

Personal: Positive attitude. Detail oriented. Ability to work independently. Ability to make accurate decisions. Confidence. Enthusiasm.

Professional: Ability to type. Good spelling, punctuation and grammar. Ability to handle advanced electronic equipment. Teamworker.

Where The Jobs Are
Law Departments
Personnel
Claims Area
Records Department
Communications
Medical Department
Word Processing Center

Education

Level	Job Title	Experience Needed
Entry	Instructor	Professional Training and/or College Degree
2	Academic Department Head	4-5 years
3	Program Director	6-8 years
3	Consultant	8-10 years

Salaries in Education
(See Salaries in Teacher Education)

Qualifications

Personal: Patience. Good communication skills. Ability to manage. Detail oriented.

Professional: Knowledge of various types of word processing equipment. Willingness to retrain as needed.

Where The Jobs Are
Schools
Consulting Firms

Vendor Companies

Level	Job Title	Experience Needed
Entry	Sales Representative	Professional Training
2	Marketing Support Representative	1-3 years
2	Sales Manager	3-5 years
3	Director of Sales & Marketing	5-7 years
3	Vice President of Marketing & Sales	7-10 years

Salaries with Vendor Companies
(See Careers in Marketing - Sales/Management)

Qualifications

Personal: Positive attitude. High energy level. Initiative. Self-motivated. Enthusiasm. Ability to work independently.

Professional: Product knowledge. Perception of customer needs. Strong sales and marketing skills.

Where The Jobs Are
Word Processing Manufacturing Firms
Office Equipment Suppliers

Consulting

Level	Job Title	Experience Needed
Entry	Training Specialist	Professional Training and/or College Degree
2	Consultant	1-5 years
3	President/Owner	6 + years

Salaries in Consulting
(See Salaries in Computer Systems-Support Services)

Qualifications

Personal: Positive attitude. Enthusiasm. Ability to work independently. Effective written and verbal communication skills. Flexibility.

Professional: Product knowledge. Perception of customer needs. Strong marketing and sales skills.

Where The Jobs Are
Freelancing
Education
Equipment Manufacturers
Private Corporations

Employment Agencies

Level	Job Title	Experience Needed
Entry	Instructor	Professional Training
2	Employment Counselor	1-3 years
3	Owner/Manager	3-6 years

Salaries in Employment Agencies vary but are usually based on a base salary plus commissions on the number of candidates successfully placed in jobs. Percentages of commission progress with salary amounts; however, compensation in Employment Agencies also can include bonuses and travel reimbursement. As an owner, compensation is earned after all of the overhead costs for running the business (rent, salaries, equipment, etc.) are paid.

Qualifications

Personal: Assertiveness. Ability to work under pressure. Good communication skills. Effective interpersonal skills. Positive attitude. Enthusiasm. Persistence. Patience. Risk-taker. High energy level.

Professional: Ability to assess clients' needs. Strong business ethics. Good business judgement. Ability to manage. Strong marketing and sales skills.

Where The Jobs Are

Temporary Employment Agencies
Permanent Placement Agencies

Trade Publications

Logos, Information Management and Processing Association, P.O. Box 16267, Lansing, M I 48901

The Word, Office Technology Management Association, 9401 West Beloit Road, Suite 101, Milwaukee, WI 53227

Professional Associations

Information Management and Processing Association
P.O. Box 16267
Lansing, MI 48901

National Association of Professional Word Processing Technicians
110 W. Byberry Road
Philadelphia, PA 19116

Office Technology Management Association
9401 W. Beloit Road
Suite 101
Milwaukee, WI 53227

Word Processing Society, Inc.
P.O. Box 92553
Milwaukee, WI 53202

Job Search Techniques

INTRODUCTION

By applying the information in ''Managing Your Career'' you have learned how to select the essential ingredients of your job. Now that you know what you want, you need a strategy for getting it. In ''Job Search Techniques,'' you will learn how to:

Now that you know what you want, you need a strategy for getting it. In "Job Search Techniques," you will learn how to:

- Apply for a job
- Interview for a job
- Accept a job offer

This is an important process to master because you will use it repeatedly throughout your career. These techniques will enable you to make successful career moves. Remember, in ''Managing Your Career,'' you saw that jobs were part of your career. You recognized that you will probably have several jobs throughout your lifetime. Just as important to choosing the right next job is knowing how to get it. The wrong move could keep you out of the running when in fact, you may be the most qualified person for the position. Even after you have considerable experience in your field, don't assume that your job search does not require careful planning and execution. The competition will remain throughout your career and using effective job search techniques is one way to stay in the running.

Competition in the Job Market

Assume the role of the personnel manager for a company. You have just run an ad in the paper for a management trainee to fill a job. The applicants must have a high school diploma; advanced schooling is desired but not required. You are really having a problem deciding which one to hire and have made the following list to help you decide.

Pat	*Terry*	*Gail*
Five minutes late to interview	On time to interview	Arrives ten minutes before interview
Well-dressed, well-groomed	Well-dressed but hair long and unkept	Clothing clean but evidence of much wear & tear
Has H.S. diploma & 2 years professional training	Has H.S. diploma	Has held part-time job
Has worked odd jobs	Has experience at local store, no pay	Has H.S. dioploma, starting post-HS education
Answers questions well & completely	Wants on-the-job training only	Has no real plans
Has no problem getting to work	Very talkative	Answers questions "yes" "no"; does not elaborate
	Lives close by	Does not have own car

1. Which candidate do you choose?

2. Give three reasons why you chose this person.

  a. _____

  b. _____

  c. _____

3. Give three reasons why you did not choose the other applicants.

_____

Name

  a. _____

  b. _____

  c. _____

_____

Name

a. _____

b. _____

c. _____

The experience each candidate brings to the job interview was only one of your considerations when evaluating which candidate is best suited for your position. When applying for a job there are a number of significant factors that affect your chances of getting the job. Lack of proper preparation and know-how can mean a missed opportunity for you as well as the employer. Both of you are concerned with the right match. How the application process is handled by both parties is a good indication of how right that match may be.

APPLYING FOR A JOB

Before attempting to apply for any job you should be able to prepare a professional resumé and a concise job application. Both documents are very often the first impression an employer has of you. Remember, you never get a second chance to make a first impression, whether on paper or in person! So take the time to do the best job you can.

The Resumé

A resumé is a factual presentation of yourself. Employers use resumés to determine your eligibility for the job. Employers can quickly see whether you have the right educational background, previous work experience and professional objectives needed to be successful in the job for which you are applying. Employers like to be able to briefly scan the resumé to find this out. Your resumé should be brief, to the point, and formatted for easy reading. The length and style of your resumé will depend on how much work experience you have. Even for someone with a lot of experience, no more than two pages is recommended.

The difference in style may be the functional resumé versus the chronological resumé. The functional resumé highlights the skills you have acquired from prior jobs that relate directly to the skills needed in the job for which you are applying. The chronological resumé highlights your employment history by dates. The chronological resumé is a useful format for applicants with a minimal amount of work experience. Following are examples of a chronological and functional resumé.

A Chronological Resumé

YOUR NAME

Permanent Address:
Street Address
City, State, Zip
Phone Number

Professional Objective:
State the type of position that you are applying for and long-term goal. You may include indications of wanting growth and challenge in your objective.

Education:
List Professional Training and/or College(s) first and then high school attended, with date of graduation along with *degree* and *major*. Underline names of schools. List the most recent program first and work backwards, in order.

Courses: *(Optional)*
List no more than six; list only those that have something to do with the position for which you are applying.

Special Skills: *(Optional)*
Skills you have developed can be *concrete* (typing, shorthand, computer operations) or *abstract* (organizational, public speaking, management, etc.) Show diversity.

Work Experience:
Include part-time and summer work with brief descriptions and dates of employment. List the most recent job first and work down. If your employment history includes many short-term, miscellaneous jobs, use the following rules:
1. List those relevant to the position for which you are applying.
2. List those you held for the longest periods of time.

Extracurricular Activities, Hobbies: *(Optional)*
List any organizations individually along with responsibilities you held. Then list hobbies and special interests that might be pertinent to the position for which you are applying. Also list others that *seem* less relevant as well as they will indicate your diversity in a variety of areas.

Personal Data: *(Optional)*
You may wish to note your general good health and marital and dependent status here.

References: *(Optional)*
List at least three or state that they are available upon request. Be sure to get permission in advance. Teachers, friends, or former employers (do not use relatives). Include names, titles, addresses, and telephone numbers with area codes.

A Functional Resumé

ROSE MARTINSON
43 Racine Avenue
Skokie, Illinois 60076
(312) 546-7898

OBJECTIVE:

To obtain an Executive Secretarial position within a major corporation which will benefit from my administrative, communication and interpersonal skills.

QUALIFICATIONS:

Production

Generated all personal and business correspondence via WANG Word Processor
Processed over 25,000 full and part-time job opportunities annually
Arranged hotel and travel accommodations for executive staff
Typing 75 wpm
Shorthand 120 wpm
Knowledge of IBM Displaywriter, WordStar and Lotus 1,2,3

Planning/Promotion

Coordination of daily schedules of management staff
Supervision of four clerical assistants
Initiated and implemented new filing system and interoffice communication procedural manual
Assisted in formulation of marketing strategies
Aided in generation of promotional materials serving as liaison among professional photographers, printers, and media personnel
Coordinated the planning and execution of a one-day conference on Stress Management

EMPLOYMENT HISTORY:

1983-present	Northwestern University, Chicago, IL *Administrative Assistant to Placement*
1980-1982	The Field Foundation, Chicago, IL *Administrative Assistant to Director of Office Services*
1976-1980	Howard T. Mack, Inc. Skokie, IL *Administrative Assistant to Associate Personnel Director*

EDUCATION:

1976	Bryant & Stratton Business Institute, Buffalo, NY. A. S. Administrative Management

REFERENCES: Available upon request

Resumé Worksheet

Resumé of _____

Permanent Address:

_____

_____

_____

Professional Objective:

_____

_____

_____

Education:

_____   _____

_____

_____   _____

_____

Courses: *(Optional)*

_____

_____

Special Skills: *(Optional)*

_____

_____

Work Experience:

_____

_____

Position: _____

Duties: _____

_____   _____

Position: _____

Duties: _____

_____   _____

Position: _____

Duties: _____

_____   _____

Position: _____

Duties: _____

Personal Data: *(Optional)*

References:
Available upon request. Have a list of at least three references printed in the
same type and on the same kind of paper. Refer to the following "Tips" section
under "References."

Tips for Preparing a Chronological Resumé

1. **Identification:** Print your first name, middle initial and last name at the top of the page.

2. **Address:** A correct address is critical information. A potential employer may want to send you an offer letter or communicate with you for some other reason. In any case, receiving that information will be extremely important to you. If you are not currently living at your permanent address, list both your present and permanent address.

3. **Telephone Numbers:** Your telephone number is a critically important item. Always include your area code. Don't assume the caller will know it. If you have no telephone or have an unlisted number that you prefer not to give out leave the telephone number of a very reliable person who is home much of the time and can take messages for you without damaging your credibility. During your job search check with that person regularly for messages.

4. **Personal Data:** The listing of personal information such as weight, height, sex, age, marital status, etc. is optional. You may wish to make a general statement such as: *Single, excellent health*. There are employers who feel that certain jobs such as sales which require a lot of traveling are more suited to single people and thus may be looking for a single person. If you know that there is certain personal data which is specific to the particular job for which you are sending your resumé, then it would be wise to specify that information.

Professional Objective: Some suggest that a professional objective is not required on a resumé because it may limit the applicant's possibilities for being considered for a wide range of jobs. On the other hand, there are those who feel your professional objective is an important part of your resumé and should be included whether you are just starting out or making a next step in your career. If properly done, a professional objective indicates direction to an employer. You've gone to the trouble of trying to decide what you want to do; now you want to show the employer that you *know* what you want. A professional objective can be stated most clearly in one sentence, no more than two sentences. Your professional objective should reflect your short and long term career goals and a realistic attitude. It should be stated so that it is broad enough to give you some flexibility but specific enough not to appear that you are floundering with your career direction.

Example:

Good Professional Objectives:

> *#1* An entry level job as Informations Coordinator leading to a career doing market research in the travel industry.
>
> *#2* An entry level job as a Store Manager Trainee leading to a career in retail operations.

Poor Professional Objectives:

> *#1* An entry level job as a Store Manager Trainee leading to a retail buying career. *This is inappropriate because it is not a correct career path. If a buying track is what you want, you must start off on a buying track, as opposed to a management track.*
>
> *#2* An entry level position with a growing company with an opportunity for advancement. *This is too general; does not indicate that real direction has been thought through.*

Use the short-term and long-term goals you developed in "Managing Your Career" to develop an effective Professional Objective.

Education: Don't leave anything out. You want to account for how you have spent your time the best you can. If you attended a school but did not complete a diploma, certificate or degree, then list it as a place you attended.

Courses: These are especially helpful to list for entry level applicants without a lot of work experience and for those people having taken highly specialized courses that will help them on the job.

Special Skills: You should list any special skills that you have that are relevant to the job you are seeking. Typing speed and computer skills are some examples. You don't want to list more personal characteristics in this area. Save talking about your personality for the cover letter.

Work Experience: Don't make assumptions for employers and leave out certain experiences because you think they won't be valuable. Chances are if you think this way, an employer won't value them either. It is important not to leave big gaps of time on your resumé. You should list most of the experiences you have had and be prepared to convince an employer that you have learned from each one of them. This is a very important point. Whether these experiences have been part-time or full-time jobs, it is very important for you to examine what you might have gained from that experience. So many times employers see someone who has worked as a waitperson for three summers and subsequently asks about the job. The employer then waits for the applicant to talk about his or her experiences as a waitperson working with the public, working under pressure, working nights, weekends and holidays, only to find the applicant apologizing for lack of work experience related to his or her chosen career. Certainly if you worked to support your college education, that should be noted on your resumé.

Example: Earned 80% of college tuition through part-time employment.

This spells, initiative, determination and responsibility.

Extracurricular Activities/Hobbies: These demonstrate leadership potential, interpersonal skills, initiative, creativity, ability to plan and organize, etc. They also show that when there's nothing to do, you choose to make valuable use of the time rather than seeing it as opportunity to do nothing. This may be an important characteristic for the manager to see who wants a secretary who will take initiative when he or she is away.

References: You should always be prepared to list references. Have the courtesy to call and ask or write to the person you'd like to be a reference for you. It is not essential to actually list references on your resumé, but you should at least indicate: "References available upon request." When you do this, type up your list of references on a separate sheet of paper headed: **REFERENCES** for *Your Name*. This does not have to be mailed out with your resumé, but should be taken with you on a job interview.

Action Word List for Constructing a Resumé

The following words should be used when writing your resumé. They are action-oriented words which concisely summarize your previous accomplishments.

administered	supervised	improved	coordinated
equipped	directed	achieved	created
constructed	reduced costs	accomplished	organized
implemented	raised profits	completed	negotiated
controlled	analyzed	recorded	conducted
guided	invented	enlarged	sold
initiated	developed	designed	wrote
created	planned	researched	expanded
established	managed	trained	produced

Writing letters as part of the job search can be one of your most valuable efforts. It can also be one of the most difficult. Some basic guidelines to remember:

Letters

1. *Be brief and to the point.*
2. *Use standard business letter writing formats.*
3. *Make sure you address the letter to the proper individual and use his/her proper title.*
4. *Make absolutely **no** errors in grammar, punctuation, spelling, and typing. An error could rule you out of consideration automatically.*

Always formalize your follow-up or preliminary activity in the job search with a letter. A cover letter should always accompany a resume that is sent by mail. It is professional, but more important, it really says a lot about you. Employers sometimes interview for days to fill a position. They may see many qualified candidates. Sending a thank-you letter for the interview expressing further interest in the position may indicate to the employer that you are really very interested in the job. It may also help the employer remember you from among a lot of other outstanding candidates. Writing letters as part of your job search may be one of the most important things you do.

The Letters You Should Write When Applying for a Job

A. *Letter Application for Specific Position: (cover letter)* This letter states your specific qualifications for the job for which you are applying. It is also known as a cover letter.

1. Always address to a specific person and use his/her full title.
2. Enclose a typed copy of your resumé.
3. State the position for which you are applying.
4. Relate how your education has made you qualified for this position.
5. State what you can offer rather than what you hope to gain.
6. Avoid any mention of salary.
7. Request an interview at the employer's convenience.
8. Follow in approximately one week with a telephone call.

B. *Letter of Inquiry:* This letter may be used if a mass mailing campaign is part of your job search. It is a letter that is similar to a "cold call" in sales. You are writing to inquire whether or not the company has a need for someone with your background. To your knowledge there is not a specific position available.

1. Always address to a specific person and use his/her full title.
2. Enclose a typed copy of your resumé.

3. State your interest in the company.
4. Briefly state how your background may benefit the company.
5. State that you would like the opportunity to discuss your qualifications in person, at the employer's convenience. (It might be useful to incorporate some of the tangible benefits you may be able to offer to the employer by applying in writing using the Proof by Example exercise you have done before.)

C. *Letter to Request a Recommendation:* This letter is written to persons who you feel will be able to recommend you satisfactorily for a position. A personal call should be made in preference to a letter.

1. Choose people you are sure will recommend you favorably.
2. Identify yourself (maiden name, etc.)
3. Ask their permission before using their names as reference.
4. Make the contact friendly, but convince the person that this is important to you.
5. Send a brief thank-you letter if reference is given.

D. *Thank You Letter Following the Interview:* This letter is written after the interview to thank the interviewer for his/her time and cooperation.

1. Send the letter right after the interview.
2. Thank the interviewer for his/her time.
3. Restate the position for which you applied, give the date and/or place of the interview.
4. Express your interest in the opportunities offered.
5. Include your telephone number and return address.
6. Show your enthusiasm.

E. *Letter Accepting a Position:* This letter is written after you have agreed to accept a specific position.

1. Answer the offer immediately.
2. Be direct about accepting.
3. Restate the specific position you have accepted.
4. Express your appreciation and good feeling about the position.

F. *Letter Refusing a Position:* This letter is written after you have definitely decided not to accept the particular position offered.

    1. Answer the offer immediately. Don't be embarrassed.
    2. Be direct with the answer, but soften the blow. Do not say "no" in the first paragraph.
    3. Be brief and concise. Make the letter simple.
    4. Express your thanks remembering that you may want to reapply for a future position with the same people.

G. *Thank You Letter for a Plant/Office Visit*

    1. Address to the specific person or people who hosted you.
    2. State your appreciation for their valuable time.
    3. Comment on what impressed you the most.
    4. Comment on what you learned from the visit.

H. *Application Letter for Cooperative Education Program*

    1. Address it to the hiring authority and/or person involved in the selection process.
    2. Enclose a typed copy of your resumé (and references if typed on a separate cover).
    3. State why you would like to be considered for the program.
    4. State the kind of professional experience you hope to gain.
    5. State what qualification you can bring to the COOP employer.

Sample Cover Letter

220 South Road
Southboro, Massachusetts 01772
March 18, 19 ____

Ms. Mary Jones, Vice President
American Insurers
2518 Brookline Avenue
Boston, Massachusetts 00215

Dear Ms. Jones:

First Paragraph. In your initial paragraph state the reason for the letter, name the specific position or type of work for which you are applying, and indicate from which resource (placement officer, news media, friend, employment service) you learned of the opening.

Second Paragraph. Indicate why you are interested in the position, the company, its products or services — above all, what you can do for the employer. If you are a recent graduate, explain how your academic background makes you a qualified candidate for the position. If you have some practical work experience, point out your specific achievements or unique qualifications. Try not to repeat the same information the reader will find in the resumé.

Third Paragraph. Refer the reader to the enclosed resumé or application form which summarizes your qualifications, training, and experiences.

Final Paragraph. In the closing paragraph, indicate your desire for a personal interview and your flexibility as to the time and place. Repeat your phone number in the letter and offer any assistance to help in a speedy response. Finally, close your letter with a statement or question which will encourage a response. For example, state that you will be in the city where the company is located on a certain date and would like to set up an interview. Or, state that you will call on a certain date to set up an interview. Or, ask if the company will be recruiting in your area, or if it desires additional information or references.

Sincerely,

Thomas L. Smith

Now that you've learned what goes into a cover letter, try to write one yourself. Choose a fictitious or real company and a position for which you are applying.

Your Cover Letter

Dear _____ :

First Paragraph: Your reason for writing.

Second Paragraph: Your qualifications.

Third Paragraph: Refer to enclosed resumé or application.

Final Paragraph: Your planned follow-up.

Sincerely,
(Written signature)
Your name typed

Samples of Other Letters

Thank You for Interview

Your Address

Inside Address
(If possible, use individual's name.)

Dear _____ :

    I appreciated the opportunity to talk with you on *(date)*. The information you shared with me about *(company name)* was excellent, and I am excited about the possibility of applying my education and experience to the position we discussed.

    If I can provide you with any additional information, please let me know. I look forward to hearing from you soon.

                         Sincerely,

                         (Written signature)

                         Your name typed

Make sure you keep current and accurate records of every interview: the date, time, location, interviewer and any special information concerning the company or job itself.

Thank You for Plant Visit

Your Address

Inside Address
(If possible, use individual's name.)

Dear _____ :

    Thank you for your letter of *(date)* suggesting a plant visit at *(time)* on the following date: *(list dates)*.

    The most convenient date for me would be *(date)*. I will arrive at your office at *(time)*.

    Enclosed is a copy of my resumé, along with the application for employment. *(If necessary.)*

    I appreciate the opportunity to visit your plant. I am very interested and eager to learn more about possible employment opportunities with *(organization name)*.

                    Sincerely,

                    (Written signature)

                    Your name typed

Make sure you arrive on time for a plant/office visit and are well prepared with extra copies of your resumé and a list of references.

Thank You for Office Visit

Your Address

Inside Address
(If possible, use individual's name.)

Dear _____

   Thank you for your letter of *(date)* suggesting a office visit at
(time) on the following dates: *(list dates)*.

   The most convenient date for me would be *(date)*. I will arrive at your
office at *(time)*.

   Enclosed is a copy of my resumé, along with the application for
employment. *(If necessary.)*

   I appreciate the opportunity to visit your office. I am very
interested and eager to learn more about possible employment opportunities with *(organization name)*.

                Sincerely,

                (Written signature)

                Your name typed

*Make sure you arrive on time for a plant/office visit and are well prepared with
extra copies of your resumé and a list of references.*

Letter of Acceptance

Your Address

Inside Address
(If possible, use individual's name.)

Dear _____ :

   I am very pleased to accept your offer *(state offer)* as outlined in your letter of *(date)*. (Include all details of offer — location, starting salary, starting date.)

   (Mention enclosures — application, resumé, employee forms, or other information — and any related commentary.)

   I look forward to meeting the challenges of the job and I shall make every attempt to fulfill your expectations.

                 Sincerely,

                 (Written signature)

                 Your name typed

Resist the temptation to sound either overly grateful or reticent about your abilities to fulfill the job requirement. A straightforward pleasant, but confident, response is all that is needed.

Letter of Rejection

Your Address

Inside Address
(If possible, use individual's name.)

Dear _____ :

After considerable thought, I have decided not to accept your offer of employment as outlined in your *(date)* letter. This has been a very difficult decision for me. However, I feel I have made the correct one for this point in my career.

Thank you for your time, effort, and consideration. Your confidence in me is sincerely appreciated.

Sincerely,

(Written signature)

Your name typed

Job Applications

You will want to ensure that your job application is the best one an employer sees. On a job application you are simply presenting information an employer needs to see in order to determine whether you should be considered for a particular job. The job application is a screening device. It does not get you the job.

Parts of a Job Application:

1. *Identification*
2. *Family relationships*
3. *Health*
4. *Education*
5. *Position desired*
6. *Experience*
7. *Miscellaneous*

Identification:

1. *Name*
2. *Social Security Number*
3. *Address*
4. *Telephone Number*
5. *Physical Traits*
6. *Date and Place of Birth*
7. *Proof of Age*
8. *Citizenship*
9. *Emergency Information*

Family Relationships:

1. *Marital Status*
2. *Dependents*
3. *Family Names and Occupations*

Health:

1. *General Health*
2. *Disabilities and Physical Limitations*
3. *Emotional and Mental Disorders*
4. *Family Illness*
5. *Workers' Compensation*
6. *Attendance*

Education:

1. *Education and Formal Training*
2. *Future Schooling*

Position Desired:

1. *Position Desired*
2. *Salary Desired*
3. *Availability*
4. *Transportation*

Experience:

1. *Work Experience*
2. *Military Experience*
3. *Volunteer Activities*
4. *Certification, Registration, and Licenses*

5. *Professional Associations*
6. *Clubs and Organizations*
7. *Hobbies, Interests, and Leisure-time Activities*
8. *Other Skills*

Miscellaneous:

1. *Future Plans*
2. *References*
3. *Arrest, Jail, and Conviction*

Points to Remember When Completing a Job Application

1. **Name:** Be sure to **print** your name where asked on the application and **sign** neatly on the signature line. You should carefully read and verify all statements on the application before signing it. Never list a nickname. Always use your complete legal name.
2. **Social Security Number:** Be sure to print your social security number so that it is readable and **correct**! Many companies use their employees' social security numbers in filing and computer systems. An error in your social security number could cause problems with your payments, benefits, taxes, retirement, and unemployment account. If you do not have a social security number, you should apply now at the nearest social security office or post office.
3. **Address:** Before you list your address, read instructions. Then be prepared to put all your data in the correct spaces. If the application does not ask for a certain order, list, in the following order: your street address, rural route or box number, city, state, and zip code. Consider your answer when asked how long you've lived at a certain address. This information will give employers an impression of your stability.
4. **Telephone Number:** A source of frustration for an employer is wanting to reach a good candidate and not being able to do so because the candidate has either forgotten to leave a telephone number or has left an incorrect one. List a phone number that is likely to be answered during the day. If no one will be answering your phone, or if you do not have a phone, list the number of someone who can accept messages for you. Choose someone who will be polite, take your message accurately, and get the message to you very quickly.
5. **Physical Traits:** Some employers need this information for insurance or security reasons. Certain jobs have specific height and weight requirements (police officer, fire fighter).
6. **Date and Place of Birth:** You may be asked to give the date of your birth on some applications. It is important that you give the right information. This date is used to compute your insurance and

retirement plans after you are hired. You can be fired for falsifying information on a job application. Remember that the law will be on your side if you are **denied** a job because of your age.

7. **Proof of Age:** You may be asked to prove your age for some employers. Most employers accept a driver's license as proof of age. If you do not have a driver's license, get a copy of your birth certificate or any other legal document that shows your age.

8. **Citizenship:** You may be asked to indicate whether or not you are a citizen of the United States. Noncitizens are usually asked to list their Visa type and number.

9. **Emergency Information:** There are two reasons why this question is asked. The first is obvious — to be sure your family will be notified of any emergencies that may arise. The second reason is to show your stability. Employers might think of you as a "drifter," and thus unreliable, if you do not list the name of someone who would be concerned about you.

10. **Marital Status:** On all applications list your marital status as EITHER MARRIED OR SINGLE. Other terms invite employers to pry into your social life. SINGLE best describes your status even if you are engaged, living with soneome, or divorced. MARRIED best describes your status even if you are separated.

11. **Dependents:** A DEPENDENT is anyone who relies on you as a source of support. Most dependents are family members (spouse, children, elderly parents). When listing your number of dependents do not list yourself. If you have no dependents, put a dash in the space.

12. **General Health:** It will benefit you the most if you can list your health as excellent. You may have a health problem that will **not** affect your ability to do the job you want. If so, do not note any negative information on your application. Leave the health sections blank if necessary and be prepared to discuss during an interview. If you have a health problem, ask your doctor if it will in any way impair your ability to perform your job. If your doctor thinks the problem would be limiting, ask for advice on how to handle this on a job application.

13. **Attendance:** The best person for the job is the one who will be there every day. The fewer days you have missed in your previous employment, the more dependable you will seem to new employers.

14. **Education and Formal Training:** You should be able to account for all the time you spent in school or in training. This information could be important in explaining gaps in your employment history. It will also clearly indicate to employers whether or not you meet one of the primary requirements for the job that is available.

15. **Salary Desired:** If you have not recently researched the job market, be careful how you answer this question. You do not want to undersell yourself or ask for such a high salary that you rule yourself out of

the competition! You can research the job market by following the suggestions below:

1. *Read want ads that list salaries for similar positions.*
2. *Call your local employment office or job placement office and ask the salary range for the type of job you are seeking.*
3. *Talk with people who do the kind of work you want.*

You may list a specific salary, a high-low range, or leave the space blank. Another alternative is to respond with the word, *open*. This is a positive word. It will not commit you to a future either too low or too high. When considering a salary offer don't forget to consider the benefits as well as the base salary. Added benefits can make one salary more valuable than a slightly higher one without benefits. Mentally adjust your desired salary according to the benefits, then state the salary you want.

16. **Work Experience:** You should be well prepared to list your work history. List the data for your most recent job first. List your next most recent job in the next form, and so on. If you have no work experience, leave the spaces blank and be prepared to offset this during an interview.

17. **Professional Organizations:** Employers may be interested in the professional organizations to which you belong. Such a membership is especially important if the organization and job are directly related.

18. **Hobbies, Interests, and Leisure-Time Activities:** What you do with your free time tells an employer much about your interests and drive. An employer may have a special interest in you if your hobby relates closely to your job.

19. **References:** Consider the following people to be your references:

1. *Former employers, supervisors, and co-workers*
2. *Former teachers, instructors, and professors*
3. *Your minister, priest or rabbi*
4. *Acquaintances who have job titles indicating responsibility*
5. *Long-time acquaintances*

Many job-seekers think that employers do **not** contact references. This is a myth. Employers **often** contact references — especially when the job includes significant responsibility.

Be Prepared

Pen: Do not use pencil; only use a black or blue pen. Your pen should let you print neatly without blobs, smudges, or smears. You may want to use a fine-point pen. Such a pen makes it easier to print small when you must write in small blanks or boxes. It is wise to carry a spare pen. Your spare pen should have the same ink color and line width as your first pen.

JIST Card: Have it handy at all times because it will show your most important job information.

Fact Card: This is an index card that can fit easily into your wallet or billfold. It will briefly contain important dates of employment that you need to list correctly on an application. For those that have trouble remembering their social security number, references, telephone numbers, etc., this is a helpful tool.

Resumé: If you prefer, you may carry an extra resumé with you to use as a reminder of important information as well. In fact, it is wise to be prepared to present a resumé should you obtain an immediate interview.

Follow Instructions

Be sure to read all of the instructions before writing any data on an application. Many applications begin with general instructions, such as "Print in ink," or "To be handprinted in ink," or "Typewritten." Separate instructions may tell you not to put any data in certain spaces.

Following instructions is important. Employers want to hire people who can follow instructions on the job! Employers will not have a high regard for your dependability and skill if you cannot follow instructions on an application.

The Dash: Some application questions *will not apply to you*. Make a short dash (-) after each of these questions. The dash is simple; it tells the employer you have read the question but it does not apply to you.

Blank Spaces: It is sometimes better to leave a blank space on your application. An application will not get you a job. However, it can keep you from being considered for a job. If an honest answer to an application question is negative or can easily be misunderstood, leave this item blank. Do not even make a dash in this space. You can explain the blank in the interview if necessary. In this way the blank will not automatically be used to screen you from a job for which you might otherwise qualify.

Expect employers to ask you questions about blank spaces. If a blank space is not mentioned in the interview, be sure to mention it after you are offered the job. This will prevent you from being possibly accused later of withholding information. An alternative to leaving a space blank is to write "will explain in interview." Decide for yourself which way is better for you. But **do** be prepared to explain it!

Review the following Job Application for employment at Sears, Roebuck, and Co. Based on the previous information how would you rate it? Then review the blank application for American Industries, Inc. Complete the application form in its entirety. As you go along, make a list in the space below of any answers that you are unsure of and would like to discuss.

_____

_____

_____

_____

_____

_____

_____

_____

_____

_____

_____

_____

SEARS, ROEBUCK AND CO.
APPLICATION FOR EMPLOYMENT

PLEASE PRINT INFORMATION REQUESTED IN INK.

Date __10 - 9 - 91__

SEARS IS AN EQUAL OPPORTUNITY EMPLOYER and fully subscribes to the principles of Equal Employment Opportunity. Sears has adopted an Affirmative Action Program to ensure that all applicants and employes are considered for hire, promotion and job status, without regard to race, color, religion, sex, national origin, age or handicap.

To protect the interests of all concerned, applicants for certain job assignments must pass a physical examination before they are hired. Alternative placement of an applicant who does not meet the physical standards of the job for which he/she was originally considered is permitted.

NOTE: This application will be considered active for 90 days. If you have not been employed within this period and are still interested in employment at Sears, please contact the office where you applied and request that your application be reactivated.

Name __Smith__   __Albert__   __Claude__   Social Security Number __411-76-2614__
 Last   First   Middle   (Please present your Social Security Card for review.)

Address __1526 North Otter Street__   __Scranton__   __PA__   __18602__
 Number   Street   City   State   Zip Code

County __Marion__   Current phone of nearest phone __555-1212__

Previous Address _____
 Number   Street   City   State   Zip Code

(Answer only if position for which you are applying requires driving.)

If hired, can you furnish proof of: Age? ☒ Yes ☐ No   U.S. Citizen? ☒ Yes ☐ No   Licensed to drive car? ☐ YES ☒ NO
or Alien legally entitled to work in U.S. ☐ Yes ☐ No   Is license valid in this state? ☐ YES ☒ NO

Have you ever been employed by Sears? ☐ YES ☒ NO   If so, when and where last employed? _____   Position _____

Former employes of Sears and certain Subsidiaries may be entitled to service credit under the Pension Plan based on prior employment with Sears, Roebuck and Co., Homart Development Co., Sears Investment Management Co., Sears Roebuck Acceptance Corp., Sears, Roebuck de Puerto Rico, Inc., Sears Roebuck Overseas, Inc., Sears Securities Sales, Inc., Terminal Freight Handling Co., Allstate Insurance Company and their Subsidiaries, Lifetime Foam Products, Pacific Installers, and Sears, S.A. (Central America).

Have you a relative in the employ of Sears in the store or unit to which you are applying? __No__

A PHYSICAL OR MENTAL DISABILITY WILL NOT CAUSE REJECTION IF IN SEARS MEDICAL OPINION YOU ARE ABLE TO SATISFACTORILY PERFORM IN THE POSITION FOR WHICH YOU ARE BEING CONSIDERED.

Do you have any physical or mental impairment which may limit your ability to perform the job for which you are applying? __No__

Do you have any Service related disability? ☐ Yes ☐ No

	School Attended	No. of Years	Name of School	City/State	Graduate?	Course or College Major	Average Grades
EDUCATION	Grammar	6	Holy Trinity	Scranton, PA		General	B
	Jr. High	3	Crestview Junior H.S.	Scranton, PA		General	B
	Sr. High	3	Warren Central. H.S.	Scranton, PA		College Prepamatory	C
	Other	—	—	—	—	—	—
	College	3	Indiana - Purdue University at Indpls.	Indpls. IN		Electronics Degree In progress	B

	BRANCH OF SERVICE	DATE ENTERED SERVICE	DATE OF DISCHARGE	HIGHEST RANK HELD	SERVICE-RELATED SKILLS AND EXPERIENCE APPLICABLE TO CIVILIAN EMPLOYMENT
MILITARY SERVICE	United States Air Force	1-2-81	4-15-82	E-2	Radio Repair Training School

What experience or training have you had other than your work experience, military service and education? (Community activities, hobbies, etc.)
__National Association of Electronic Salespeople, Big Brother__

I am interested in the type of work I have checked:

Sales __✓__ Office ___ Mechanical ___ Warehouse ___ Other (Specify) __Repair__
Or the following specific Job __Sales Representative, Electronics Repair__

I am seeking (check only one):   I am available for (check only one):

☐ Temporary   ☐ Part-Time
☒ Permanent Employment   ☒ Full-Time Work

If temporary, indicate dates available _____.

If part-time, indicate maximum hours per week ___, and enter hours available in block to the right.

Have you been convicted during the past seven years of a serious crime involving a person's life or property?

NO ☒   YES ☐   If yes, explain _____

HOURS AVAILABLE FOR WORK		
Sun	8 a.m. To	Close
Mon	8 a.m. To	Close
Tues	8 a.m. To	Close
Wed	8 a.m. To	Close
Thurs	8 a.m. To	Close
Fri	8 a.m. To	Close
Sat	8 a.m. To	Close

10534 Rev. 1-81   (SEE REVERSE SIDE)

REFERENCES

LIST BELOW YOUR FOUR MOST RECENT EMPLOYERS BEGINNING WITH THE CURRENT OR MOST RECENT ONE. IF YOU HAVE HAD LESS THAN FOUR EMPLOYERS USE THE REMAINING SPACES FOR PERSONAL REFERENCES. IF YOU WERE EMPLOYED UNDER A MAIDEN OR OTHER NAME PLEASE ENTER THAT NAME IN THE RIGHT HAND MARGIN. IF APPLICABLE ENTER SERVICE IN THE ARMED FORCES ON THE REVERSE SIDE.

NAMES AND ADDRESSES OF FORMER EMPLOYERS BEGINNING WITH THE CURRENT OR MOST RECENT	Nature of Employer's Business	Name of your Supervisor	What kind of work did you do?	Starting Date	Starting Pay	Date of Leaving	Pay at Leaving	Why did you leave? Give details
NOTE State reason for and length of inactivity between present application date and last employer: *Doing odd/independent jobs, college courses – 6 months*								
1 Name Fred Willis Address 1275 East 11th Street Tel No 555-2121 City Indianapolis, State Indiana Zip Code 46156	Electrical Subcontractor	Rafael Castillo	Electricians Assistant	Month 8 Year 91	$310.00 Per Week	Month 10 Year 91	$325.00 Per Week	Work slowdown, limited schedule.
NOTE State reason for and length of inactivity between last employer and second last employer: *Doing odd/independent jobs, college courses – 5 months*								
2 Name Indianapolis Public Schools Address 593 Walnut Ave. Tel No 555-3131 City Indianapolis State Indiana Zip Code 47304	Maintenance of school buildings	Eric Burgess	Custodian	Month 7 Year 90	$250.00 Per Week	Month 3 Year 91	$260.00 Per Week	Desired a more demanding position
NOTE State reason for and length of inactivity between second last employer and third last employer: *Traveled the United States – 7 months*								
3 Name Wayne Construction Address 1436 West Anderson Drive Tel No 555-4141 City Indianapolis Indiana Zip Code 48139	Heavy/light construction and wiring	Kim Lenski	Electrical and electronic equipment installer	Month 5 Year 86	$230.00 Per Week	Month 12 Year 89	$269.00 Per Week	Company went out of business.
NOTE State reason for and length of inactivity between third last employer and fourth last employer:								
4 Name Address Tel No City State Zip Code				Month Year	Per Week	Month Year	Per Week	

I certify that the information contained in this application is correct to the best of my knowledge and understand that any misstatement or omission of information is grounds for dismissal in accordance with Sears, Roebuck and Co. policy. I authorize the references listed above to give you any and all information concerning my previous employment and any pertinent information they may have, personal or otherwise, and release all parties from all liability for any damage that may result from furnishing same to you. In consideration of my employment, I agree to conform to the rules and regulations of Sears, Roebuck and Co., and my employment and compensation can be terminated with or without cause, and with or without notice, at any time, at the option of either the Company or myself. I understand that no unit manager or representative of Sears, Roebuck and Co. other than the President or Vice-President of the Company, has any authority to enter into any agreement for employment for any specified period of time, or to make any agreement contrary to the foregoing. In some states, the law requires that Sears have my written permission before obtaining consumer reports on me, and I hereby authorize Sears to obtain such reports.

Applicant's Signature *Albert C. Smith*

NOT TO BE FILLED OUT BY APPLICANT

INTERVIEWER'S COMMENTS	Date of Emp		Tested		(Store will enter dates as required.)		Mailed	Completed
	Dept. or Div.	Regular ☐ Part-Time ☐	Physical examination scheduled for			REFERENCE REQUESTS		
			Physical examination form completed			CONSUMER REPORT		
	Job Title					With. Tax (W-4)		
	Job Title Code	Job Grade				State With. Tax		
	Compensation Arrangement		Review Card prepared	Minor's Work Permit				
			Timecard prepared	Proof of Birth				
Prospect for	Manager Approving			Training Material Given to Employe				
1 2	Employe No	Rack No						
			Unit Name and Number _____					

Reprinted with permission of Sears, Roebuck and Co.

AMERICAN INDUSTRIES, INC. — APPLICATION FOR EMPLOYMENT

LAST NAME		FIRST	MIDDLE		SOCIAL SECURITY NO.	
PRESENT ADDRESS					TELEPHONE	
CITY		STATE	ZIP		HEIGHT	WEIGHT
PERMANENT ADDRESS					TELEPHONE	
CITY		STATE	ZIP		U.S. CITIZEN	
REFERRED BY:						
RELATIVE EMPLOYED BY COMPANY? NAME/DEPT.						

IN EMERGENCY: NAME/ADDRESS		TELEPHONE
PERSONAL PHYSICIAN: NAME/ADDRESS		TELEPHONE

EDUCATION

		YEARS ATTENDED	DATE GRADUATED	
	ELEMENTARY SCHOOL - NAME/LOCATION			
MIDDLE	HIGH SCHOOL -NAME/LOCATION	YEARS ATTENDED	GRADUATE? ☐ Yes ☐ No	WHEN
		MAJOR SUBJECT AREA		
	COLLEGE/TECHNICAL	YEARS ATTENDED	DATE GRADUATED	
		MAJOR	DEGREE RECEIVED	
FIRST	COLLEGE/TECHNICAL	YEARS ATTENDED	DATE GRADUATED	
		MAJOR	DEGREE RECEIVED	
	MEMBER PROFESSIONAL ORGANIZATION	REGISTRATION NUMBER		
	MEMBER PROFESSIONAL ORGANIZATION	REGISTRATION NUMBER		
	SUBJECTS OF SPECIAL STUDY/RESEARCH			
LAST NAME	BUSINESS MACHINES YOU CAN OPERATE			

Use this application for practice.

HEALTH INFORMATION

GENERAL CONDITION OF HEALTH	HOW MANY DAYS MISSED LAST YEAR DUE TO ILLNESS?
☐ POOR ☐ FAIR ☐ GOOD	

CHECK THE APPROPRIATE BOX "YES" OR "NO" TO INDICATE WHETHER OR NOT YOU HAVE HAD ANY OF THE LISTED PHYSICAL CONDITIONS:

	Yes No		Yes No		Yes No		Yes No		Yes No
ASTHMA	☐ ☐	HEADACHE	☐ ☐	DIABETES	☐ ☐	SKIN DISORDER	☐ ☐	STOMACH TROUBLE	☐ ☐
HEART TROUBLE	☐ ☐	HIGH BLOOD PRESSURE	☐ ☐	HEARING DEFECT	☐ ☐	VISION DEFECT	☐ ☐	SPEECH DEFECT	☐ ☐

LIST ANY OTHER PHYSICAL DEFECTS OR ALLERGIES:

HISTORY OF BACK TROUBLE?	WHEN?	WHERE?
☐ YES ☐ NO		

DESCRIBE CIRCUMSTANCES:

ANY LIFTING RESTRICTIONS?	PHYSICIAN'S NAME/ADDRESS
☐ YES ☐ NO	

WERE YOU EVER INJURED?	WHEN?	WHERE?
☐ YES ☐ NO		

DESCRIBE CIRCUMSTANCES:

EVER COLLECT WORKERS' COMPENSATION?	WHEN?	WHERE?
☐ YES ☐ NO		

DESCRIBE CIRCUMSTANCES:

HOW LONG OFF WORK?

EMPLOYER'S NAME/ADDRESS	PHYSICIAN'S NAME/ADDRESS

Use this application for practice.

EMPLOYMENT RECORD
Include Military Experience if Applicable

EMPLOYER — NAME/ADDRESS	JOB TITLE	REF. CHK'D OFF. USE ONLY
	NAME OF SUPERVISOR	
	EMPLOYED FROM / TO / SALARY	
	NAME WORKED UNDER	
	REASON FOR LEAVING	
EMPLOYER — NAME/ADDRESS	JOB TITLE	REF. CHK'D OFF. USE ONLY
	NAME OF SUPERVISOR	
	EMPLOYED FROM / TO / SALARY	
	NAME WORKED UNDER	
	REASON FOR LEAVING	
EMPLOYER — NAME/ADDRESS	JOB TITLE	REF. CHK'D OFF. USE ONLY
	NAME OF SUPERVISOR	
	EMPLOYED FROM / TO / SALARY	
	NAME WORKED UNDER	
	REASON FOR LEAVING	
EMPLOYER — NAME/ADDRESS	JOB TITLE	REF. CHK'D OFF. USE ONLY
	NAME OF SUPERVISOR	
	EMPLOYED FROM / TO / SALARY	
	NAME WORKED UNDER	
	REASON FOR LEAVING	

REFERENCES

NAME	BUSINESS	REF. CHK'D OFF. USE ONLY	
ADDRESS	YEARS KNOWN	FROM	TO
CITY	STATE	ZIP	
NAME	BUSINESS	REF. CHK'D OFF. USE ONLY	
ADDRESS	YEARS KNOWN	FROM	TO
CITY	STATE	ZIP	
NAME	BUSINESS	REF. CHK'D OFF. USE ONLY	
ADDRESS	YEARS KNOWN	FROM	TO
CITY	STATE	ZIP	

Use this application for practice.

HIRING INFORMATION

Position Wanted			If Employed, May We Contact Present Employer?	How Much Notice Given Last Employer?
Date Able To Start	Indicate Shifts You Can Work	Can You Work Week-ends?	Distance From Home To Work	Method of Trans-portation
Salary Desired	Ever Apply This Company Before? Where?	When?	Ever Collect Unemploy-ment Compensation?	Ever Convicted of a Felony or Misdemeanor?

I authorize investigation of all statements contained in this application. I understand that misrepresentation or omission of facts called for is cause for dismissal. Further, I understand and agree that my employment is for no definite period and may, regardless of the date of payment of my wages and salary, be terminated at any time without previous notice.

DATE	APPLICANT'S SIGNATURE

DO NOT WRITE BELOW THIS LINE!

TELEPHONE REFERENCES CHECKED

REFERENCE 1	Excellent	Good	Average	Fair	Poor	REFERENCE 2	Excellent	Good	Average	Fair	Poor	REFERENCE 3	Excellent	Good	Average	Fair	Poor
Integrity	☐	☐	☐	☐	☐	Integrity	☐	☐	☐	☐	☐	Integrity	☐	☐	☐	☐	☐
Neatness	☐	☐	☐	☐	☐	Neatness	☐	☐	☐	☐	☐	Neatness	☐	☐	☐	☐	☐
Conscientious	☐	☐	☐	☐	☐	Conscientious	☐	☐	☐	☐	☐	Conscientious	☐	☐	☐	☐	☐
Intelligence	☐	☐	☐	☐	☐	Intelligence	☐	☐	☐	☐	☐	Intelligence	☐	☐	☐	☐	☐
Skill in position	☐	☐	☐	☐	☐	Skill in position	☐	☐	☐	☐	☐	Skill in position	☐	☐	☐	☐	☐
Cooperation	☐	☐	☐	☐	☐	Cooperation	☐	☐	☐	☐	☐	Cooperation	☐	☐	☐	☐	☐
Absenteeism	☐ Average			☐ High		Absenteeism	☐ Average			☐ High		Absenteeism	☐ Average			☐ High	

REASON FOR SEPARATION	REASON FOR SEPARATION	REASON FOR SEPARATION
WOULD YOU RECOMMEND APPLICANT?	WOULD YOU RECOMMEND APPLICANT?	WOULD YOU RECOMMEND APPLICANT?
WOULD YOU RE-EMPLOY?	WOULD YOU RE-EMPLOY?	WOULD YOU RE-EMPLOY?

REMARKS

INTERVIEWED BY			DATE
REPORT FOR DUTY (DATE)	DEPARTMENT	POSITION	SALARY

Reprinted with permission of American Industries, Inc.

You can probably see after having now completed this exercise that it would have been extremely useful for you to have written down on a small index card, dates of employment and education and previous salaries, etc., so that you could easily and accurately complete a job application at any company pesonnel office.

Classified ads in local newspapers are obviously a direct source of leads for your job search. There are some points to be aware of when using classified ads.

The Classifieds

Ads. There are three kinds of ads: *Straight Classified, Display Ads* and *Blind Ads.* The first two ads are pretty straightforward and you can easily decide whether or not you are interested in applying. The Blind Ad indicates no company name, address or telephone number. When you respond to that ad you have no idea where your resumé is going. This is not necessarily bad. For instance, a company may not have announced a new position that has become available and wishes to keep it confidential so that other people in similar positions don't start thinking they are loosing their jobs.

On the other hand, watch a blind ad that appears repeatedly. The company may experience a high turnover rate in that position and not wish to list its name each time the ad runs for a new replacement. Also, be careful! It has happened that people answer blind ads run by their own company, only to inadvertently let their employer know they are seeking employment elsewhere. Here's an example of this scenario:

You are a Department Manager in XYZ Department Store and are unchallenged in your current position. You decide you are interested in moving into personnel work so you answer a blind ad in the newspaper for a Personnel Assistant at a local retail store. Unknown to you the store in the ad is **your** XYZ Department Store and your supervisor in the personnel department receives your letter and resume applying for the job. In some instances this could have favorable results, you could get the job. If your employer feels differently he or she may be upset that you were not honest about looking for another job. This doesn't happen often, but you should be prepared if it does.

Employment Agencies. Agencies run ads regularly in local newspapers to attract qualified candidates for placement. There is nothing wrong with sending your resumé along if you are interested in the position, however, you should look for those ads that indicate the words "Fee Paid" or "No Fees". This means that if you are placed in a job through an employment agency, your employer will be required to pay the placement fee, not you. If this is not indicated in the paper, ask the agency about it before accepting a job. Should you have to pay the fee, it could be a substantial amount of your salary. You may choose to do this if the job is worth it to you but you should be aware of it first.

Jobs listed under "Sales" also vary tremendously. You should read the fine print. *For example,* a recent listing under the Sales area looked like this:

Sales
Sales person needed for local retail store.

Does this job pay an hourly rate at minimum wage, salary plus commissions or straight commission? The ad didn't say..

Sales
Now is the time to own your own business.

Here the word sales was used as a catagory of business that was itself up for sale. This ad was for a direct mail advertising business available for sale. Finally an ad appeared that read:

SALES/Route Service
Must be mechanically inclined.

This was actually a customer service job for a technical company. These three jobs are distinctively different, yet all three appeared together under the general heading of Sales.

To better understand the skills needed to do the job you are reading, pick out the "Action Words" (organize, coordinate, implement, etc.) used in the ad. Refer to the Glossary of Terms used in Job Descriptions to clarify in your mind what skills an employer is looking for when using these terms.

The classified ads are a great source of leads for your job search. Just be sure that you read the ads thoroughly before sending in your resumé.

The Hidden Job Market

If there is anything true about finding a job it is that you should not depend on any one source for results. Even if your school boasts of a high placement rate for its graduates, you always need to explore all of your options before making a final decision.

The placement office may be the source of several good job offers, but the job you take may be one that came from somewhere else. Many, many good jobs are never advertised in the newspaper and never called into your school's placement office. The way you find out about these jobs are through:

Networking   *Independent Mass Mailing Campaigns*
Professional Associations   *Telemarketing Campaigns*

NETWORKING: Spread the word that you are job hunting. Talk to friends, relatives, teachers, current employers (if appropriate), employees at different companies that you think you would like to work for and your school's alumni. Many people will be able to let you know about jobs at their own company because of internal job posting systems.

PROFESSIONAL ASSOCIATIONS: Some of the Professional Associations in your career field are listed in the CAREER PATHS section. They can be an extremely valuable source of information to you throughout your career. For more contacts like this refer to the *Encyclopedia of Associations* in the reference area at your local library. Some professional associations publish job bulletins, some actually provide placement services, some do not. The only way you will know is to write and ask. If you are a member of the Future Business Leaders of America or the Distributive Education Clubs of America, write and ask for advice and any career literature they may have.

INDEPENDENT MASS MAILING CAMPAIGNS: At first, you may think they are a waste of time, but your chances of unearthing the job you want at a company you really never thought of are good through this method. Visit your placement office, go to the library, use the yellow pages — find lists of potential employers. First identify at least twenty that you may really be interested in and from there — it's up to you. Mailing out two hundrerd resumés and cover letters is not a bad idea if your field is especially competitive. When using the mass mailing campaign you may want to adjust your cover letter to suit particular types of employers.

Example: When applying for a job as a chef in a large hotel, you may use a different approach than if you were applying to a small fine dining establishment. The menus will be different, the clients will be different, the employer's needs will be different even though both are in need of same type of professional. If you receive a lot of rejection letters, don't panic. If many of the companies you write to don't reply right away, *DON'T GET DISCOURAGED!* It is not a reflection on you. The employer hasn't even met you! It is an indication that your background is not appropriate at the current time. Pay attention to the positives. One of the few answers you get might be just what you're looking for. When a company sets up an interview with an unsolicited candidate, there is a good chance, that there either is an opening suited to your background or one may be coming soon.

EMPLOYMENT AGENCIES: Agencies are especially helpful to you once you have a few years of work experience. Some agencies are able to assist with entry level positions, but most deal with advanced positions requiring at least two to three years experience. It won't hurt to select one or two reputable employment agencies to submit resumés to during an entry level job search. If you do have a lot of experience, use them more heavily. Just do not fall into the trap of depending solely on the agency to find you a job. And remember, be sure to ask if the employer will pay the placement fee if you are hired.

TELEMARKETING CAMPAIGNS: Get on the telephone and do some preliminary work for your job search. Call companies directly to see if they are actively seeking applicants in any particular area of the company. Find out the person's name, title and address that may be responsible for the hiring. You can create a job for yourself over the telephone if you are smart! When you call, know what you are going to say, be prepared to announce your qualifications, what you have to offer the company, rather than just asking if there are any jobs available. Many times employers will call candidates in for informational interviews if the candidate sounds like a person who might fit into the company somewhere. When you speak to someone on the telephone, you have an opportunity to create an impression that you cannot produce on a resumé or a job application.

The Jist Card

If you are thinking of using the telemarketing approach in your job search, make use of the *JIST CARD* you prepared earlier as part of putting the Sales Process to work (see page #26). Take the JIST CARD and read it carefully. Does it briefly summarize your strongest skills, abilities and personality traits? If it doesn't, rework it until it does. If you believe what it says, it will come through when you use it. Make it accurate.

Recite what you've written on the JIST CARD several times. Listen to yourself speak confidently about your skills, abilities and personality traits. When you call an employer to search out a job,

> **1.** Introduce yourself by name
> *"Good morning, my name is _____ . May I have the Personnel Department please?"*
> **2.** When speaking to the Personnel Department, first ask to speak to a hiring authority. Then introduce yourself again and state the purpose of your call.
> *"I am calling because I am very interested in working for XYZ stores."*
> *"I am interested in a position as* (what is on your JIST CARD?) *I* (proceed to recite your qualifications briefly and concisely but with confidence)." *End by saying that you would like an opportunity to meet with that person at his or her convenience.*

Like the mass mailing campaign the telemarketing campaign will have its share of rejections, but it will also have its share of successes. Pay attention to the positives. One of the few positive responses you get may be just what you are looking for. Looking for a job is a lot of work. It requires patience, persistence, originality, creativity and confidence. Most of all it requires exploring every possibility available to you. The worst thing that can happen is that you might get a job offer!

INTERVIEWING TECHNIQUES

Successful interviews are the result of good preparation. Preparation not only gives you the information, and the appearance you need to succeed, but more important, it gives you the confidence to succeed.

Think of preparing for an interview like preparing for a final exam. If you start studying well in advance it helps. If you get enough of a head start on studying you may not have to cram the night before. What this means is that you can get to sleep on time, probably get up in time to have breakfast and freshen up properly so that you will arrive on time and feel good when you sit down for the exam. There will be an air of calmness and confidence that will help you think straight throughout the exam. You will leave knowing that regardless of the outcome, you gave it your best shot, You did the best you could do. The same preparation given to an interview will result in the same satisfaction.

In "Interviewing Techniques" you will receive practical hints on how to interview successfully. You will be introduced to:

Types of interviewing preparation
Questions most frequently asked on an interview
Legal issues regarding job interviews
Mock interview evaluation
"On-the-interview" strategies
How companies rate applicants
Proper follow-up after an interview

But first you need to get the interview. The following are some suggested vehicles for getting those interviews:

1. *Mass Mailings*
2. *Posted Jobs in Your School's Placement Office*
3. *Listen & Read*
4. *On-Campus Interviews*
5. *Career Fairs*
6. *Company Visits*
7. *Effective Cover Letters*
8. *Classified Ads*
9. *Networking*
10. *Telephone Calls*
11. *Employment Agencies*

```
┌─────────────────────────────────────────────────────────┐
│                                                           │
│                PREPARING FOR AN INTERVIEW                 │
│                                                           │
│    The three keys to interviewing success                 │
│                                                           │
│    ❶ PREPARATION        ──→        Know yourself          │
│    ❷ PREPARATION        ──→        Know your career goals │
│    ❸ PREPARATION        ──→        Know your employer     │
│                                                           │
└─────────────────────────────────────────────────────────┘
```

How to Research a Company

1. *Company Standings*
   - Look at the company's annual financial report and determine the following: private or publicly owned? What information can I obtain from privately owned companies? Growth rate? Expansion?
   - Analyze the competition: Who's the leader? How much competition? Reputations?

2. *Organizational Framework*
   - Look at the company's organizational chart thoroughly and determine: degree of individual responsibility? Centralized vs. decentralized? What is the chain of command?
   - What is the system for promotions within the company?

3. *Philosophies and Policies*
   - Consider the philosophies of the company: Are they practiced as stated? Do you agree with what is practiced? Is the company production or people oriented? Is the management traditional or progressive?
   - Are you allowed to read the company's policies? Do you agree with them?

4. *Geographic*
   - Where is the company's market? (international/national) Direction and rate of expansion?
   - Do you know where you will be located? How often is relocation required for promotion? How much travel is involved?

5. *Management Development*
   - How much training is provided by the company? Is continuing education endorsed? Does the company have a Human Resources program? What support groups are available?

6. *Salary and Benefits*
   - How open is the company about salary? How does it compare with the industry average? How are raises determined? What is the maximum earning potential?
   - Read the company's benefits and consider the following: insurance package (reputation of insurance company), travel pay, sick leave,

training pay, overtime, vacation, pregnancy leave, relocation fee, holidays, continuing education, profit sharing and retirement.

- On the average, benefits will average about 25-30% of the salary. Remember, benefits are non-taxable.

7. *Miscellaneous Advice*

- Talk to someone employed by the company who is where you would like to be in 2 years, and ask:
  How honest has the company been?
  How strictly are policies followed?
  Any questions your interviewer avoided or was unable to answer.

8. *References and Resources*

- Information available from the company's:
  Financial reports
  Charts of corporate structure
  Company literature
- Other sources
  Professors
  Employees of the company
  Alumni
  Journals

One of the best ways to learn about a company is to thoroughly read their Annual Report. That is often easier said than done. The following should enable the student to read and understand a typical Annual Report.

How To Decipher Annual Reports

This step-by-step guide offers insight and explains business and technical jargon.

To many employees and shareholders, reading an annual report is about as enlightening as hieroglyphics.

The average shareholder or company employee spends only 5 to 10 minutes looking at an annual report, according to an article in *The Courier,* employee magazine at First Citizens Bank & Trust Company, Raleigh, N.C. The article, "Reading your annual report: Beyond the pictures," appeared in conjunction with the mailing of First Citizens' 1981 annual report.

The reason for this is simple: Most people don't know what to look for when they read an annual report, the article explains. Yet, for many companies, the annual report is the only document concerning the firm's financial health that is distributed widely on a regular basis.

To help employees (and others) make sense out of First Citizens' or any company's annual report, *The Courier* offered these tips:

- If you do nothing else, look at the "Highlights" section, usually outlined on the first page of the report. These numbers tell at a glance how the company did for the year and offer some comparisons to the prior year.
- The first thing to look for is net income, often called "the bottom line." Earnings per share tell how much profit is earned by each share of stock and is of particular interest to shareholders. Shareholders' equity tells what the company is worth. This number is produced simply by subtracting liabilities (what the company owes) from assets (what the company owns). "Be wary if liabilities ever exceed assets — it means your company is bankrupt."
- After reading the highlights, read the chairman's message to shareholders. It's a good summary of how the company did and why, and it gives the general outlook for the coming year.
- Now you're ready for more financial details, so turn to the page in the financial section entitled "Analysis of Earnings." This section analyzes in detail the company's performance for the year. Charts, graphs and tables usually accompany a narrative discussion.
- Finally, unless your brain has overheated from the strain, you're ready to study the most significant part of the report . . . the audited financial statements. Each of the audited financial statements previews current period information along with comparable data for the prior year.
- The Balance Sheet gives a detailed look at the company's financial position at the end of the year.
- The Statement of Income is a more detailed report of revenues, expenses, taxes, gains and losses on sales of securities and the amount of money earmarked for retained earnings.
- The Statement of Changes in Shareholders' Equity provides a summary of changes in stock, surplus, undivided profits and shareholders' equity.
- The Statement of Changes in Financial Position provides a summary of the sources of funds and how they were spent during the year.
- An integral part of the audited financial statements are the footnotes, which present more details and explain information contained in the basic financial statements.

"The annual report is a specialized publication which talks the language of stockbrokers and business executives," the article concludes. "But that doesn't mean you have to be left in the dark." (Danita Morgan, editor, *The Courier,* First Citizens Bank & Trust Company, P.O. Box 151, Raleigh, NC 27602)

(Reprinted with permission from **Communication World** *— a monthly publication of the International Association of Business Communicators.)*

Possible Sources for Researching a Company

1. *Write for information*
2. *Research information*
3. *Know the sources that are available to you*

Reference Volumes:

American Men of Science
College Placement Annual
Dictionary of Corporate Affiliations (National Register Publishing
Company, Inc.)
Dun & Bradstreet Directories (Million Dollar Directory, Middle Market
Directory)
Encyclopedia of Associations, Vol. 1 (National Organizations, Gale
Research Company)
Encyclopedia of Business Information Sources (Two Volumes)
Fitch Corporation Manuals
Fortune Magazine's Directories
Foundation Directory
Investor Banker, Broker Almanac
Mac Rae's Blue Book
Moody Manuals
Research Centers Directory
Register of Manufacturers (For different states, e.g. California Manufac-
turers Register)
Standard and Poor's
Standard Register of Advertisers
Thomas' Register of American Manufacturers
Walker's Manual of Far Western Corporations & Securities

Periodicals:

Advertising Age
Business Week
Dun's Review
Forbes Magazine
Fortune Magazine
Wall Street Journal
New York Times

Interview Preparation

The various forms of preparation for your interview are situational knowledge,
mental preparation, physical preparation, and written preparation.

Situational Knowledge

1. Do you know where the company is located?
2. Do you know how long it will take you to get there?
3. Do you know where you will park?
4. Do you know what office to go to?
5. Do you know the name and title of the person with whom you will be interviewing?
6. Do you have the phone number of the company so that you can call if you are going to be late for any reason?
7. Do you know if you will be interviewing with more than one person?

Mental Preparation

Mental preparation for a job interview involves several areas. It involves your knowledge of the company, the position for which you are applying, the career path you wish to follow, as well as your mental attitude about work in general, your expectations about the job, and your confidence in your ability to do the job.

You have seen the kind of information you should research about the company with which you are to interview. Knowledge about the company serves many purposes on a job interview. *First,* it confirms your real interest in working for the company. *Second,* it provides you with a frame of reference for the interview. For example, if you are extremely nervous about your interview, you may want to jot down some questions about the information you read. Maybe it is to clarify something you did not really understand or maybe it is to find out something you want to know that could not be found in the literature. By having a frame of reference from which to ask questions on the interview, you will feel more relaxed. You will be able to pick up the ball when there is a lag in conversation during the interview or have something to respond to if the interviewer asks you if you have any questions. The interview should be a **conversation** between two people. You shouldn't let yourself be talked at because you are too shy to ask questions. Remember this is an investment for both you and the company. You have as much right to evaluate the opportunities being discussed as the interviewer has to evaluate you.

Third, knowledge of the company before the interview puts you in a convincing position that shows the employer you really want to work with that company. Equipped with the proper knowledge, you can bring the company name into your responses and conversations. You can clearly and specifically state the reasons you want to work with that company and the reasons you would be an asset to the company. This is most difficult to do without being able to incorporate specific information about the company. You already learned how to use the sales process on a job interview. *Convincing* is the key word. **Genuinely convincing** is most important.

Part of mental preparation for an interview is having a clear understanding about the job for which you are interviewing. Time after time, interviewers comment that applicants don't really understand the nature of the job for which they are applying. Typically, the employer may ask, "What do you see yourself doing every day as a *(title of the job)?*" It was pointed out to you in **Managing Your Career** that the one area in which applicants fall short is lack of specific information available to really answer questions effectively. And yet, isn't it critical to know what you are getting into when you choose a career field? The information provided in **Career Paths** and in the **Index of Job Descriptions** should give you the information you need about the job for which you are interviewing. You used this information once in deciding on your career goal; use it again to make yourself more convincing on your job interview. Be able to speak comfortably about the job you are applying for as it relates to your career field and the professional objectives you have developed. Let the interviewer know that you have thought about the big picture and that the decisions you are making are a part of an overall plan. Employers like to see applicants that have *career direction.*

Next, your mental attitude about work will be evaluated in your interview. You should be enthusiastic about the challenges your career presents to you, as opposed to the person who does not see the value of work beyond the paycheck. Emanating motivation and enthusiasm about work relates a work ethic and a belief on the part of the employer that you might be able to make some valuable contributions to the company. Your attitude about work is important.

The employer will evaluate your expectations about the job as well. Demonstrate realistic attitudes about the responsibilities and authority you hope for as well as the starting salary you expect to earn. Be confident in your ability to do the job.

Physical Preparation

Physical preparation for a job interview reinforces your mental preparation. You could have spent a lot of time thinking through all you will be discussing on the interview, but if you feel sick, tired, or sloppy, your mental attitude and alertness will be diminished.

Some important guidelines include:

1. Start with cleanliness, good grooming and hygiene.
2. Get proper rest the night before.
3. Eat breakfast.
4. Wear a professional outfit that still relates your own personal style.
5. Present a professional image — enhance it! Along with the clothing you wear, bring your resumé and references in a leather-bound folder. Properly arrange your portfolio if this is part of your presentation;

have a pen with you and bring extra copies of your resumé along. Also have with you the small index card you prepared earlier with all pertinent dates and salaries so that you can quickly and efficiently complete a job application if you are required to do so.

6. Wear little jewelry, perfume or cologne — just enough to enhance your presentation of yourself but not so much that it becomes the focal point of attention. The same applies to makeup.

7. Remember to have clean hair neatly and stylishly groomed.

8. Arrive ten minutes early.

9. Relax.

10. Smile.

11. Be energetic.

Written Preparation

Make sure you have the proper street directions to the company. It is not inappropriate to bring notes with you on an interview. Bring notes from your company research in case you need it. Prepare a brief list of questions to have with you. Write down any miscellaneous information that does not appear on your resumé that you feel might be worth bringing up at the interview. Summarize the details of the job as you perceive them from the ad you read or the information you have researched. This information should not prove to be a distraction on the interview, but rather a help should you need it. Remember how important eye contact is as an indicator of listening and interest level.

Finally, as a wrap-up to preparation in general, review the Proof by Example Exercise in Section II, "Managing Your Career." The information you have outlined through this simple exercise is the most valuable information you can impart during your interview.

> *Study it.*
> *Review it.*
> *Rehearse it mentally.*
> *Rehearse the information in a conversational style that is clear, confident, and convincing.*

Preparing for a Job Interview: *Summary*

1. Is my **goal** clear to me? If not, it will not be clear to an employer! **Repeat the steps in the career planning process** until you can answer this question comfortably.

2. Have I decided if and **where** I am willing to relocate?

3. Have I decided **how much** I need to earn to meet my living expenses?

4. Have I **researched** the company so that I know the company's:
   a. Relative size

b. *Plans or potential for growth*
c. *Array of product lines or services*
d. *Potential new products, services, locations*
e. *The competition? What makes this company different?*
f. *Age and style of management*
g. *Number of plants and stores or properties*
h. *Geographic locations, including location of home office*
i. *Parent company or subsidiaries*
j. *Structure of the training program*
k. *Recruiter's or department manager's name*

5. Can I now explain to an employer why I want to work for **them**?
6. Can I also explain to an employer why they should **hire me**?
7. Do I have the proper **outfits** to wear on my interviews?
8. Will I be **well-groomed, alert, and on time** for my interview?
9. Is my **resumé** ready?
10. Have I developed a **positive attitude** so that the interview will be successful?
11. Have I remembered the key to the sales process — why people buy, how to sell — the features and benefits way!

Stages and Topics Covered During the Initial Interview

The Interview

Stages	Interviewer Topics	Interviewer Looks For
FIRST IMPRESSIONS	Introduction and greeting Small talk about traffic conditions, the weather, the record of the basketball team	Firm handshake, eye contact Appearance and dress appropriate to the business, not college setting, Ease in social situations, good manners, poise
YOUR RECORD	*Education* Reasons for choice of school and major Grades, effort required for them Special areas of interest Courses enjoyed most and least, reasons Special achievements, toughest problems Value of education as career preparation Interaction with instructors High school record, important test scores	Intellectual abilities Breadth and depth of knowledge Relevance of course work to career interests Special or general interest Value placed on achievement Willingness to work hard Relation between ability and achievement Reaction to authority Ability to cope with problems Sensible use of resources (time, energy, money) High energy level, vitality, enthusiasm
	Work Experience Nature of jobs held Why undertaken Level of responsibility reached Duties liked most and least	Leadership, interest in responsibility Willingness to follow directions Ability to get along with others Seriousness of purpose

	Supervisory experience Relations with others	Ability to motivate oneself to make things happen Positive "can do" attitude
	Activities and Interests Role in extracurricular, athletic, community, and social service activities Personal interests — hobbies, cultural interests, sports	Diversity of interests Awareness of world outside the lab Social conscience, good citizenship
YOUR CAREER GOALS	Type of work desired Immediate objectives Long-term objectives Interest in this company Other companies being considered Desire for further education, training Geographical preferences and limitations Attitude toward relocation Health factors that might affect job performance	Realistic knowledge of strengths and weaknesses Preparation for employment Knowledge of opportunities Seriousness of purpose: career-oriented rather than job-oriented Knowledge of the company Real interest in the company Work interests in line with talents Company's chance to get and keep you
THE COMPANY	Company opportunities Where you might fit Current and future projects Major divisions and departments Training programs, educational and other benefits	Informed and relevant questions Indicators of interest in answers Appropriate, but not undue, interest in salary or benefits
CONCLUSION	Further steps you should take (application form, transcript references) Further steps company will take, outline how application handled, to which departments it will be sent, time of notification of decision Cordial farewell	Candidate's attention to information as a sign of continued interest

20 Questions *(Typically asked by interviewers)*

1. What kind of company or work environment are you looking for?
2. What kind of job or duties/responsibilities are you looking for?
3. Tell me a little bit about professional training and/or your college experience.
4. Describe some of the part-time/summer jobs you've had in the past.
5. What is your academic/school record up until now?
6. Describe some of your extracurricular/student activities.
7. What do you consider some of your strong points?
8. What are some of your short- and long-term job goals?
9. Tell me about your past employers.

10. What do you know about this company?
11. What led you to choose your major field of study?
12. Why did you select your institution for your education?
13. What are the three most important accomplishments thus far in your life?
14. What is the most difficult assignment you have tackled and how did you resolve it?
15. Why should I hire you?
16. How would a friend/former employer/instructor describe you?
17. Will you relocate/does relocation bother you?
18. Are you willing to travel?
19. What are your salary expectations?
20. Are you willing to spend at least six months as a trainee?

Interview Strategies

1. *When you meet the recruiter . . .*
   Shake his/her hand firmly, maintaining eye contact with the person, offer a pleasant but professional smile and say, "Hello, I'm *(your name)*. It's good to meet you *(Mr., Ms., or Mrs. recruiter's name)*." Wait for the recruiter to indicate you should sit down or wait for him/her to sit down before you do so.

2. *During the interview maintain . . .*
   A positive attitude
   Good posture
   An interested manner
   A good appearance
   A pleasant look on your face
   Eye contact with the recruiter
   Confidence
   Be yourself — This is what recruiters look for!

3. *Make the interview a two-way conversation . . .*
   Ask questions, as well as answering them!

4. *The recruiter will be assessing . . .*
   Why this kind of employment?
   Ultimate goal?
   Relocation?
   Social, civic activities?
   Future career goals?
   Job or career?
   Reason for wanting to work for the company?
   Quality of professional training?
   Past experiences?
   How you heard about this company?

What to Find Out During an Interview

- The exact job: its title, responsibilities and department in which you would work?
- The fit of the department into the company structure: its purpose, its budget, and other departments with which it works?
- Reporting structure: one or more bosses?
- Type of formal or informal training you would be given?
- Working on your own or as a member of a team?
- Will skills you learn on this job prepare you for higher level jobs?
- How job performance is measured?
- What your opportunities for advancement are and where those who previously held your position are now?
- What the salary for this position is?

Guide to Appropriate Pre-Employment Inquiries

ACCEPTABLE	SUBJECT	UNACCEPTABLE
"Have you worked for this company under a different name?" "Have you ever been convicted of a crime under another name?"	NAME	Former name of applicant whose name has been changed by court order or otherwise
Applicants place of residence How long applicant has been resident of this state or city?	ADDRESS OR DURATION OF RESIDENCE	
"Can you, after employment, submit a birth certificate or other proof of US citizenship or age?"	BIRTHPLACE	Birthplace of applicant Birthplace of applicant's parents, spouse or other relatives Requirements that applicant submit a birth certificate, naturalization or baptismal record
"Can you, after employment, submit a work permit if under eighteen?" "Are you over eighteen years of age?" "If hired, can you furnish proof of age?" /or/ Statement that hire is subject to verification that applicant's age meets legal requirements.	AGE	Questions which tend to identify applicants 40 to 64 years of age
	RELIGIOUS	Applicant's religious denomination or affiliation, church, parish, pastor or religious holidays observed "Do you attend religious services /or/ a house of worship?" Applicant may not be told "This is a Catholic/Protestant/Jewish/ atheist organization."
Statement by employer of regular days, hours or shift to be worked	WORK DAYS AND SHIFTS	
	RACE OR COLOR	Complexion, color of skin, or other questions directly or indirectly indicating race or color
Statement that photograph may be required after employment	PHOTOGRAPH	Requirement that applicant affix a photograph to his application form Request applicant, at his option, to submit photograph Requirement of photograph after interview but before hiring
"If you are not a U.S. citizen, have you the legal right to remain permanently in the U.S.?" "Do you intend to remain permanently in the U.S.?" Statement by employer that if hired, applicant may be required to submit proof of citizenship	CITIZENSHIP	Whether applicant or his parents or spouse are naturalized or native-born United States citizens Date when applicant or parents or spouse acquired U.S. citizenship Requirement that applicant produce his naturalization papers or first papers Whether applicant's parents or spouse are citizens of the U.S.
"Languages applicant reads, speaks or writes fluently	NATIONAL ORIGIN OR ANCESTRY	Applicant's nationality, lineage, ancestry, national origin, descent or parentage Date of arrival in United States or port of entry; how long a resident Nationality of applicant's parents or spouse; maiden name of applicant's wife or mother Language commonly used by applicant, "What is your mother tongue?" How applicant acquired ability to read, write or speak a foreign language
Applicant's academic, vocational, or professional education; schools attended	EDUCATION	Date last attended high school
Applicant's work experience Applicant's military experience in armed forces of United States, in a state militia (U.S.) or in a particular branch of U.S. armed forces	EXPERIENCE	Applicant's military experience (general) Type of military discharge
"Have you ever been convicted of any crime?" If so, when, where, and disposition of case?	CHARACTER	"Have you ever been arrested?"
Names of applicant's relatives already employed by this company Name and address of parent or guardian if applicant is a minor	RELATIVES	Marital status or number of dependents Name or address of relative, spouse or children of adult applicant "With whom do you reside?" "Do you live with your parents?"
Name and address of person to be notified in case of accident or emergency	NOTICE IN CASE OF EMERGENCY	Name and address of relative to be notified in case of accident or emergency
Organizations, clubs, professional societies, or other associations of which applicant is a member, excluding any names the character of which indicate the race, religious creed, color, national origin, or ancestry of its members	ORGANIZATIONS	List all organizations, clubs, societies, and lodges to which you belong"
"By whom were you referred for a position here?"	REFERENCES	Requirement of submission of a religious reference
"Do you have any physical condition which may limit your ability to perform the job applied for?" Statement by employer that offer may be made contingent on passing a physical examination	PHYSICAL CONDITION	"Do you have any physical disabilities?" Questions on general medical condition Inquiries as to receipt of Worker's Compensation
Notice to applicant that any misstatements or omissions of material facts in his application may be cause for dismissal	MISCELLANEOUS	Any inquiry that is not job-related or necessary for determining an applicant's eligibility for employment

There are two ways to sharpen your interviewing skills: mock interviews and informational interviews.

Mock Interviews

A mock interview is simply a practice interview. It is conducted by someone other than a potential employer. You can ask several people to give you a mock interview: an instructor, a friend, a relative or, of course, a member of your school's placement office. First, go through the following steps:

- Review "20 Questions."
- Rehearse the answers mentally.
- Review the Proof by Example exercise.
- Review your JIST card.
- Look over your resumé.

Give the person who will interview you the list of questions most frequently asked on an interview. Let them conduct the interview and evaluate you by using the following Mock Interview Evaluation form. Go through as many mock interviews as you think necessary to master the interviewing process.

Mock Interview: *Evaluation*

	Out-standing	Very Good	Good	Needs Improvement	Unsatisfactory
Communication Skills					
Appearance					
Proof By Example					
Enthusiasm					
Initial Impression/ Clothing					
Poise/Confidence					
Preparation					

Comments and Evaluation

Interviewed by:

_____

Date:

_____

Informational Interviews

An informational interview is one in which you interview someone who is already working in your chosen career. Preferably it is someone who actually has the same type of job that you are seeking. The following list of questions for informational interviews will give you an idea of the kind of information you can obtain. You can actually use this form to collect information when conducting the interview.

Questions for Informational Interviews

Occupation: _____

Person to be interviewed: _____

Write comments and additional interview questions in the space.

   1. What do you like about your occupation? Why?

   _____

   _____

   _____

   2. What are the activities and responsibilities connected with your job? Could you describe your job routine for a typical day or week?

   _____

   _____

   _____

   3. Do the activities and responsibilities of your occupation vary depending on the employer, or are they generally the same? In what ways could your job situation be different from those of others in your occupation?

   _____

   _____

   _____

4. Do the number of responsibilities in your occupation remain constant or increase over time?

_____

_____

_____

5. What skills are necessary to perform your job activities?

_____

_____

_____

6. What training and education does your occupation require?

_____

_____

_____

7. Do the training requirements for your occupation vary from employer to employer?

_____

_____

_____

8. How much variety is connected with your work routine?

_____

_____

_____

9. How would you describe your actual work setting or workplace?

_____

_____

_____

10. What opportunities are there in your job for sharing ideas, acquiring new skills and learning from your co-workers or supervisors?

_____

_____

_____

11. How competitive is entry into your field? What is the outlook for openings in your field over the next few years?

_____

_____

_____

12. What is the usual progression for jobs and assignments for people in your occupation? What career paths can people follow?

_____

_____

_____

13. Is yours considered a staff or a line position? If a line position, what other people do you supervise?

_____

_____

_____

14. What qualities do employers look for in job applicants who want to enter your occupation?

_____

_____

_____

15. What are the goals of your organization? How would you describe its overall philosophy and objectives?

_____

_____

_____

16. This interview began with the question, "What do you like about your occupation?" What do you *not* like about your occupation? What job frustrations and negative points should I know about before deciding whether to enter this field?

_____

_____

_____

17. To what extent are the advantages and disadvantages of your particular job attributable to your particular place of employment?

_____

_____

_____

18. Do you know the names of employers other than your own who hire people in your occupation? Do you know of any sources I could consult to locate still more employers?

_____

_____

_____

19. Can you recommend the names of other people I can consult to find
out more about your field? May I use your name to introduce myself?

_____

_____

_____

Procedures for Arranging and Conducting Informational Interviews

1. Compile a list of employers for the occupations in your career field.
Use business directories, the *Encyclopedia of Associations*, the yellow
pages of cities across the United States, the *College Placement Annual*,
or other sources. Note employers' locations, phone numbers, types
of businesses, product lines, and other relevant information that you
discover. Include alumni from your school on your list. Check with
your alumni or placement office for names of past graduates who
would be willing to help you out.

2. Review your list of employers and mark those you consider the most
attractive.

3. If possible, compare employer locations with other members of your
class. Coordinating trips to visit the same city with a classmate may
reduce travel costs.

4. Mark those employers on your list located where you are able to
travel and visit.

5. Draft a separate list of employers to contact for arranging interviews.
Base your new list on the occupations you are considering the most
seriously, the new employers that appear the most attractive to you,
and your ability to travel.

6. Before contacting employing organizations consider the following
issues:

- When can the interviews be conducted? Other commitments may
conflict or need to be rescheduled. Interviews should be scheduled
to allow more than adequate time to locate destinations, accommo-
date delays, conduct the interviews, and take advantage of
invitations to extend your visit or tour employers' facilities.
- What people are available for interviews? This can be checked by
telephoning the employer to explain your needs. Public relations
or personnel offices are good sources for this information.

- How can you know if the person you ask for an interview is able to give you the kind of information you are seeking? Verify that the person you contact actually works in the occupation you are assessing. Clearly explain your needs and objectives before requesting an interview.
- Where should the interviews be conducted? Request that interviews be conducted in locations allowing privacy and freedom from distraction. The people you interview may agree to provide tours of their work places. Your interviews should be conducted close enough to actual work settings for you to be able to observe them at some point during your visits.

7. Schedule your informational interviews. Whenever possible make your arrangements directly with the people you plan to interview. Explain the nature of this class and your reasons for requesting an interview. You should find most people open to talking with you about their occupation.

9. Leave your phone number or address to give your interview subjects the ability to contact you if rescheduling becomes necessary.

10. If you have not had experience in interviewing for information, you may want to practice doing mock interviewing with a classmate, friend, or relative.

11. Review the information you want to obtain about your interview subjects' occupations. You can use the previous interview, Questions for Informational Interviews, or draft questions of your own. You should be familiar enough with the questions you want to ask so that you will not need to continually refer to a list during the interviews. This will help achieve a more natural, relaxed, and spontaneous conversation with your interview subjects. This style of interview is likely to provide more honest, candid, and complete information than a straight question and answer interview format.

12. Reconfirm interview times, dates, and locations on the day before each scheduled interview.

13. At the conclusion of each visit, ask your subject for the names of other people who can provide information about the occupations in your targeted range of occupations. Obtaining permission to use your subjects' names can help in arranging future interviews.

14. After each interview take time to send a thank-you letter to your subject. Courtesy is a good habit, and you may want to be remembered favorably by your subjects' organizations.

Post Interview

HOW COMPANIES RATE APPLICANTS

Evidence of Ability	→	Grades
Desire to Work	→	Part-Time & Summer Jobs
Ambition	→	Future Career Plans
Ability to Communicate	→	Interview
Acceptable Personality	→	Interview

HOW EMPLOYERS RATE APPLICANTS

Appearance and Manner	→	Well-groomed
		Professional presence
		Considerate
		Polite
Personality	→	Warm and friendly
		Attract or repel
		Attentive
		Responsive
		Enthusiastic
Intelligence	→	Mental organization
		Alertness
		Judgement
		Understanding
		Show imagination
Attitude	→	Loyal
		Tactful
		Constructive
		Cooperative
		Reasonable
Self-Expression	→	Clear and interesting
		Convincing
		Pleasant voice
Effectiveness	→	Reliable
		Trustworthy
		Industrious

Employer's INTERVIEW EVALUATION

Appearance

Grooming	___A ___B ___C
Posture	___A ___B ___C
Dress	___A ___B ___C
Manners	___A ___B ___C

Preparation for Interview

| Asked pertinent questions | ___A ___B ___C |
| Resumé | ___A ___B ___C |

Verbal Communication

| Conversational ability | ___A ___B ___C |
| Expression | ___A ___B ___C |

Direction

Well-defined goals	___A ___B ___C
Confidence level	___A ___B ___C
Realistic and practical	___A ___B ___C

Maturity

Responsible	___A ___B ___C
Self-reliant	___A ___B ___C
Decisive	___A ___B ___C
Leader-School	___A ___B ___C
Leader-Work	___A ___B ___C

Sincerity

| Genuine attitude | ___A ___B ___C |
| Artificial attitude | ___A ___B ___C |

Personality

Enthusiastic	___A ___B ___C
Extrovert	___A ___B ___C
Motivation	___A ___B ___C
Aggressive	___A ___B ___C
Unresponsive	___A ___B ___C
Noncommittal	___A ___B ___C

Qualifications

Academic preparation	___A ___B ___C
Work experience	___A ___B ___C
Position match	___A ___B ___C

Overall Evaluation

Long-range potential	___A ___B ___C
Drive and ambition	___A ___B ___C
Ability and qualification	___A ___B ___C

A - *Outstanding*
B - *Average*
C - *Below Average*

Post-Interview Company Evaluation

Company Name _____

Company Standing	**Yes**	**No**	**Comments**
Is the company public?	___	___	_____
Is the company private?	___	___	_____
Is the company an industry leader?	___	___	_____
Is the company growing?	___	___	_____
Does the company have a positive reputation?	___	___	_____

Organizational Framework	**Yes**	**No**	**Comments**
Is the company mainly centralized management?	___	___	_____
Is the company mainly decentralized management?	___	___	_____

*Is the company's advancement
   vertical?*
   horizontal?
   frequent?

Philosophies and Policies	**Yes**	**No**	**Comments**
Do I agree with the company philosophy?			
Is the company production oriented?			
Is the company people oriented?			
Is the company's management traditional?			
Is the company's management progressive?			

Geography	**Yes**	**No**	**Comments**
Is the job in a desired location?			
Is relocation required?			
Is travel required?			

Management Development	**Yes**	**No**	**Comments**
Is there a formal training program			
Is the majority of training "Hands On"?			
Is there a continuing education program?			
Is there a remedial training program?			
Is the evaluation system used as a management tool?			
Are there criteria to be met before salary increases are given?			
Are salary increases given on the basis of merit?			
Is there a maximum earning level?			
Does the company provide health insurance?			
dental insurance?			
sick leave?			

Salary and Benefits	**Yes**	**No**	**Comments**
Does the company provide			
vacations?	____	____	_____
holiday leave?	____	____	_____
automobile?	____	____	_____
expense account?	____	____	_____
retirement plan?	____	____	_____
profit sharing?	____	____	_____
relocation expenses?	____	____	_____
pregnancy leave?	____	____	_____
other?	____	____	_____

Starting Salary _____

Post-Interview Self Evaluation

Preparation	**Yes**	**No**
Did I know the interviewer's name?	____	____
Did I research the company?	____	____
Did I write down questions to ask?	____	____
Did I choose proper attire prior to the interview?	____	____
Did I pick a comfortable outfit?	____	____

Interview		
Was I on time?	____	____
Was my handshake firm?	____	____
Did the interviewer seem pleased to see me?	____	____
Did I help the greeting go smoothly by being cheerful?	____	____
Was the interview rushed?	____	____
Did the interviewer actively listen?	____	____
Did I carry the conversation?	____	____
Did I ask my questions?	____	____
Were all my questions answered?	____	____
Did I keep eye contact consistent?	____	____
Did the interviewer quickly say goodbye?	____	____
Was I rushed out of the office?	____	____
Did the interviewer seem interested in me?	____	____

Conclusion of Interview		
Did I show enthusiasm about the company?	____	____
Was the atmosphere comfortable?	____	____
Were my objectives satisfied during the process of the interview?	____	____
Was I alert during the interview?	____	____

Follow-up After an Interview

Your evaluation by the employer doesn't stop when you leave your interview. How you follow up after the interview is just as important as the preparation you did beforehand.

Follow-up begins as you end your interview with the employer. If it is unclear to you what will happen next — *Ask.* The employer may indicate that he or she will get back to you in two or three weeks or by a certain date. If that is the case, you may want to ask if that will be by telephone or in writing. If by telephone, you will want to be sure to leave a number where you can be easily reached.

If the employer says that he or she would like you to get back to him or her after thinking about the interview and indicate if you would like to pursue things further, *Do It!* They are not giving you the run around but may be testing your initiative and your genuine interest in the company. The employer may even ask that you visit one of the company's locations if you have not done so already before pursuing a second interview. This is to be sure that you will understand the company style and the type of environment in which you may be working. If you are unsure of your interest in the company, this visit could be a deciding factor for you. In that case, it is a benefit to both you and the employer.

If an employer asks you to take initiative in any way — *Do It!* If you are absolutely sure the job or the company is not right for you, don't waste their time by taking the next step, but **do** send a thank-you letter acknowledging the time given to your first meeting. You do not want to burn any bridges as you move through your career. If an employer says nothing about follow up — *Ask* what you should do or expect next. If an employer does not get back to you in the time they indicated, call the employer. Be sure to wait for the designated amount of time to go by before calling.

Always send a thank-you letter immediately after an interview. If you are interested in the job, the letter will jog the employer's mind about you as an applicant and will relate your interest in the job. If you are not interested in the job, still send a thank-you letter for the time the employer took with you. A few years from now that employer may be one that you want to work for and you would not want to have created a negative first impression of your professionalism.

Follow-up after an interview is part of your evaluation process as a candidate. Be conscientious in this area. It will benefit you in the long run.

ACCEPTING A JOB

Accepting a job is a big step. It is a commitment. Among the things you will want to consider are the type of position, the salary, and the location of the job. As you seek your first job, it is not likely that you will get your first choices in all three areas. If you want to stay in a particular geographic area, your salary may be less than what you could earn somewhere else. If type of position is your first choice, you may have to be willing to relocate anywhere for that opportunity. Your first job will involve a choice. On the lines that follow, prioritize these three components — *location, type of position, salary* — in order of their importance.

1. _____

2. _____

3. _____

These priorities will change throughout your career, but also as you gain experience, your chances of getting your first choice in all three areas will be better. Make this decision first before accepting a job.

Budgeting Your First Salary

1. Put yourself at the top of the list.

Charles Lefkowitz, Chairman of the *International Association for Financial Planning* recommends that, "You should put away between 5% to 20% of every paycheck before you do anything else. If you can learn that discipline early on, you'll be way ahead." Payroll deduction plans are a great way to do this. This is because the money never touches your hands, so the temptation to spend it is not there. Also some employers offer special benefits, such as IRA's, 401K's, or matching programs, to payroll deduction savers.

2. Have your own slush fund.

Having at least a month's salary in a liquid, money market-type account works well.

3. Get out of debt.

Student loans that are paid off early give you the opportunity to invest your money.

4. Plan a good tax strategy.

Seeking professional help in this area may pay off. Keeping track of what is and is not fully deductible is the job of a professional. The key for you is to find out what deductions you are entitled to as well as the limitations involved. A free information packet including a state-by-state directory of certified financial planners is available from the *International Association of Financial Planning, (IAFP), 2 Concourse Parkway, Suite 800, Atlanta, GA 30328.* A typical consultant's fee is $250. Depending on your needs and interests, the fee may be well worth the return.

5. Invest.

Early in your career, investments in the stock market, mutual funds or other sources won't be as important as your initial basic investments such as clothing and a car. Exercise discipline and pay off these debts as soon as possible. A working wardrobe and a vehicle are investments because they will get you to the job on time, looking good — leverage that you will need at the beginning of your career.

*Compute Your Net Cash Flow

Monthly Income

Wages & Salary   _____
Interest on Savings, CD's, Bonds   _____
Other   _____
        Total Monthly Income $_____

Monthly Expenses

Rent   _____
Automobile Loans   _____
Personal Loans *(Student Loans)*   _____
Charge Accounts   _____
Income Taxes   _____
Social Security   _____
Savings & Investments   _____
Contributions   _____
Household Maintenance   _____

Furniture   _____
Gas   _____
Electricity   _____
Telephone   _____
Water   _____
Transportation   _____
Food   _____
Clothing   _____
Medical   _____
Entertainment   _____
Other Expenses   _____

      Total Monthly Expenses $ _____

      Total Monthly Income   _____

      Total Monthly Expenses   _____

      Discretionary Monthly Income $ _____
      (Subtract your expenses from your income.)

*SOURCE: International Association of Financial Planning

Cost of Living

Throughout your career, a job offer may vary in salary and location. You may
not be sure if you should relocate for a job because you may not know what
the cost of living is in that area. You may decide to take a job offer because it
pays more than another and be willing to relocate to wherever that job is. The
American Chamber of Commerce Researchers Association recommends:

Don't jump at a high starting salary unless you know what it is really worth!

Very often a high salary in one city will buy you much less than a lower salary
somewhere else. It all depends on the cost of living in each locale. Here's how
to decide between a job offer, with identical duties and titles, in Indianapolis
starting at $22,000 and another in New York City starting at $28,000 a year.

*(City #1)	Index #	X	Starting	= $
(City #2)	Index #		Salary	_____

SAMPLE EQUATION:

● What is the New York equivalent of a
$22,000 offer in Indianapolis?

$$\frac{New\ York}{Indianapolis} \quad \frac{141.2}{96.6} \quad X \quad \$22,000 \quad = \$32,157$$

● What is the Indianapolis equivalent of a
$28,000 offer in New York City?

$$\frac{Indianapolis}{New\ York\ City} \quad \frac{96.6}{141.2} \quad X \quad \$28,000 \quad = \$19,156$$

*Reprinted with the permission of National Business Employment Weekly, Spring, 1987.

This means that to have the same buying power in New York that $22,000 would get in Indianapolis, you would need to earn $32,157 a year. On the other hand, a $28,000 starting salary in New York would buy you only as much as a $19,156 salary in Indianapolis. To calculate equivalent offers for any two locations of your choice:

First: Find the index numbers for the two locations in the table below.
Then: Insert those numbers into the adjacent formulas.
You will then find how each job offer compares in worth according to the location of the job.

AVERAGE CITY, U.S.A.   100.0

Alabama			
Birmingham	99.5	Riverside	111.2
Mobile	96.1	Sacramento	108.3
Tuscaloosa	94.9	San Diego	119.9
		San Jose	111.6
Arizona			
Phoenix	109.5	**Colorado**	
Tucson	100.6	Colorado Springs	96.4
		Denver	100.1
Arkansas		Ft. Collins	97.4
Fayetteville	92.4		
		Connecticut	
California		Hartford	120.2
Fresno	105.7		
Los Angeles	115.3	**Delaware**	
Orange County	117.9	Dover	94.9

Florida

Fort Lauderdale	112.9
Gainesville	97.6
Miami	110.3
Tallahassee	101.7

Georgia

Atlanta	110.6
Columbus	95.1
Macon	98.6

Illinois

Quad Cities	93.3
Rockford	104.2
Springfield	102.4

Indiana

Ft. Wayne	94.8
Indianapolis	96.6
South Bend	91.3

Iowa

Cedar Rapids	99.9
Sioux City	96.8

Kansas

Wichita	96.4

Kentucky

Bowling Green	97.7
Lexington	101.5
Louisville	96.9
Owensboro	97.2

Louisiana

Baton Rouge	97.0
New Orleans	96.6

Maine

Portland	105.9

Maryland

Baltimore	106.9

Michigan

Jackson	93.4
Lansing	105.6

Minnesota

St. Paul	103.1

Mississippi

Gulfport	98.4

Missouri

Columbia	92.0
Kansas City	101.9
St. Louis	98.6

Montana

Billings	103.5
Great Falls	97.9

Nebraska

Lincoln	96.7
Vermillion	92.4

Nevada

Las Vegas	109.4

New Jersey

Newark/Elizabeth	127.6

New Mexico

Albuquerque	101.6

New York

Binghamton	104.2
Buffalo	97.1
New York City	141.2
Syracuse	95.5

North Carolina

Chapel Hill	106.0
Charlotte	98.7
Greensboro	97.8
Raleigh	101.4

Ohio

Akron	101.2
Cleveland	99.2
Columbus	103.1
Youngstown	93.4

Oklahoma

Oklahoma City	96.6

Oregon

Portland	108.7

Pennsylvania

Erie	101.5
Lancaster	105.2
Philadelphia	120.5
Wilkes-Barre	94.9

South Carolina

Columbia	101.1
Greenville	97.3

South Dakota

Rapid City	96.7
Vermillion	92.4

Tennessee

Memphis	98.5
Nashville/Davidson	102.0

Texas		**Virginia**	
Austin	105.0	Hampton	103.3
Brownsville	91.3	Richmond	102.4
Dallas	108.9	Roanoke	96.7
Houston	102.0		
Lubbock	94.3	**Washington**	
San Antonio	96.5	Seattle	105.2
Waco	94.7	Spokane	95.6
		Tacoma	103.3
Utah			
Salt Lake City	100.2	**West Virginia**	
Provo	90.6	Charleston	98.1
Vermont		**Wisconsin**	
Montpelier/Barre	103.1	Fond du Lac	100.4
		Green Bay	97.4
Virgin Islands		Janesville	91.6
St. Thomas	135.9	La Crosse	92.8
		Wyoming	
		Caper	95.9

Source: American Chamber of Commerce Researchers Association Inner-City Cost of Living Index.

Exercise

$$\frac{(City\ \#1)}{(City\ \#2)} \quad \frac{Index\ \#}{Index\ \#} \quad X \quad \frac{Starting}{Salary} \quad = \$ \underline{\hspace{2cm}}$$

EQUATION:

■ What is the _____ equivalent of a
$_____ offer in _____ ?

_____ _____ X $ _____ = $

■ What is the _____ equivalent of a
$_____ offer in _____ ?

_____ _____ X $ _____ = $

Company Standing

Before you accept a job, you should feel comfortable about the stability of the company. Review the information in How to Research a Company and you see that the important areas to consider when evaluating an employer are:

- *The company's financial condition*
- *The age/history of the company*
- *The stability of its workforce*
- *The company's plans for expansion*
- *The company's philosophies and policies*
- *The company's organizational framework*
- *The company's standing with respect to its competition*
- *The company's leadership*
- *The company's view of its employees*
- *The company's compensation, employee assistance programs, training and promotional programs*
- *The company's involvement in the community*

Total Compensation Packages

> *Salary & Benefits* = Total Compensation

It's true that you need to earn a certain salary to meet cost of living expenses and still have enough discretionary income to enjoy life. You have already learned how to evaluate a job offer based on the worth of the salary being offered and the cost of living in different geographic areas. But there is more to consider. In addition to salary, benefits constitute a major portion of total compensation packages.

Bruce Serlen talks about "The $8,000 Question" in his article in *National Business Employment Weekly*. Serlen says that, "Benefits, even at starting management levels, can easily be worth $8,000 a year. Specifically, $8,166. That's what companies spend annually on benefits for the average worker, according to the U.S. Chamber of Commerce. While the value of different benefits packages varies, they can amount to more than 40% of a job's total compensation." Most companies have a wide range of benefits that go beyond the traditional health coverage and retirement plan. These additional benefits may include:

Tuition reimbursement
Legal & financial counseling

"When considering an offer, think of benefits and salary as two parts of the total compensation. One can't really be divorced from the other," advises Sheila H. Akabas, Director of the Center for Social Policy and Practice in the Workplace at Columbia University's School of Social Work.

National Business Employment Weekly, Spring, 1987.

Parental leave
Dependent care for elderly relatives
Day care for children
Stock options
Company cars
Club membership
First-class travel
Time off
Company vacations
Housing
Discounts
Meals

Medical coverage seems to be the most expensive benefit. Because younger employees often have minimal health care needs while older workers need more coverage, many companies offer their employees options for medical coverage. This is frequently done in the form of a "cafeteria-style benefits program." In this case, a person can tailor a program to fit his or her individual needs. By choosing less medical coverage you may free up a number of credits, which can then be used for benefits you choose or a cash alternative.

In any case, you see that there is more to the worth of a job offer than just the salary. Take into consideration what that salary is worth in the particular geographic location and then add the accompanying benefits in order to make the best decision.

Promotional Opportunity

Some companies have more predictable promotional routes than others. Some move employees through different grades or levels of jobs based on their seniority with the company. Others base promotions strictly on performance. The large ones may offer many employees the chance to move up while other, smaller companies, have less room at the top. There are those that have a formal, internal job posting system to which employees may respond by applying for posted positions. Other companies go directly to employees selected on the basis of good performance to fill positions. Knowing the procedures regarding promotional opportunities at a company before you accept a job will help you understand your chances for advancement with that company.

Training Programs

Training programs vary from company to company. Before accepting a job, find out about any formal training the company may have. You should know:

1. *Duration of the program*
2. *Salary during training phase*
3. *Location of the training (possibly a distant home office site)*
4. *Existence of ongoing training (some companies have continuing Career Development programs)*

If training is done on-the-job as opposed to a formal program, this is fine in most cases. Just be sure to ask enough questions to get the feel of whether or not the training will be structured enough for your needs. If an employer offers you a lower salary to begin training on the job and says that it will go up to a certain amount after your training period, ask how long that will be. If you are accepting this as a condition of employment, you should be able to measure the time frame within which the change should occur. This will be important to you from a financial stand point. You will then have an idea as to how long you will be working within a particular budget and be able to plan your personal and financial responsibilities based on that knowledge.

LIFELONG CAREER PLANNING

The strategies you have learned in "Job Search Techniques" are an important part of managing your career. Career planning is a lifelong process involving periodic assessment of your job to see if a change may be appropriate. Don't make a move for the sake of change. Don't move just for any opportunity. Move because it is the next logical step along the career direction you have mapped out for yourself. When you decide to change jobs you will see that you will use these strategies that you are applying now in applying for a job and interviewing. By mastering these skills now you will know that you are in control of managing your own career throughout your lifetime.

Contemporary Issues in the Workplace

INTRODUCTION

There is evidence that the world of work is changing toward increasing integration between personal and professional lifestyles. The overlap of personal interests affecting the workplace is a result of changing personal value systems. For example, there is a trend for workers to value free time more than ever before. Personal problems such as alcoholism or drug addiction affect a person's performance in the workplace. Career women now wanting to raise families are faced with conflicts in priorities.

These contemporary issues in the workplace affect the way we live and work. Personal value systems are changing the workplace. You should be aware of some of the issues that will affect you during your career. Following are updates on:

- Drug Testing
- Smoking in the Workplace
- Parental Leave
- Day Care
- Alternative Work Arrangements
- Employee Assistance Programs

DRUG TESTING

An increasing number of employers — including the *U.S. Postal Service, General Motors, Alcoa,* the *New York Times* and *American Airlines* — are requiring pre-employment urine or blood tests to screen for the presence of cocaine, barbiturates, amphetamines, marijuana and opiates. Some companies fire workers with drug problems. Other companies attempt to help an experienced employee ovecome the problem. It is often more cost effective for the company to do that because there really is no guarantee that a new worker won't have the same problem. Through Employee Assistance Programs (EAP's), companies offer on-site or off-site confidential counseling and treatment. Other companies' insurance plans cover drug programs, and some offer paid leaves of absence. When AT&T evaluated its EAP after three years, it found that 86% of those who had been treated were completely rehabilitated.

Drug and alcohol testing of employees and job applicants continues to increase. Some companies fire workers with drug problems.

The Realities of Substance Abuse in the Workplace

- Alcohol and drug abuse is estimated to raise insurance costs $50 billion annually.
- Nearly 30% of employers are said to test college recruits for drug use.
- An employer's decision not to promote an employee because her husband was a drug abuser has been upheld.
- The Attorney General has called on employers to conduct "surveillance" of areas where employees may be using drugs.

SMOKING

The Surgeon General estimates that cigarettes cause 350,000 fatalities in the U.S. every year from lung cancer, heart disease, and various respiratory ailments. That's roughly seven times the total deaths suffered by Americans in the Vietnam War. The Surgeon General further concludes that the combination of smoking and pollutants in the work environment has produced a health disaster. There is heavy pressure to forbid smoking in more and more work sites. Local ordinances are being enacted to require employers to provide a smoke-free workplace. When executives were asked to choose between two job candidates with equal qualifications, and only one smoked, they were fifteen times more likely to hire the nonsmoker. *Accountemps,* a temporary service for the accounting industry, had 100 corporate vice presidents and personnel directors surveyed. Results indicated that smoking during a job interview may reduce your chances of getting hired. Employees who smoke cost their company a substantial amount of money. In addition, there are negative social reactions attached to smoking in the workplace. These perspectives and others on smoking in the workplace are presented in "Hire a Non-Smoker."

Forty-six percent of personnel directors at the nation's largest corporations prefer to hire nonsmokers over smokers.

Hire a Non-Smoker

- ***Non-Smokers*** . . . have less absenteeism than smokers. The U.S. Public Health Service Studies show that smokers are absent from work because of illness 30 percent more often than non-smokers.
- ***Non-Smokers*** . . . have fewer illnesses. Smokers are particularly susceptible to invading viruses and bacteria. They catch the common cold one and one-half times more often than non-smokers.
- ***Non-Smokers*** . . . have fewer chronic diseases leading to early disability. Smoker's diseases such as lung cancer, emphysema and coronary heart disease often turn workers into permanent invalids, necessitating early retirement and costly disability payments.

- ***Non-Smokers*** . . . have fewer work accidents. Smoking is often a distraction and can lead to accidents. *(Example: Many car accidents occur because the driver was searching for, lighting, or disposing of a cigarette and his or her attention was diverted.)*
- ***Non-Smokers*** . . . tend to be more productive. They don't take time out for "smoking breaks," trips to the cigarette machine, nor do they fumble with matches, lighters and ashtrays.
- ***Non-Smokers*** . . . make a better impression with the general public. Receptionists, salespeople and executives present a better image if they don't smoke. They smell better, look better and don't risk offending nonsmokers who don't like smoke.
- ***Non-Smokers*** . . . are less destructive of company property. Fire damage caused by careless smokers represents huge financial losses. A conservative estimate by the National Fire Protective Association is that one-quarter of all fires resulting in property losses are caused by smoking materials. In fires where lives are lost, more than one half are smoking-related. Destruction, such as cigarette burns in rugs, on desks, trash-can fires and damaged merchandise adds up!
- ***Non-Smokers*** . . . do not offend fellow workers. No need to elaborate on this! Any non-smoker who has had to work with smokers will tell you what it's like.
- ***Non-Smokers*** . . . are less subject to many occupational health hazards. When an industrial condition such as airborne contaminants already exists, non-smokers do not further endanger their health with tobacco smoke.
- ***Non-Smokers*** . . . can work around sensitive machinery. Smokers may foul instruments, making them inaccurate or, at best, necessitate frequent cleaning.

*The High Cost of Workplace Smoking	Annual Cost Per Smoker
On-the-job time lost	$1,820
Morbidity and early mortality (lost earnings)	765
Passive smoking	664
Property damage and depreciation	500
Maintenance	500
Medical care	230
Absenteeism	220
TOTAL	$4,699

A smoking ban in the workplace can result in savings of up to 75 percent in personnel costs, insurance premiums, maintenance charges, and other expenses, according to William L. Weis, professor of accounting in the Albers School of Business at Seattle University.

SOURCE: "NO IFS, ANDS, OR BUTTS — WHY WORKPLACE SMOKING SHOULD BE BANNED" BY WILLIAM L. WEIS, *MANAGEMENT WORLD*, SEPTEMBER 1981.

From "Best of Business Quarterly, Summer, 1986

PARENTAL LEAVE

According to a survey by the *Catalyst Career and Family Center* in New York, barely half of the nation's firms offer even unpaid maternity leaves. Catalyst also reports that 36.8 percent of American corporations participating in a recent survey offer paternity leave. Yet of these, only 2.7 percent give men even partial pay for their time off. Although the number of companies offering parental leave is on the rise, most leaves are non-paid. Despite the strong interest many men and women have in staying home to care for their children, many of them simply cannot afford to. Some studies interpret the low number of men taking leave as a lack of interest when it appears likely that the absence of pay is the real issue. In Sweden, a parent-insurance benefit program was established by law in 1974. Men are paid up to 90% of their salaries during their leaves. Today, according to Shelia Kamerman, Ph.D., a professor at the Columbia University of Social Work, about 25% of eligible men make some use of the parent insurance. Perhaps if American men knew that their jobs would not be threatened and they could be paid for their time off, more would ask for leave.

---

*Mothering Laws

In only five states is a new mother entitled by law to take a paid maternity leave. Elsewhere in the world the benefits are far more liberal.

	Maximum Weeks of Parental Leave	Job Security	Maximum Weekly Benefits
In the United States			
California	10	No	$224
New Jersey	10	No	$213
Hawaii	8-10	No	$212
Rhode Island	8-10	No	$171
New York	8	No	$145
Abroad			
Sweden	52	Yes	90% of weekly salary for 38 weeks
Italy	44	Yes	80% for 22 weeks
West Germany	40	Yes	100% for 18 weeks
Chile	18	Yes	100% for 18 weeks
Canada	17	Yes	60% for 15 weeks

SOURCES: INTERNATIONAL LABOUR OFFICE, GENEVA; SHEILA KAMERMAN, COLUMBIA UNIVERSITY; NOW LEGAL DEFENSE AND EDUCATION FUND.

*From Newsweek, January 26, 1987

DAY CARE

"Seventy-seven percent of women and 73% of men surveyed report that they take time away from work attending to their children — making phone calls or ducking out for a long lunch to go to a school play. That alone translates into hundreds of millions of dollars in lost output for U.S. corporations," says John P. Fernandez, manager of personnel services at AT&T. Dana Friedman, senior research associate at the Conference Board, says, "Child care is likely to be the fringe benefit of the 1990's because what's good for employees becomes good for business."

Quality day care varies enormously. States license and monitor the private for-profit and not-for-profit centers. In some states, important matters such as learning activities or the teacher-child ratio are ignored. The tremendous amount of time being spent by workers on child care and the inconsistent quality of day care centers is creating a new push toward the corporate on-site day care center. There are advantages to such centers. Parents can drop in any time. Companies benefit in the recruitment and retention of employees. One of the most innovative efforts recently made was by Levi Strauss & Co. When children get sick, traditional day care centers are not the answer for working parents because sick children are not allowed in day care centers. To enable parents of sick children not to miss work, Levi Strauss & Co. funded a 17-bed children's infirmary that is attached to an independent day care center in San Jose, California.

Problems with child care are the most significant predictors of absenteeism and unproductive time at work.

Chicken Soup is a sick-child day care operation in Minneapolis. First Bank System, a Minneapolis bank holding company, pays 75% of the $26.26 a day for each employee's child who checks into Chicken Soup. First Bank loses $154 a day if a $40,000-a-year middle manager misses work to take care of a sick child. Chicken Soup saves the company 87% or almost $135 a day.

Companies are realizing the advantages of day care centers. About 3,000 companies offer subsidized day care centers, financial assistance for child care, or child care referral services.

*What Working Parents Say About Child Care	Men	Women
Report that both spouses share equally in child care responsibility	55.1%	51.9%
Say the job inteferes with family life	37.2%	40.9%
Sought less demanding job to get more family time	20.5%	26.5%
Refused a job, promotion, or transfer because it would mean less family time	29.6%	25.7%
Felt nervous or under stress in past three months	49.2%	70.2%
Missed at least one workday in the past three months due to family obligations	37.8%	58.6%
Think children of working parents benefit by having interesting role models for parents	77.5%	86.3%
Think children of working parents suffer by not being given enough time and attention	55.4%	58.2%
Would like their companies to provide a subsidized child care center	38.5%	54.1%
Would like their companies to offer flexible working hours	34.8%	54.1%
Think companies can do more to help manage work/family responsibilities	34.5%	30.9%

Though working fathers and mothers pretty much agree that they share equally in child care responsibilities and that their jobs interfere with family life, more fathers say they have refused a new job, promotion, or transfer that would take away from family time. Mothers are more likely to report that they feel stress. Only 30.9% of the women polled in FORTUNE's nationwide survey of 400 working parents wanted more child care help from their companies. But over half said they would like their employers to offer flexible working hours and provide subsidized day care centers.

*From Fortune, February 16, 1987

Though working fathers and mothers pretty much agree that they share equally in child care responsibilities and that their jobs interfere with family life, more fathers say they have refused a new job, promotion, or transfer that would take away from family time. Mothers are more likely to report that they feel stress. Only 30.9% of the women polled in FORTUNE's nationwide survey of 400 working parents wanted more child care help from their companies. But over half said they would like their employers to offer flexible working hours and provide subsidized day care centers.

*From Fortune, February 16, 1987

ALTERNATIVE WORK ARRANGEMENTS

Seven point six million work under one of several types of alternative (flexible) work arangements. The reasons for this trend are:

1. *The growing number of single parent families*
2. *The high cost of commuting*
3. *The desire for larger blocks of personal time*
4. *The desire of older workers to reduce their hours yet still continue to work*
5. *The growing number of professional career women now taking time to raise their children while still remaining involved with their careers.*

Alternative work arrangements reduce the stresses caused by conflict between job demands, family needs, leisure values and educational needs. Organizations enhance their recruiting attractiveness by offering alternative as well as standard work arrangements.

Standard Work Schedule: These include the standard day, evening, and night work sessions and 40 hour per week schedules. Standard work schedules also include overtime work, part-time work, and shift work over a 40-hour week.

Flex Time: Flex time is a work schedule that gives employees daily choice in the timing of work and nonwork activities. Core time is when the employee has to work. Flexible time allows the employee freedom to *choose* the remaining time to work.

Compressed Work Weeks: Provisions for employees who want to work fewer than five days a week have led to compressed work weeks. By extending the workday beyond the standard eight hours, employees generally need to work only three to four days per week for a standard 40-hour work week.

Permanent Part-Time Work and Job Sharing: A permanent part-time work schedule may be a shortened daily schedule *(Ex: 1 to 5 p.m.)*, or an odd hour shift *(From 5 to 9 p.m.)*. Job sharing is a particular type of part-time work. In job sharing, two people divide the responsibility for a regular full-time job. Both may work half the job, or one could work more than the other. Traditional part-time workers generally receive little or no benefits but workers on permanent part-time and job sharing schedules often do.

Advantages and Disadvantages of Standard Work Schedules		
Type of Schedule	**Advantages**	**Disadvantages**
Regular	Allows for standardization, predictability, and ease of administration; consistent application for all employees	Doesn't fit needs of all employees, not always consistent with preferences of customers
Shift	More effective use of plant and equipment: allows continuous operation and weekend work	Can be stressful, especially if rotating shifts; lower satisfaction and performance
Overtime	Permits more efficient utilization of existing work force; cheaper than alternatives: allows flexibility	Job performance may decline; may not be satisfying and may contribute to employee fatigue
Parttime	Allows scheduling flexibility to the organization, enabling it to staff at peak and unusual times; cheaper than fulltime employees	Applicable to only a limited number of jobs; increased costs of training; no promotion opportunities

Source: From "Part-time and Temporary Employees," ASPA-BNA Survey 25. Bulletin to Management, December 5, 1974, p. 5. Reprinted by permission from Bulletin to Management, copyright © 1974 by The Bureau of National Affairs, Inc., Washington, D.C.

EMPLOYEE ASSISTANCE PROGRAMS (EAPs)

EAP is a confidential counseling-referral service provided for any company employee wishing help with a personal problem. It is a service provided by the Personnel Department and deals with personal problems affecting job performance. The following is an example of a company's perspective about the existence of its EAP.

Why Is This Service Being Offered?

Each of us, regardless of the job we perform, has a variety of problems in our daily lives. Most of the time we work them out ourselves, but occasionally, a problem becomes too much for us to handle. It affects our job performance, our personal happiness, our health, and family or friends. When that happens, we need professional help in working out the problem, otherwise, the situation gets worse . . . with consequences that are costly and unpleasant. The purpose of our program is to help prevent personal problems from interfering with job performance. We offer confidential counseling and assistance in locating appropriate professional services.

EAPs assist employees with chronic personal problems which hinder their job performance, attendance, and even off-the-job behaviors. They are often used with employees who are alcoholics or who have severe marital or drug related problems. The philosophy of most EAPs is to help individuals help themselves within a context of fairness yet firmness. A company which establishes an EAP generally thinks they have a responsibility to the employee and that the employee should be given a chance to correct any undesirable job behavior. Nevertheless, it is the employee who must help him or herself. If he or she fails to participate in an EAP or recover through other means, the employer may have no other choice than to terminate the employee. The success rate of those attending EAPs is high. It is estimated that 65 to 80 percent of those who have received treatment for chemical dependency return to the workforce and do a satisfactory job in the opinion of their supervisors.

Glossary of Terms Used in Job Descriptions

GLOSSARY OF TERMS USED IN JOB DESCRIPTIONS

accept	To receive with consent; to take without protest.
accountability	The state of being subject to judgment for an action or result which a person has been given authority and responsibility to perform.
act	To exert one's power so as to bring about a result; to carry out a plan or purpose. See **execute, implement,** and **perform.**
add	To affix or attach; to find the sum of figures.
administer	To direct the application, execution, use, or general conduct of.
adopt	To take and apply or put into action.
advise	To give recommendations to. See **propose** and **recommend.** To offer an informed opinion based on specialized knowledge.
affirm	To confirm or ratify.
align	To arrange or form in a line.
amend	To change or modify.
analyze	To study the factors of a situation or problem in order to determine the outcome or solution; to separate or distinguish the parts of a process or situation so as to discover their true relationships.
anticipate	To foresee events, trends, consequences, or problems in order to deal with them in advance.
apply	To adjust or direct; to put in use.
appraise	To evaluate as to quality, status, or effectiveness of.
approve	To sanction officially; to accept as satisfactory; to ratify thereby assuming responsibility for. *(Used only in the situation where the individual has final authority.)*
arrange	To place in proper or desired order; to prepare for an event. See **prepare.**
ascertain	To find out or learn with certainty.
assemble	To collect or gather together in a predetermined order or pattern. See **collect, compile,** and **coordinate.**
assign	To give specific duties to others to perform. See **delegate.**
assist	To lend aid or support in some undertaking or effort. *(No authority over the activity is implied.)*
assume	To take upon oneself; to undertake; to take for granted.
assure	To confirm; to make certain of. See **ensure.**

attach	To bind, fasten, tie, or connect.
attend	To be present for the purpose of listening or contributing.
audit	To examine and review a situation, condition, or practice, and conclude with a detailed report on the findings.
authority	The power to influence or command thought, opinion, or behavior.
authorize	To empower; to permit; to establish by authority.
balance	To arrange or prove so that the sum of one group equals the sum of another.
batch	To group into a quantity for one operation.
calculate	To ascertain by mathematical processes; to reckon by exercise of practical judgment.
cancel	To strike or cross out.
carry	To convey through the use of the hands.
center	To place or fix at or around the center; to collect to a point.
chart	To draw or exhibit in a graph.
check	To examine for a condition; to compare for verification. See **control, examine, inspect, monitor,** and **verify.**
circulate	To distribute in accordance with a plan. See **disseminate.**
classify	To separate into groups having systematic relations.
clear	To get the agreement or disagreement of others.
close	To terminate or shut down.
code	To transpose words or figures into symbols or characters. Also **encode.**
collaborate	To work or act jointly with others.
collate	To bring together in a predetermined order.
collect	To gather facts or data; to assemble; to accumulate. See **assemble** and **compile.**
compile	To collect into a volume; to compose out of materials from other documents.
compose	To make up, fashion, or arrange.
concur	To agree with a position, statement, act, or opinion.
conduct	To lead, guide, or command the efforts of others toward producing a chosen result.
confer	To converse with others to compare views. See **consult, discuss,** and **negotiate.**
consolidate	To combine separate items into a single whole.
construct	To set in order mentally; to arrange.
consult	To seek advice of others; to confer.
control	To exert power over in order to guide or restrain; to measure, interpret, and evaluate for conformance with plans or expected results.
cooperate	To work jointly with others. See **collaborate.**
coordinate	To bring into common action or condition so as to harmonize by regulating, changing, adjusting, or combining. See **assemble.**

copy	To transfer or reproduce information.
correct	To rectify; to make right.
correlate	To establish a mutual or reciprocal relationship; to put in relation to each other.
cross foot	To add across, horizontally.
cross off	To line out, strike out.
cross out	To eliminate by lining out.
date stamp	To affix or note a date by stamping.
decide	To choose from among alternatives or possibilities so as to end debate or uncertainty.
delegate	To entrust to the care or management of another; to authorize or empower another act in one's place. See **assign, authorize,** and **represent.**
delegation	Assigning to a subordinate the responsibility and commensurate authority to accomplish an objective or specific result.
delete	To erase; to remove.
design	To conceive and plan in the mind for a specific use; to create, fashion, execute, or construct according to a plan. See **develop, devise, formulate,** and **plan.**
determine	To make a decision; to bring about; to cause; to decide and set limits to, thereby fixing definitely and unalterably. To find out something not before known as a result of an intent to find defined and precise truth.
develop	To conceive and create; to make active, available, or usable; to set forth or make clear, evident, or apparent.
development	The result of developing.
devise	To come up with something new, especially by combining known ideas or principles. See **design, develop, formulate,** and **plan.**
direct	To lead, guide, or command the efforts of others toward producing a chosen result. See **conduct, manage,** and **supervise.**
direction	Guidance or supervision of others.
disassemble	To take apart.
discover	To find out something not known before as a result of chance, exploration, or investigation. See **ascertain** and **determine.**
discuss	To exchange views for the purpose of convincing or reaching a conclusion.
dissemble	To take apart.
disseminate	To spread information or ideas. See **circulate, distribute, issue,** and **release.**
distribute	To divide or separate into classes; to pass around; to allot; to deliver to named places or persons. See **circulate, disseminate, issue,** and **release.**
divide	To separate into classes or parts. subject to mathematical division.

draft	To compose or write papers and documents in preliminary or final form, often for the approval or clearance of others.
duty	Assigned task.
edit	To revise and prepare for publication.
endorse	To express approval of; to countersign.
ensure	To make safe or certain. See **assure.**
establish	To set up or bring into existence on a firm basis.
evaluate	To ascertain or determine the value of.
examine	To investigate; to scrutinize; to subject to inquiry by inspection or test.
execute	To put into effect; to follow through to the end.
exercise	To employ actively, as in authority or influence.
expedite	To accelerate the movement or progress of, to remove obstacles.
facilitate	To make easy or less difficult.
feed	To supply material to a machine.
figure	To compute.
file	To lay away papers, etc., arranged in some methodical manner.
fill in	To enter information on a form.
find	To locate by search.
flag	To mark distinctively.
follow up	To check the progress of; to see if results are satisfactory.
formulate	To develop or devise a plan, policy, or procedure; to put into a systemized statement.
furnish	To give or supply. See **provide.**
goal	An objective.
guidance	Conducting or directing along a course of action.
implement	To carry out; to perform acts essential to the execution of a plan or program; to give effect to.
inform	To instruct; to communicate knowledge.
initiate	To originate; to introduce for the first time.
insert	To put or thrust in.
inspect	To examine carefully for suitability or conformance with standards. See **check, control, examine, monitor,** and **verify.**
instruct	To impart knowledge to; to give information or direction to; to show how to do.
instructions	To furnish with directions; to inform.
	Specific Precise and detailed directions that closely limit what can be done or how it can be done.
	General Directions that are merely outlined, hence do not closely limit what can be done or how it can be done.
intensive	Exhaustive or concentrated.
interpret	To explain or clarify; to translate; to elucidate.

interview	To question in order to obtain facts or opinions.
inventory	A list of items; stock on hand.
investigate	To study closely and methodically.
issue	To distribute formally.
itemize	To set or note down in detail; to set by particulars.
line	To cover the inside surface of; to draw lines on.
list	To itemize.
locate	To search for and find; to position.
maintain	To keep up to date or current; to keep at a given level or in working condition.
manage	To control and direct; to guide; to command the efforts of others toward producing a chosen result. See **supervise.**
measure	To find the quality or amount of; to ascertain dimension, count, intensity, etc.
merge	To combine.
mix	To unite or blend into one group or mass.
monitor	To observe or check periodically for a specific purpose.
multiply	To perform the operation of multiplication.
negotiate	To exchange views and proposals with an eye to reaching agreement by sifting possibilities, proposals, and pros and cons.
nonroutine	Irregular or infrequent situations that arise relating to business or official duties. Characteristic of higher-level jobs.
note	To observe, notice, heed.
notify	To give notice to; to inform.
objective	A desired result. See **goal.**
observe	To perceive, notice, watch.
obtain	To gain possession of; to acquire.
open	To enter upon; to spread out; to make accessible.
operate	To conduct or perform activity.
organization	Individuals working together in related ways within a specific structure toward a common end.
organize	To arrange in interdependent parts; to systemize.
originate	To produce as new; to invent.
outline	To make a summary of the significant features of a subject.
participate	To take part in.
perform	To carry out; to accomplish; to execute.
place	To locate an employee in a job.
plan	To devise or project a method or course of action.
policy	A definite course or method of action selected from among alternatives and in light of given conditions, to guide and determine present and future decisions.
position description	A document which describes the purpose, scope, duties, responsibilities, authorities, and working relationships

	associated with a position or entity to be occupied and performed by one person.
position specification	A document which describes the physical characteristics, knowledge, skill, experience, and education requirements of a person who would be ideally suited to perform a specific job.
post	To announce by public, written notice; to transfer or carry information from one record to another.
practice	To work repeatedly to gain skill.
prepare	To make ready for a special purpose.
principle	A governing law of conduct; a fundamental belief serving as a responsible guide to action; a basis for policy.
procedure	A particular way of accomplishing something or of acting; a series of steps followed in a regular, definite order; a standardized practice.
proceed	To begin or carry out.
process	To subject to some special treatment; to handle in accordance with prescribed procedures.
program	A series of planned steps toward an objective.
promote	To act so as to increase sales or patronage; to advance someone to a higher level or job.
propose	To offer for consideration or adoption; to declare an intention.
provide	To supply for use; to make available; to furnish.
purchase	To buy or procure.
purpose	Something set up as an objective or end to be attained; a reason.
rate	To appraise or assess; to give one's opinion of the rank or quality of.
receive	To take something that is offered or sent.
recommend	To advise or counsel a course of action or to suggest for adoption a course of action.
reconstruct	To restore; to construct again.
record	To register; to make a record of.
refer	To direct attention to.
register	To enter in a record or list.
release	To authorize the publication of, dissemination of.
remit	To transmit or send money as payment.
render	To furnish, contribute.
report	To supply or furnish organized information.
represent	To act for or in place of; to serve as a counterpart of; to substitute in some capacity for.
request	To ask for something.
require	To demand as necessary or essential.

requisition	A document making a request.
research	Inquiry into a specific subject from several sources.
responsibility	The quality or state of being accountable for.
responsible for	Having caused; accountable for.
review	To examine, usually with intent to approve or dissent; to analyze results in order to give an opinion.
revise	To change in order to make new, to correct, to improve, or bring up to date.
route	To prearrange the sending of an item to the location to which it is to be sent.
routine	Regular procedure, or normal course of business or official duties.
scan	To examine point by point; to scrutinize.
schedule	To plan a timetable; to set specific times for.
screen	To examine so as to separate into two or more groups or classes, usually rejecting one or more.
search	To look over and through for the purpose of finding something.
secure	To get possession of; to obtain; to make safe.
select	Chosen from a number of others of a similar kind.
separate	To set apart from others for special use; to keep apart.
serve	To hold an office; to act in a capacity; to discharge a duty or function.
sign	To authorize by affixing one's signature.
sort	To put in a definite place or rank according to kind, class, etc.
stack	To pile up.
standard of performance	A statement of the conditions that will exist when a job is acceptably done.
	Whenever possible the elements of the statement include specific reference to quantity, quality, cost, and time.
stimulate	To excite, rouse, or spur on.
study	To consider attentively; to ponder or fix the mind closely upon a subject.
submit	To present information for another's judgment or decision.
subtotal	An interim total.
subtract	To deduct one number from another.
summarize	To give only the main points.
supervise	To oversee a work group, leading, guiding, or commanding its efforts to produce a chosen result.
support	To provide service, assistance, or supplies to another person or department.
survey	To ascertain facts regarding conditions or the condition of a situation usually in connection with the gathering of information.
tabulate	To form into a table by listing; to make a listing.

trace	To record the transfer of an application or document; to copy as a drawing.
train	To increase skill or knowledge by capable instruction.
transcribe	To make a typed copy from shorthand notes or dictated record; to write a copy of.
transpose	To transfer; to change the usual place or order.
underline	To emphasize or identify by drawing a line under the characters or subject.
verify	To prove to be true or accurate; to confirm or substantiate; to test or check the accuracy of.

This Glossary was developed in 1981 by Richard B. Shore and Patricia Alcibar for American Management Associations. Used by permission.

From: "Job Descriptions in Human Resources" by JoAnn Sperling 1985, N.Y., Amacom (A Division of American Management Association)

General Index of Job Descriptions

GENERAL INDEX OF JOB DESCRIPTIONS

Academic Department Head
Administers affairs of an academic department. May administer department's budget and recruit academic personnel. Conducts meetings to discuss current teaching strategies and obtains recommendations for changes within the department.

Accountant
Helps businesses and individuals set up financial recordkeeping. Examines, analyzes, and interprets accounting records for the purpose of giving advice or preparing statements. Estimates future revenues and expenditures to prepare budget.

Account Executive
Responsible for the development of and service of a customer account. Brings business to the firm. Consults with the client and collaborates with associates to find best strategies for servicing clients.

Account Executive (Advertising)
Meets with clients. Participates in meetings with other departments on the ideas for a campaign. Plans overall strategy for clients. Keeps up-to-date on media rate changes and new media outlets. Serves as a link between the agency and the clients.

Account Executive (Public Relations)
Meets with clients to determine needs for public relations program. May review company strategies and goals, current customer base and reputation with the public. Recommends public relations program. Keeps up-to-date on new and existing programs and policies. Serves as a link between the public relations firm and the clients.

Account Executive (Telemarketing)
Organizes and manages a program internally once it has been brought in by a telemarketing representative. Coordinates script writing, script testing, list preparation, forms design (to record sales and customer data), and client reports. Monitors the project and provides regular reports for the client.

Account Executive Trainee (Advertising)
Fields material from other departments. Takes calls from clients. Keeps in touch with traffic department on schedules for ads and spots.

Account Manager
Develops an efficient coverage pattern for the territory. Decides on the call frequency for major accounts. Develops a sales plan for the territory. Promotes,

sells, and services product line. Reviews customer-call reports. Coordinates activities at individual key customer locations.

Account Representative
(See Account Executive)

Account Supervisor
(See Account Manager)

Accounts Supervisor/Manager
(See Account Manager)

Activities Coordinator *(Cruiselines)*
Plans and implements activities for passengers on cruiselines.

Actuarial Trainee
Works for insurance companies analyzing statistics to determine probabilities of accident, death, injury, earthquake, flood, fire, etc., so that the rates charged for insurance policies will bring in profits for the company while still being competitive with those of other insurance carriers.

Actuary
Uses mathematical skills to predict probabilities of events that will be used for insurance plans and pension programs.

Adjuster
Investigates and settles claims of losses suffered by policy holders of all kinds of insurance.

Adjuster Trainee
Assists with investigations and settling claims of losses suffered by policy holders of all kinds of insurance.

Administrative Analyst/Planner
Responsibilities include developing any new systems and setting up any long-range planning systems; responsible for the planning group, which actually plans each day's shipment to distribution centers. Works on product allocation and inventory control. Responsible for anything that might affect the distribution area.

Administrative Assistant
An administrative support job performed with little or no supervision, and one that is a step higher than an executive secretary. Handles dissemination of contract information or works with a chief officer of a company in preparing corporate reports. Often involves supervision of others.

Administrative Dental Assistant
Checks office and laboratory supplies; maintains waiting, reception, and examination rooms in a neat and orderly condition, answers telephones, greets patients, and other callers, records and files patient data and medical records, fills out medical reports and insurance forms, handles correspondence, schedules appointments and arranges for hospital admission and laboratory services. May transcribe dictation and handle the bookkeeping and billing.

Administrative Manager

Provides maximum support to all divisions through the regional or district distribution centers and ensures that timely, cost-effective service is provided to those units and their customers. Supervises personnel, equipment, materials, facilities, product handling, inventory control, building services, customer relations, order processing, office services, and district operations.

Administrative Medical Office Assistant

(See Administrative Dental Assistant)

Administrative Secretary

Handles everything except dictation and typing. Duties range from filing and setting up filing systems, routing mail, and answering telephones to more complex work such as answering letters, doing research and preparing statistical reports.

Administrative Support Manager *(Word Processing)*

Responsible for the operation of the entire word processing center.

Administrator *(Education)*

Directs the administration of an educational institution, or a division of it, within the authority of the governing board. Develops or expands programs or services. Administers fiscal operations such as budget planning, accounting, and establishing costs for the institution. Directs hiring and training of personnel. Develops policies and procedures for activities within area of responsibility.

Advertising Manager

Plans and executes advertising policies of an organization. Confers with department heads to discuss possible new accounts and to outline new policies or sales promotion campaigns. Confers with officials of newspapers, radio, and television stations and then arranges billboard advertising contracts. Allocates advertising space to department. May authorize information for publication.

Agent *(Insurance)*

Sells traditional life insurance to clients. May also sell mutual funds and other equity-based products. Many agents also qualify as financial planners after obtaining certification. Explains financial products in detail to prospective clients. Processes necessary paperwork when closing a sale.

Airline Schedule Analyst

Reviews schedules for all incoming and outgoing flights. Makes recommendations for changes in schedules to ensure maximum service while still maintaining strict procedures.

Airport Manager

Responsible for operating a safe facility and fund raising. Keeps the public informed on safety decisions affecting the area surrounding the airport.

Airport Operations Agent

Customer service agent responsible for assigning boarding times, lifting tickets; coordinates baggage service; announces flight arrivals to main desk.

Airport Security Officer
Notes suspicious persons and reports to superior officer. Reports hazards.
Inspects baggage of passengers. Assists passengers with lost luggage claims.
Directs passengers to appropriate boarding areas. Warns or arrests persons
violating ordinances. Issues tickets to traffic violators. Maintains overall
security of the airport.

Analyst *(Marketing)*
(See Market Research Analyst)

Area Manager *(Retail)*
Manages a selling center within a store. This would include a small group of
departments carrying related merchandise.

Architect
Involved with all aspects of the planning, designing, and construction of
buildings. Prepares proposals which include illustrations and scaled drawings.
Draws the structural system as well as the other elements that go into the
project. Provides advice about choosing contractors.

Assistant Actuary
(See Actuary)

Assistant Buyer *(Production)*
(See Buyer-Production)

Assistant Loan Officer
(See Loan Officer)

Assistant Marketing Director *(Travel)*
Assists with the development of competitive strategies for clients. Reviews
services and products being offered and evaluates client's market position.
Assists companies with monitoring themselves to make sure they are delivering
what is promised.

Assistant Media Planner
Learns to interpret rate cards of various media. Analyzes audience ratings.
Writes letters and memos. Compares media alternatives. Prepares and delivers
presentations to clients. Talks with sales representatives from various media.
Evaluates media buying.

Assistant Purchasing Agent
(See Purchasing Agent)

Assistant Quality Assurance Manager
(See Quality Assurance Manager)

Assistant Store Manager
(See Store Manager)

Assistant Travel Editor
(See Travel Editor)

Assistant Underwriter
(See Underwriter)

Associate Analyst *(Marketing)*
(See Market Research Analyst)

Associate Media Director
Makes decisions on media buying. Reviews alternative selections' and results of ratings to determine decision.

Associate Research Director *(Advertising)*
Evaluates information published by the government, trade or other groups as relates to individual ad campaigns. Evaluates suggestions and findings of the research account executive to determine best approach to each ad campaign. Keeps campaigns operating within specified guidelines.

Attractions Specialist
Has specific knowledge of local attractions and how to promote them. Provides input on target population for promotional effort.

Bank Manager
Manages, directs, and coordinates activities of workers engaged in accounting and recording of financial transactions, setting up trust or escrow accounts, probating estates, and administering trust or mortgage accounts. Develops relationships with customers, business, community and civic organizations to promote goodwill and generate new business.

Bank Officer Trainee
Gains experience in the main functions of the banking business. These include the trust department, where money is invested for families, institutions, or other businesses; the credit department, where decisions are made on loaning money to customers and operations, where all of the normal business functions (data processing, personnel, public relations and accountants) are monitored.

Benefits Coordinator
Administers various employee benefit programs such as group insurance — life, medical, and dental; accident and disability insurance; pensions; investment savings, and health maintenance organizations. Initiates medical and option forms and/or affidavits; arranges for their completion and submission within time limits. Implements new benefit programs; arranges and conducts employee information presentations and enrollments. Ensures program compliance with governmental regulations.

Branch Manager
Plans, coordinates, controls the work flow, updates systems, strives for administrative efficiency, and is responsible for all functions of a branch office.

Branch Sales Manager
Makes a direct sales effort to the customers in the area to sell a product line. Provides management with sales and booking forecasts on a monthly, quarterly, and annual basis. Keeps abreast of prices and performance of competitors' products in his or her territory. Handles service and related problems as they arise. Trains and supervises sales staff.

Broadcast Technician
Performs the work of an electronics technician specifically on various types of broadcast equipment. *(See Electronics Technician)*

Buyer *(Production)*
Responsible for placing orders, expediting back orders and processing paperwork for stock and non-stock supplies. This includes processing requisitions, researching products, clarifying specifications, typing purchase orders, following up on back orders, selecting vendors, maintaining up-to-date product information files and utilizing computer terminals and hand held order entry devices to place order.

Buyer *(Retail)*
Selects the goods to be sold by retail stores or wholesale outlets. They also help to plan the selling programs for the goods they have purchased. Buyers normally specialize in one type of goods such as men's clothing, housewares and accessories.

Buyer Trainee *(Retail)*
Assists supervising buyer. Places orders and speaks with manufacturers by telephone. Supervises the inspection and unpacking of new merchandise and overseeing its distribution.

Camp Manager
Directs and coordinates activities of workers concerned with preparation and maintenance of buildings and facilities in residential camp; coordinates through staff or personally directs staff in preparing and maintaining such camp facilities as dining halls, etc. used by resident employees. Schedules purchase and delivery of food supplies. Enforces safety and sanitation regulations.

Chief Accountant
Responsible for the supervision and control of the general accounting functions. This includes general ledger, payables, payroll, property, budget reporting and statistical accumulation. Responsible for financial statement and report preparation and budget reviews. Supervises and trains employees in accounting, payroll and accounts payable.

Chief Actuary
Oversees the calculation of probabilities of death, sickness disability, injury, property loss, fire and other hazards. Evaluates and analyzes relevant statistics. Determines the rate of expected losses due to the issuance of various types of policies. Determines the various provisions contained in insurance policies.

Chief Financial Officer
Develops corporate financial objectives. Establishes policies and procedures for the effective recording, analyzing, and reporting of all financial matters. Directs the controller, treasury, and corporate financial services activities to assure that each of these functions meets established goals and provides effective service to the corporation as a whole.

Chief Internal Auditor
(See Internal Auditor)

Chief Tourism Officer
Oversees the staff engaged in tourism development for a particular area. Works within established budgets. Approves promotional campaigns.

Central Region Sales Manager
Responsible for sales function in the central region. *(See Regional Sales Manager)*.

City Manager
Responsible for managing inbound business for a car rental company.

City Mortgage and Real Estate Secretary
Works with real estate investment officers and provides secretarial support for an investment team. Prepares commitment letters, various reports, maintains files and handles telephone communications.

Claims Examiner
Analyzes insurance claims to determine extent of insurance carrier's liability and settles claims with claimants in accordance with policy provisions. Investigates questionable inquiries.

Claims Representative
Reviews insurance claim forms for completeness; secures and adds missing data and transmits claims for payment or for further investigation.

Clinical Dental Assistant
Reviews patient's records and presents them to the dentist; obtains information needed to update medical histories; takes patient X-rays; assists the dentist in examining patients; instructs about medications.

Clinical Medical Assistant
Receives patient's height, weight, temperature and blood pressure; obtains medical histories; performs basic laboratory tests; prepares patients for examination or treatment; assists the physician in examining patients. Instructs patients about medication and self treatment, draws blood, prepares patients for X-rays, takes EKG's and applies dressings.

Coder
Converts routine items of information obtained from records and reports into codes for processing by data typing using predetermined coding systems.

Coder-Editor
Synthesizes the results of questionnaires or mail or telephone surveys. The results are then reviewed by the research analyst.

Coding Clerk Supervisor
Supervises and coordinates activities of workers engaged in converting routine items of information from source documents into codes to prepare records for data processing. Modifies, revises, or designs forms and initiates procedures to develop more efficient methods of data input.

College Recruiter
Interviews college graduates on-campus. Works in conjunction with the policies and standards approved by the Employment Manager.

Commissioner of Tourism

Promotes overall tourism efforts. Generates new sources for funding. Interfaces with businesses in the community to gain support for tourism development.

Communications Equipment Technician

Performs the work of an electronics technician specifically on various types of communications equipment. *(See Electronics Technician)*

Communications Technician

May direct activities of production, circulation or promotional personnel. May prepare news or public relations releases, special brochures and similar materials. Assigns staff member, or personally interviews individuals and attends gatherings, to obtain items for publication, verify facts, and clarify information.

Computer Operator

Operates computer equipment to insure that tasks are processed in accordance with a schedule of operations. Maintains and completes daily logs. Maintains an accurate report of equipment and/or software malfunctions.

Concierge

Handles guests' problems in a hotel, makes reservation requests with restaurants and transportation facilities, arranges tours, procures theatre tickets, and handles a host of other activities.

Conference and Meeting Coordinator

Coordinates the planning and execution of conferences and meetings on and off site. Notifies attendees of details. Makes necessary facilities arrangements. Makes travel arrangements if required. Oversees the function and conducts post meeting evaluation.

Conference Planner

Compiles list of individuals or groups requesting space for activities and schedules needed facilities. Notifies program participants of locations assigned. Maintains schedules and records of available space, space used and cancellations. Requisitions needed equipment. Arranges for services during the conference. Follows up with client after the conference for evaluation of services provided.

Conference Reporter

Attends conferences at the request of the conference coordinator. Records minutes of the meetings and activities that occur during the conference. Types up summaries and distributes to requesting parties.

Conference Service Coordinator

Books the meetings, services them and follows up with a post meeting evaluation.

Consultant

Consults with client to determine need or problem, conducts studies and surveys to obtain data, and analyzes data to advise on or recommend a solution. Advises client on alternate methods of solving problem or recommends a specific solution. May negotiate contract for consulting service.

Consultant/Advisor *(Paralegal)*

Assists the legal publisher in planning new kinds of books to be written either about the paralegal profession or the procedures utilized by paralegals in law offices.

Controller

Directs financial affairs of an organization. Prepares financial analyses of operations for guidance of management. Establishes major economic objectives and policies for the company. Prepares reports which outline company's financial position in areas of income, expenses and earnings based on past, present and future operations. Directs preparation of budgets and financial forecasts.

Convention Center Manager

Manages the building, does marketing and public relations for events at the center. Responsible for entire budget for the center and supervises personnel.

Convention Planner

Arranges space and facilities for convention. Keeps exhibitors and attendees informed of procedures and policies for participation. Assigns trouble shooters to be available to provide needed services during the convention and minimizes situations that may result in a safety, legal, or logistical problem.

Convention Sales Manager

Responsible for generating convention business at hotel, civic center or other appropriate facility. Oversees sales staff. Approves advertising and rate packages. Handles projections on business and expected income. Works within established budgets.

Coordinator of Membership Sales

Maintains prospect lists for membership in travel clubs, or travel associations. Coordinates marketing programs to solicit new membership. Explains membership policies and benefits and receives payment of membership dues. Makes decisions on appropriateness of membership.

Coordinator/Scheduler *(Word Processing)*

Sees that there is an even flow of work to the word processor.

Coordinator of Scheduling *(Retail)*

Prepares production schedules. Determines type and quantity of material needed to process orders. Issues work orders. Calculates costs for manufacturing.

Coordinator/Travel Information Center

Supervises and coordinates activities of workers engaged in greeting and welcoming motorists at state highway information center. Provides information, such as directions, road conditions, and vehicular travel regulations. Provides maps, brochures and pamphlets to assist motorist in locating points of interest or in reaching destination. May direct tourists to rest areas, camps, resorts, historical points or other tourist attractions.

Copy Chief

Supervises one or more copy writers in an advertising agency, department, or service, whose function it is to assign the work of preparing the textual matter for advertisements; supervises the actual writing and transmits the completed work in accordance with the existing traffic arrangement in the firm. Coordinates copywriting activities with the layout, art, and production departments of the organization.

Copywriter

Writes original advertising material about products or services for newspapers, magazines, radio and television, posters, or other media.

Corporate Recruiter

Recruits corporate level staff for the organization. Works in conjunction with the policies and standards approved by the Employment Manager.

Corporate Travel Manager

Sets up travel budget, establishing policies for employees to follow, acts as a liaison with an outside travel agency that actually handles the arrangements; also involves personnel relocation as well as meetings and convention planning. May administer corporate aircraft, transportation to training programs, the car pool, and possibly group recreational trips or vacations for employees; may also negotiate discounts with travel suppliers.

Court Reporter

Makes accurate records of what is said during proceedings of all types. Memorizes and then reproduces the appropriate symbols that are involved in shorthand and machine reporting. All types of recordings, manual, machine and tape are transcribed accurately and typed in the required format.

Creative Director

Develops basic presentation approaches and directs layout design and copy writing for promotional material. Reviews materials and information presented by client and discusses various production factors to determine most desirable presentation concept. Confers with heads of art, copy writing and production departments to discuss client requirements and scheduling, outlines basic presentation concepts, and coordinates creative activities.

Credit Manager

Responsible for the collection of accounts deemed to be delinquent and for determining when the accounts should be referred to an outside agency for further collection efforts. Generates reports on a daily and monthly basis. Posts cash on a daily basis.

Cruise Director

Supervises all activity on board the cruiseline. Responsible for overall safety and service of passengers. Oversees staff on board.

Customer Service Agent (Travel)

Arranges for car rental on-site at rental company by phone with travel agent or in person with individual customer. Processes contracts and arranges billing upon return of the rental vehicle.

Customer Service Manager (Retail)

Responsibilities include making certain that shipments take place as scheduled.

Acts as a liaison between customers and the sales force. Spends most of the time on administrative duties including reviewing performance standards. Also trains personnel.

Customer Service Representative

Responds to customer inquiries and performs a variety of duties related to customer service. Works with customers to offer alternatives to unresolvable problems. Receives, researches, and answers customer inquiries and requests regarding accounts, products, rates and services. Develops and maintains company's image and corporate philosophy in the community.

Customer Service Representative *(Airlines)*

Duties include booking onward flight reservations, securing hotel and car rental reservations, and ticketing passengers in flight.

Customer Service Representative *(Retail)*

Resolves customer complaints and requests for refunds, exchanges and adjustments. Provides customers with catalogs and information concerning prices, shipping time and costs. Approves customer's checks and provides check-cashing service according to exchange policy. Issues temporary charges. Keeps records of items in layaway, receives and posts customer payments and prepares and forwards delinquent notices.

Customs Inspector

Inspects baggage, articles worn or carried by persons, and vessels, vehicles, or aircraft entering or leaving the United States to enforce customs and related laws.

Data Entry Operator

Operates keyboard machine to transcribe data onto magnetic tape for computer input. Examines codes on forms and source documents to determine work procedures.

Data Entry Supervisor

Accountable for quality, productivity, cost effectiveness, and timeliness of work to ensure efficient and effective conversion and verification of data into computer readable forms. Directs distribution of work; prioritizes allocation of resources to meet schedules. Sets performance standards and reviews policies for data entry personnel.

Dean

Develops academic policies and programs for college or university. Directs and coordinates activities of academic department heads within the college. Participates in activities of faculty committees and in the development of academic budgets. Serves as a liaison with accrediting agencies which evaluate academic programs.

Demographer

Plans and conducts demographic research and surveys to study the population of a given area and affecting trends.

Dental Assistant
Helps dentist during the examination and treatment of patients. They set up and maintain instruments, arrange appointments, and keep records of patients.

Dental Hygienist
Licensed to clean teeth under the supervision of a dentist. Instructs patients in dental care, diet and nutrition for proper mouth care.

Dentist
Helps patients take care of their teeth and gums, either to correct dental problems or to advise patients on ways to prevent future cavities and gum problems.

Department Manager (Office)
Directs and coordinates departmental activities and functions utilizing knowledge of department functions and company policies, standards, and practices. Gives work directions, resolves problems, prepares work schedules, and sets deadlines to insure completion of operational functions. Evaluates procedures and makes recommendations for improvements. Assigns or delegates responsibility for specific work.

Department Manager (Retail)
Supervises and coordinates activities of personnel in one department of a retail store. Assigns duties to workers and schedules lunch, breaks, work hours and vacations. Trains staff in store policies, department procedures and job duties. Evaluates staff. Handles customer complaints. Ensures that merchandise is correctly priced and displayed. Prepares sales and inventory reports. Plans department layout. Approves checks for payment and issues credit and cash refunds.

Deputy Commissioner of Tourism Development
Establishes goals, policies, and procedures of tourism development for a given area.

Design Assistant
Researches colors by contacting color forecasting services. Visits color forecasters to see presentations. Finds new garments on the market and in stores. Contacts fabric salespeople by phone for fabric samples. Keeps records, does patterns, and keeps design room organized.

Design Technician
Tests and assists in the design of all kinds of electronics equipment developed by Electronics-Design Engineers. Performs the work of an electronics technician. *(See Electronics Technician)*

Designer (Drafting)
Makes design drawings to assist in developing experimental ideas evolved by research engineers, using specifications and sketches, and employing knowledge of engineering theory and its applications to solve mechanical and fabrication problems.

Destination Promoter
Sells meeting and convention planners, tour operators, and wholesalers on

the idea of choosing a destination for their program. Services individual travelers with information and products that will make their business or pleasure trips more satisfying.

Director of Escort Services
Responsible for the hiring, training, and assignment of tour escorts. Trains the escorts on the areas for which they will be responsible.

Director of Human Resources
Oversees the day to day activities of the human resource staff. Ensures that staff complies with policies set and approved by the Vice President of Human Resources and senior management. *(See Vice President of Human Resources).*

Director of Marketing and Sales
Supervises sales department. Coordinates sales and marketing departments to develop and implement an effective marketing effort. Responsible for increasing sales volume through direct sales efforts and by assisting sales reps in the field. Coordinates future market growth plans with regard to products, services, and markets. May plan and implement advertising and promotion activities.

Director of Marketing/Sales *(Cruiselines)*
Develops pricing strategies for packages sold to groups and individuals. Establishes advertising and promotion programs. Reviews competition's strategies for attracting clients and implements competitive strategies.

Director of Media Advertising
Defines corporate media objectives. Provides media information and advice to the company. Measures media costs against industry standards. Searches for new creative ways to use media. Recommends controls, quality and cost of media purchases.

Director of Public Relations
Plans, directs, and conducts public relations program designed to create and maintain a public informed of employer's programs, accomplishments and point of view.

Director of Public Safety
Responsible for the safety of the people and equipment in a city, town or state.

Director of Research and Development
Directs and coordinates activities concerned with research and development of new concepts, ideas, basic data on, and applications for, organization's products, services, or ideologies. Reviews and analyzes proposals submitted to determine if benefits derived and possible applications justify expenditures. Develops and implements methods and procedures for monitoring projects. May negotiate contracts with consulting firms to perform research studies.

Director of Sales and Marketing
(See Director of Marketing and Sales)

Director of Tour Guides
Responsible for the hiring, training and assignment of tour guides.

Director of Training
Oversees training function for an entire company at all locations. Responsible for approval of recommended programs and proposed budgets. *(See Training Manager)*.

Director of Transportation
Responsible for getting convention goers from their hotels to and from the center; trafficking trucks in and out of the building; working with the city to make sure street lights are working; dealing with city's Taxi and Limousine Commission to ensure there are adequate services for the center.

Display Coordinator
Designs and implements the window decorations and interior displays that are so important in promoting sales. Must work well within limitations of time, space and money.

Display Director
Supervises the display of merchandise in windows, showcases and on the sales floor of retail stores. Schedules plans for displays and ensures staff follows store plan. Often responsible for several stores within a designated division.

Distribution Manager *(Retail)*
Oversees the routing of merchandise from one branch store to another on the basis of sales. Analyzes reports of stock on hand and kind and amount sold.

District Manager
Manages personnel for an assigned district, ensuring the development and accomplishment of established objectives. Trains, develops, and motivates staff. Recruits new hires. Maintains good business relationships with customers through periodic contacts and proper handling of administrative functions.

District Sales Manager
Actually carries out "cold calls," maintains reporting forms and proper business files, holds periodic meetings with sales staff.

District Sales Manager *(Travel)*
Administers city ticket and reservations offices and promotes and develops airline passenger and cargo traffic in the district.

Divisional Manager *(Banking)*
Responsible for the activities of a related group of departments in a bank such as all departments involved with customer service versus operations or systems.

Divisional Manager *(Retail)*
Retail executive responsible for the activities of a related group of selling departments or divisions.

Doctor *(Medical)*
Examines patients, orders or executes various tests and X-ray's to provide information on patient's condition. Analyzes reports and findings of tests and of examinations and diagnoses condition. Recommends treatment.

Documentation Specialist

Makes computer technology accessible to people who have no computer background. Translates the technology into plain, comprehensive English. Writes promotional brochures and advertising copy.

Drafter

Develops detailed design drawings and related specifications of mechanical equipment, according to engineering sketches and design-proposal specifications. Often calculates the strength, quality, quantity, and cost of materials. Usually specializes in a particular field of work such as MECHANICAL, ELECTRICAL, ELECTRONIC, AERONAUTICAL, STRUCTURAL, or ARCHITECTURAL drafting.

Drafter (Computer Assisted-CADD)

Drafts layouts, drawings and designs, for applications in such fields as aeronautics, architecture, or electronics, according to engineering specifications, using the computer. Locates file relating to projection data base library and loads program into computer. Retrieves information from file and displays information on cathoderay tube (CRT) screen using required computer languages. Displays final drawing on screen to verify completeness after typing in commands to rotate or zoom in on display to redesign, modify, or otherwise edit existing design. Types command to transfer drawing dimensions from computer onto hard copy.

Economic Development Coordinator

Directs economic development, planning activities for city, state or region. Negotiates with industry representatives to encourage location in an area. Directs activities, such as research, analysis, and evaluation of technical information to determine feasibility and economic impact of proposed expansions and developments.

Editor

Reads the manuscripts and rough drafts of author and other writers which are to be published in a magazine, book or newspaper. Corrects grammatical errors, and makes suggestions improving readability and consistency of style.

Editor (Word Processing)

Helps design the overall package and rough out the information to be contained on each page of a videotex display. Once the information is set up, the page creator takes over.

EDP Auditor

Monitors computer functions of the entire company and operational procedures and reports their findings back to top management with recommendations for improvements. EDP Auditors make specific recommendations for improved accuracy, procedures, and security.

Education Consultant

Develops programs for in-service education of teaching personnel. Reviews and evaluates curricula used in schools and assists in adaptation to local needs.

Prepares or approves manuals, guidelines, and reports on educational policies. Conducts research into areas such as teaching methods and strategies.

Electronics Engineer

Works on research and development, production, and quality control problems. The electronics engineer is highly specialized and may work in a specific area such as the design and implementation of solid-state circuitry in radar, computers or calculators.

Electronics Technician

Repairs and maintains machines and equipment used in processing and assembly of electronic components. Starts equipment or machine. Reads blueprints and schematic drawings to determine repair procedures. Dismantles machine. Removes and sets aside defective units for repair or replacement. Starts repaired or newly installed machines and verifies readiness for operation.

Employment Agency Owner

Manages employment services and business operations of private employment agency. Directs hiring, training, and evaluation of employees. Analyzes placement reports to determine effectiveness of employment interviewers. Investigates and resolves customer complaints.

Employment Counselor (Word Processing)

Screens and places word processing professionals in available jobs.

Employment Interviewer

(See Interviewer)

Employment Manager

Oversees the recruiting function. This includes soliciting qualified applicants through various sources including advertising and college recruiting. Oversees screening, interviewing, and selection procedures. Responsible for overseeing the hiring of all personnel.

Employment Recruiter

Matches job seekers with job openings that employers have listed with placement firms, employment agencies, or governmental employment offices.

Engineer

Applies the theories and principles of science and mathematics to practical technical problems. Designs and develops consumer products. Determines the general way the device will work, designs and tests all components, and fits them together in an integrated plan. Evaluates overall effectiveness of the new device, as well as its cost and reliability.

Engineering Technician

Develops and tests machinery and equipment, applying knowledge of mechanical-engineering technology, under direction of engineering and scientific staff.

Equal Employment Opportunity Coordinator

Monitors and enforces governmental regulations concerning equal employment practices in all levels of the organization. Maintains required records to verify adherence to approved affirmative action plan.

Executive Director

Develops and coordinates an administrative organization plan and staff to carry out the plan. Delegates authority and responsibility for the execution of the organization's many departments and functions. Establishes operating policies and procedures; standards of service and performance. Involved with fund raising. Serves on various civic committees.

Executive Administrator *(Education)*

Makes projections for future needs; oversees curriculum and policy decisions. Hires and supervises personnel, prepares school budget. Works with local groups to ensure the best interest of the community is being met.

Executive/Administrator *(Telemarketing)*

Directs the planning and operations of telemarketing function. Sets goals and objectives for telemarketing programs and establishes budgets as well as sales goals. Guides development of telemarketing programs and evaluates available systems applications.

Executive Assistant

Member of the management team that is responsible for overseeing the overall administrative functions of an office. Ensures productivity of office staff. Makes recommendations for improved systems. Supervises staff. Handles special projects and confidential materials. Assists executive. Represents the company at professional and community events on a regular basis. Often acts as a spokesperson for the executive.

Executive Director, Associations

Directs and coordinates activities of professional or trade associations in accordance with established policies to further achievement of goals, objectives and standards of the profession or association. Directs or participates in the preparation of educational and informative materials for presentation to membership or public in newsletters, magazines, news releases or on radio or television.

Executive Director, Chamber of Commerce

Directs activities to promote business, industrial and job development, and civic improvements in the community. Administers programs of departments and committees which perform such functions as providing members with economic and marketing information, promoting economic growth and stability in the community, and counseling business organizations and industry on problems affecting local economy. Coordinates work with that of other community agencies to provide public services. Prepares and submits annual budgets to elected officials for approval. Studies governmental legislation, taxation, and other fiscal matters to determine effect on community interests, and makes recommendations based on organizational policy.

Executive Director, Convention Bureau

Directs activities of convention bureau to promote convention business in the area. Administers promotional programs. Coordinates efforts with local hotels, restaurants, transportation companies, exhibit centers and other related facilities. Works within specified budgets. Serves on various civic and community boards to enhance the position of the bureau.

Executive Director, Department of Economic Development

Directs activities of the department. Ensures that demographic and economic information is maintained. Decides on research projects to be conducted. Directs publications prepared for public information. Works in conjunction with local and national agencies.

Executive Secretary

Schedules meetings, takes minutes at meetings and then transcribes and types them, composes letters, evaluates priority of incoming mail and telephone calls. Organizes and executes special projects and reports. May prepare budget reports. Works with a minimum of supervision, initiates much of own work according to office priorities.

Expeditor

Ensures that merchandise and supplies that have been ordered are received when and where needed.

Fashion Coordinator

Offers advice to the buying staff in large department stores on changing tastes, trends and styles. Works with buying staff to be sure that the store's merchandise is completely up-to-date.

Fashion Designer

Creative specialist responsible for designing coats, suits, dresses, as well as other lines of apparel. Adapts higher priced merchandise to meet the price range of the customers.

Fashion Display Specialist

Responsible for designing display windows and display units within department or clothing stores. May have supervisory responsibilities as a coordinator for chain of stores.

Fashion Writer

Writes articles on the subject of fashion. Writes press releases and complete public relations projects. Writes about projected fashion trends, designers, new store openings. Writes newsletters for stores and buying offices. Covers fashion shows and does research.

Finance Manager

Directs activities of workers engaged in performing such financial functions as accounting and recording financial transactions. Establishes procedures for control of assets, records, loan collateral and securities.

Financial Analyst

Performs the quantitative analysis required for strategic planning and investments. Evaluates the financing and refinancing of certain projects and lines of credit. Prepares various reports for management. Collects data for financial comparisons with similar companies and securities.

Flight Attendant

Directly responsible for making passengers' flight comfortable, enjoyable and safe. Ensures cabin is in order and that supplies and equipment are on board. Greets passengers as they board the plane. Helps passengers with carry-on luggage and with finding their seats. Instructs passengers before take-off in the location and proper usage of oxygen masks and other emergency equipment and exits. Serves meals and beverages.

Freelancer *(Travel)*

Submits articles to travel editor for publication. Works independently. Initiates own stories and also writes specific articles or stories for publications upon request.

Freelancer *(Visual Merchandising)*

Initiates own designs and plans and offers services to Designers and Display Directors.

Freelance Reporter *(Court Reporting)*

Reporters who are in business for themselves. Develop their own contracts, follow up on recommendations of those for whom they may already have worked and generally initiate their own assignments.

Front Desk Clerk

Responsible for direct personal contact with the guests, handling reservations, special needs, check in and check out. Familiarizes guests with a facility as well as the surrounding area. Prepares status reports on available rooms for manager. Receives guests' complaints and makes appropriate decisions about how to resolve them.

General Accountant

Handles daily business needs, such as payroll, budgeting, accounts receivable, accounts payable, general ledger, and financial statements. Must pay close attention to all laws and regulations affecting daily business operations. They are involved in sending out all payments, royalties, dividends, rents and other necessary expenditures.

Group Manager *(Retail)*

Supervises many departments within a retail operation.

Group Sales Manager

Concentrates on managing group sales efforts including planning and forecasting sales and supervising sales staff. Identifies target markets and assigns specific groups to specific sales personnel. Devises and implements promotions and training programs.

Group Sales Representative *(Travel)*

Promotes sale of group season tickets for sports or other entertainment events. Telephones, visits, or writes to organizations, such as chambers of commerce, corporate-employee-recreation clubs, social clubs, and professional groups, to persuade them to purchase group tickets or season tickets to sports or other entertainment events, such as baseball, horseracing, or stage plays. Quotes group-ticket-rates, arranges for sale of tickets and seating for groups on specific dates, and obtains payment. May arrange for club to sponsor sports event, such as one of the races at horseracing track.

Health Club Director *(Cruiselines)*

Oversees uses of the health club on cruiseline. Ensures passenger understanding of use of the equipment and exercise available. Ensures safety and cleanliness of equipment. Supervises staff and approves recommended programs.

Health Technician *(Electronics)*

Performs the work of an electronics technician, specifically on various types of health equipment. *(See Electronics Technician)*

Hearing Reporter

Follows up and records all that is said during various types of proceedings whether they be court trials or informal meetings. Hearings are presided over by a commissioner and there is no jury. Hearings may be conducted by various governmental agencies and departments with differing functions and responsibilities.

Incentive Travel Specialist

Travel specialists responsible for developing special packages for trips that have been won as a prize or premium.

Information Broker *(Word Processing)*

Responsible for formulating specifications on the basis of which information is pulled from the database and then relayed to the client company.

Information Coordinator *(Travel)*

Coordinates organization and communication of travel information as needed. Responsible for providing accurate information to telephone inquirers and visitors about a destination, attraction, activity or program. Participates in and conducts surveys.

Information Manager

Involves specializing in database management. Besides having a general knowledge of how organizations work and how information flows through them, knowledge of how to set up and improve information systems is important. Knowledge of library referencing and indexing systems is applied. Helps a technical expert set up an electronic filing system or corporate database. Sorts and updates database files, advises how to design the automated office system that would best fit with the organization's style, workflow and procedures.

Information Packager

Edits word processing systems and their software, applies working knowledge of word processing and text and finds imaginative opportunities in which to further apply that knowledge and those related skills.

Information Specialist *(Paralegal)*

Consolidates legal information after research for easy accessibility. Lists resources for future research by subject and sets up reference library to maintain information in sequential order. Advises users on how to extract the information they need quickly and efficiently.

Informer
Person assigned by an organization as the contact person for the press or other media for obtaining desired information on an as-needed basis.

Instructor *(Education)*
Instructs students in commercial subjects (typing, accounting, computer systems), communications courses (reading and writing) and personality development in business schools, community colleges, or training programs. Instructs students in subject matter, utilizing various methods, such as lecture, and demonstration, and uses audiovisual aids and other materials to supplement presentation. Prepares or follows teaching outline. Administers tests. Maintains discipline.

Insurance Agent
(See Agent, Insurance)

Internal Auditor
Conducts independent appraisal from within the organization by analyzing, criticizing, and recommending improvements to internal financial practices. Ensures the safety and profitability of investments and assets, and seeks to uncover sources of waste and inefficiency.

International Group Secretary
Provides secretarial support for a team headed by an account executive. Duties include transcribing letters and memos from dictaphone tapes and typing comprehensive multi-country proposals for clients; preparation of travel arrangements and assisting with clients, brokers, and foreign visitors.

Interpreter
Translates spoken word from one language to another. Provides consecutive or simultaneous translation between languages. Usually receives briefing on subject area prior to interpreting session.

Interviewer
Interviews job applicants to select persons meeting employers' qualifications. Searches files of job orders from employers and matches applicants' qualifications with job requirements and employer specifications.

Inventory Control Manager
Ensures that all stock units are in adequate supply, both components and finished goods. Responsible for overall quality of the product. Maximizes customer service levels, inventory investment and manufacturing efficiencies.

Inventory Coordinator
Prepares reports of inventory balance, prices, and shortages. Compiles information on receipt or disbursement of goods and computes inventory balance, price and costs. Verifies clerical computations against physical count of stock and adjusts errors in computation or count. Investigates and reports reasons for discrepancies.

Inventory Manager
Supervises compilation of records of amount, kind and value of merchandise,

material, or stock on hand in establishment or department of establishment. Compares inventories taken by workers with office records or computer figures from sales, equipment shipping, production, purchase or stock records to obtain current theoretical inventory. Prepares inventory reports. Makes planning decisions.

Investment Banker

Analyzes the needs of clients and makes recommendations to them on the best way to obtain the money they need. Obtains permission from each of the state governments to sell the issue in their state.

Job Analyst

Reviews all job functions within the company to continuously maintain updated details on job requirements, specific functions and qualifications needed.

Junior Accountant

(See Accountant)

Junior Account Executive *(Telemarketing)*

(See Account Executive-Telemarketing)

Junior Analyst *(Marketing)*

(See Market Research Analyst)

Junior Buyer *(Retail)*

Performs duties of buyer trainee and also becomes involved in deciding on products for purchase and evaluating the store's needs. Learns to study the competition on a regular basis so as to evaluate and predict decisions.

Junior Copywriter

Studies clients from printed materials and past correspondence. May answer phone, type, file or draft simple correspondence. May write some descriptive copy and come up with concepts for new ad campaigns. Works with the art department on presentations.

Junior Consultant

(See Consultant)

Junior Drafter

Copies plans and drawings prepared by drafters by tracing them with ink and pencil on transparent paper or cloth spread over drawings, using triangles, T-square, compass, pens or other drafting instruments. Makes simple sketches or drawings under close supervision.

Keypunch Operator

Operates alphabetic and numeric keypunch machine, similar in operation to electric typewriter, to transcribe data from source material onto magnetic tape and to record accounting or statistical data for subsequent processing by automatic or electronic data processing equipment.

Labor Relations Specialist

Responsible for being fully knowledgeable of current contracts or established policies affecting the working environment of all personnel including such areas as hiring requirements, pay policies, performance standards, leave of absence authorizations, and disciplinary procedures. When dealing with bargaining units, negotiates contracts as needed.

Law Library Manager

Manages the ordering and organization of all materials to be housed in the law library. Responsible for keeping up-to-date on changes in the law and for obtaining new literature describing most current laws. Supervises staff. Trains staff and library users on how to use the library. Oversees telephone information service.

Law Office Administrator

Designs, develops and plans new procedures, techniques, services, processes, and applications in the office; plans, supervises and assists in the installation and maintenance of relatively complex office equipment; plans production, operations of service for the efficient use of manpower, materials, money, and equipment in the office.

Lawyer

Conducts civil and criminal law suits; draws up legal documents, advises clients as to legal rights, and practices other phases of the law.

Lead Agent *(Travel)*

A car rental agent responsible for answering customers' questions.

Lead Analyst

Assists higher level personnel in analytical studies of complex and important problems involving existing and proposed systems and their costs. Develops, examines and implements reporting systems and procedures which provide significant contribution in terms of time saved and increased efficiency or reduced costs.

Lead Programmer

Provides specialized advice on programming languages and documentation. Maintains up-to-date knowledge of all programming language. Makes provisions for the orderly processing of changes, updatings, and modifications of programs. Coordinates all company programming efforts.

Lead Word Processing Operator

Coordinates work priorities and assigns work to word processors. May train and supervise word processors. Ensures quality of work output.

Legal Assistant

Oversees the work of other paralegals in a firm. Delegates work, handles personnel related problems, writes appraisals of other paralegals and supervises the hiring of paralegals when needed. Works on special projects.

Legal Secretary

Schedules appointments, court appearances; prepares documents, billing, bookkeeping, and record-keeping. Handles subpoenas, mortgages, deeds, closings, pleadings, briefs, wills, proxies and abstracts. May also review law journals and assist in other ways with legal research.

Legal Technician

Initiates and composes standardized legal forms routinely as needed for specific legal actions. Accepts service of legal documents, reviews for correct form and timeliness, annotates case files and status records to reflect receipt and due dates for responses. Establishes, maintains, and closes out case files or systems of legal records. Maintains tickler system, coordinates schedules with court clerks, notifies witness of appearances and reminds attorneys of court appearance and deadlines for submitting various actions or documents.

Legislative Reporter

Records events, speeches and debates that take place in the different state legislatures. Attends and reports committee meetings.

Litigation Paralegal

Organizes and manages documents for civil or criminal trials. Organizes and prepares pleadings, case outlines, manuals for complex litigation, discovery requests and index documents; operates computers, and drafts pretrial and post trial memoranda.

Loan Manager

Supervises loan personnel and approves recommendations of customer applications for lines of credit when loan officer is not able to do so. Communicates changes in policies and regulations regularly to loan personnel and customers.

Loan Officer

Interviews applicants applying for loans. Prepares loan request paper, obtains related documents from applicants. Investigates applicant's background and verifies credit and bank references. Informs applicants whether loan requests have been approved or rejected. Processes the loans.

Mail and Information Coordinator

Coordinates the information and mail services, usually at the front desk. Responsible for ensuring that outgoing and incoming mail for the facility as well as for guests is properly routed. Advises guests on most efficient procedures for receiving or sending important mail. Ensures that messages get to hotel personnel and guests on a timely and accurate basis. May also provide guests with general information about the facility and the area.

Manager *(Accounting)*

Organizes and directs all general accounting activities. Maintains accounting systems that insure the proper accounting and recording of company resources, provides financial statements, analysis, and other key management reports.

Manager *(Banking)*
(See Bank Manager)

Manager Trainee

Performs assigned duties, under direction of experienced personnel, to gain knowledge and experience needed for management position. Receives training and performs duties in various departments to become familiar with personnel functions and operations and management viewpoints and policies that affect each phase of the business.

Manager Trainee *(Finance)*

Works with financial manager while gaining an overall exposure to all aspects of the finance function the company. Assists with budgets, purchase options and expenses. Helps review financial reports for different product lines and assists with consolidating financial data for updated reports. May interview other department heads, customers, vendors and other key people dealing with the finance area.

Manager Trainee *(Retail)*

Works with store manager organizing and managing the store on a daily basis. Spends time on the selling floor, learning customer service techniques and computerized systems. Assists with managing, merchandising and analyzing stock. Directs and physically puts stock out on the floor and presents merchandise. May work with buyer learning financial planning, vendor negotiations and branch store communications.

Manager of Programming

Trains operations staff, programmers and systems analysts in the use of new computer equipment and software. Develops programming and systems as required, specifically in critical areas. Develops documentation standards. Anticipates and foresees future requirements for user departments.

Manager of Tour Operations

Supervises support functions related to the execution of a successful tour. Areas of responsibility include the bookkeeping, secretarial, telex, and computer operations areas.

Manager *(Recreation)*

Manages recreation facilities, such as tennis courts, golf courses or arcade, and coordinates activities of workers engaged in providing services of the facility. Determines work activities necessary to operate facility, hires workers and assigns tasks and work hours accordingly. Initiates promotion to acquaint public with activities of the facility. Maintains financial records.

Manager of Systems Analysis

Evaluates advances in computer equipment and software capabilities in light of the company's future system requirements. Coordinates the formulation of short- and long-range technical systems development plans, with special emphasis on technical feasibility. Organizes, schedules, and conducts training programs for data processing personnel and users of computer services.

Manufacturing Manager

Coordinates all manufacturing operations to produce products of high quality and reliability at optimum cost, and in accordance with customer shipping schedules. Participates in the preparation of the manufacturing budget. Ensures safety of employees in their exposure to varied manufacturing process hazards. Resolves various manufacturing and production problems.

Market Research Analyst

Researches market conditions in local, regional, or national area to determine potential sales of product or service. Examines and analyzes statistical data to forecast future marketing trends. Gathers data on competitors and analyzes prices, sales, and methods of marketing and distribution. Formulates surveys, opinion polls or questionnaires.

Market Research Director

Oversees market research for a company. Sets goals and objectives for projects. Sets timetables for completion and assigns personnel to projects. Keeps appropriate administrators informed on findings and makes recommendations and proposes marketing strategies based on results.

Marketing Analyst (Paralegal)

Examines and analyzes statistical data to forecast future marketing trends in the paralegal field. *(See Market Research Analyst)*

Marketing Director

Directs and coordinates the development of marketing programs assigned to attain maximum penetration in the required market segments. Directs the creation, writing, and publishing of market and product plans. Explores development of product line offerings.

Marketing Support Representative

Backs up the sales force by demonstrating the equipment and working with the customers after the equipment is installed; teaches the customer's word processing specialists to use the equipment and helps them find the best methods of doing the company's particular tasks.

Marketing Representative (Paralegal)

Promotes and sells law-related books. Works in the marketing division of legal publishing companies.

Materials Manager

Studies receiving or shipping notices, requests for movement of raw materials and finished products and reports of warehousing space available to develop schedules for material handling activities. May confer with supervisors of other departments to coordinate flow of materials or products. Supervises activities of shipping and receiving personnel.

Media Director of Planning

Plans media relations in line with company goals. Reports and analyzes industry media trends. Communicates with product development to determine product market plans as they relate to media proposals and media scheduling. Oversees Media Planners.

Media Planner

Plans and administers media programs in advertising department. Confers with representatives of advertising agencies, product managers, and corporate advertising staff to establish media goals, objectives and strategies within corporate advertising budget. Studies demographic data and consumer profiles to identify target audiences of media advertising.

Medical Assistant
Works in hospitals or clinics cleaning and sterilizing equipment, performing various tests and helping to maintain records.

Medical Claims Examiner
Claims examiner for the medical field. *(See Claims Examiner)*

Medical Claims Representative
Claims representative for the medical field. *(See Claims Representative)*

Medical Librarian
Records, arranges, and makes medical information available to people. Handles books, films, periodicals, documents and other media related to the medical field.

Medical Records Administrator
Plans, develops, and administers medical record systems for hospital, clinic, health center, or similar facility, to meet standards of accrediting and regulatory agencies. Assists medical staff in evaluating quality of patient care and in developing criteria and methods for such evaluation. Develops and implements policies and procedures for documentation, storing, and retrieving information and for processing medical/legal documents.

Medical Records Technician
Gathers all information on patients' condition and records it on permanent files that become the history and progress of treatment of a patient's illness or injury. Accumulates the results of a physician's examinations, information on laboratory tests, and electrocardiograms, and records these results in the records. Accuracy is particularly important because much of this information is referred to during malpractice cases and it is also vital when processing insurance claims.

Medical Secretary
Processes many kinds of complex health insurance forms. Responsible for patient billing, records management, medical and office supply organization and appointments. Takes dictation and transcribes on dictaphone. Deals with medical supply vendors and pharmecutical houses. Prepares correspondence and assists physicians with reports, speeches, articles, and conference proceedings.

Medical Technician *(Electronics)*
Performs the work of an electronics technician, specifically on various types of medical equipment. *(See Electronics Technician)*

Meeting Planner
Establishes objectives of the meeting, selects the site hotel and facilities, negotiates rates, sets budgets, makes air and hotel reservations, chooses speakers, plans food and beverage, arranges for all audio-visual equipment. Arranges meeting registration, exhibits, promotion and publicity scheduling, room set-up and arranges post meeting evaluation. Planners are involved with negotiations that save the organization money.

Membership Coordinator

Solicits membership for club or trade association. Visits or contacts prospective members to explain benefits and costs of membership and to describe organization of club or association. May collect dues and payments for publications from members.

Membership Secretary

Compiles and maintains membership lists, records the receipt of dues and contributions, and gives out information to members of the organizations and associations. Sends out newsletters and other promotional materials on a regular basis. Answers telephone inquiries and coordinates mass mailings.

Merchandise Analyst

Evaluates available merchandise in different locations and identifies when transfers might be appropriate. Evaluates quality of merchandise from the vendors for price paid with the buyer.

Merchandise Manager

Takes charge of a group of departments, usually organized by merchandise. Coordinates and oversees the efforts of the buyers. Develops merchandise plans, divides up the buyer's merchandise assignments and reviews their selections. Visits the manufacturers' showrooms and travels abroad.

Merchandise Planner

Allocates merchandise from distribution point to stores as requested by buyers and merchandise managers. Ensures that merchandise is shipped properly and on a timely basis from the distribution center.

MIS Director

Recommends and initiates programs and/or systems which support the desired corporate profit objectives. Issues business data and management information that facilitates the businesses' planning and decision-making process at all levels. Responsible for total information service provided to user departments.

MIS Manager

Responsible for coordinating the short-term planning for MIS/EDP efforts in systems development and computer processing; for establishing guidelines for measurement of division activity to these plans; and for monitoring Division MIS/EDP performance to assure that information is made available to all levels of management on a complete, reliable, economic and timely basis.

MIS Specialist

Has specific knowledge of and provides service to a specialized area in the company. May concentrate on such areas as accounting, sales, production, or any other function requiring the services of the MIS department to meet their particular need.

MIS Supervisor

Assures timely and accurate processing of incoming orders through the order preparation and data processing areas, to assist in achieving a high level of customer service. Maintains external relationship with vendors of paper supplies and forms, equipment manufacturers, equipment maintenance representatives, and leasing companies. Maintains contact with all company departments using the services of the MIS department.

National Sales Manager *(Marketing)*
Devises and implements sales strategies, forecasts sales, supervises in-house salespeople; establishes and attains sales goals; trains and develops sales personnel. Develops and implements marketing and advertising strategy.

Night Auditor
Brings all of the establishment's accounts up-to-date so that a day's revenue report can be made to upper management. *(In a hotel, a revenue report includes such items as a detailed account of room revenues, number of rooms occupied, average room revenue, percentage of occupancy figures, and the like).* The night audit process is usually augmented by a computerized system. The night auditor often plays the role of the night manager.

Night Shift Supervisor *(Word Processing)*
Supervises work of word processing department during the night shift. Schedules the staff for the shift. Prioritizes work that must be completed. Responsible for maintaining the equipment and resolving routine problems that may occur in processing.

Nurse
Cares for ill, injured, convalescent and handicapped persons in hospitals, clinics, private homes, sanitariums, and similar institutions. Observes patient and reports adverse reactions to medical personnel in charge. Administers specified medications, and notes time and amount on patient's chart. Performs routine laboratory work.

Office Manager
(See Department Manager, Office)

Operations Manager *(Computer Systems)*
Assures that all jobs adhere to established conventions and may cancel any job which deviates from these conventions. Controls the processing of jobs and is responsible for obtaining the maximum utilization of the computer.

Operations Manager *(Retail)*
Oversees all functions of store operations which include personnel, credit, payroll, shipping and receiving, customer service, warehousing and distribution, security and maintenance.

Operations Research Analyst
Conducts analyses of management and operational problems and formulates mathematical or simulation models of the problem. Analyzes problems in terms of management information and conceptualizes and defines problems. Studies information and selects plan from competitive proposals that afford maximum profitability or effectiveness in relation to cost or risk.

Outside Sales Agent *(Travel)*
Brings new business to an agency on a referral basis.

Owner/Manager *(Employment Agency)*
An owner who also manages the agency. *(See Employment Agency Owner)*

Owner/Operator *(Travel Agency)*
Delegates responsibilities to qualified managers. Encourages creative marketing and sales activities. Manages budget for the overall operation.

Page Creator *(Word Processing)*
Composes actual pages of catalogs relayed to home televisions or telephones. Involves word processing, text editing, and formatting together with computer graphics. The system plus its computer graphics is called videotex.

Paralegal
Assists lawyer with routine legal assignments. Maintains legal volumes to make sure they are up-to-date, assists with legal research. Helps administer estates, draft wills, and trusts, complete federal and state tax returns, prepare initial and amended articles of incorporation, stock certificates and other securities. Helps prepare court related forms. Performs a variety of related duties upon request of the attorney.

Paralegal *(Publishing House)*
Assists the general counsel in the company's legal department with the areas of law that affect publishing, such as contract law and copyright law. May assist the legal publisher in planning new books about the paralegal profession or the procedures utilized by paralegals in the office.

Paralegal Instructor
Teaches paralegal students the legal procedures used by paralegals in the law office.

Paralegal Supervisor
Oversees work of paralegal responsible for researching law, investigating facts and preparing documents to assist lawyers.

Partner *(CPA Firm)*
Responsible for major audit accounts. Solves complex accounting problems for clients, using standard accounting principles. Also responsible for quality of client service and volume of new business brought in to the firm. Achieves objectives through the effective management of the technicians and sales staff in the firm.

Passenger Service Agent
Provides passengers with information; assists passengers with information, assists passengers when boarding the plane.

Peripheral Equipment Operator
Operates on-line or off-line peripheral machines, according to written or oral instructions, to transfer data from one form to another, print output and read data into and out of digital computer. Mounts and positions materials, such as reels of magnetic tape or paper tape onto reader-sorter. Sets, guides, keys, and switches according to instructions to prepare equipment for operations. Separates and sorts printed output forms.

Personnel Assistant
Performs diversified duties in the processing and monitoring of employee benefits programs, maintenance of all employee personnel files. Sets up files on new employees. Records changes on all employee status as necessary and forwards to payroll department.

Personnel Clerk
Prepares job postings and determines eligibility to bid and successful bidder(s). Prepares monthly absenteeism reports. Prepares monthly accident reports. Assists applicants with filling out employment applications appropriately. Acts as a backup for the department secretary, performs a variety of basic personnel and clerical functions.

Personnel Director
Supervises the hiring and firing of company employees. Prepares performance reports and sets up personnel policies and regulations. In a large corporation, oversees the entire personnel function.

Personnel Manager
Responsible for developing, implementing and coordinating policies and programs covering the following: employment, labor relations, wage and salary administration, fringe benefits administration, indoctrination and training, placement, safety, insurance, health benefits, and employee services.

Placement Director *(Paralegal)*
Responsible for employment orientation, job development, and may act as a liaison between the employer and the paralegal graduate seeking a position.

Plant Manager
Responsible for manufacturing of products in the required quantity and quality and for performing this function safely at a minimum cost. Recommends improvements in manufacturing methods. Sets up and approves production schedules. Regularly reviews inventories of required materials. Directs and approves all requisitions for maintenance and repair of building and equipment and for machine parts and manufacturing supplies.

Plant Safety Specialist
Coordinates safety programs. Communicates policies, programs, and regulations to appropriate personnel. Ensures compliance with governmental regulations. Enforces safety policies for chemical use, fire codes, equipment and ventillation systems. Ensures proper guarding of machinery to avoid operator injury. Maintains records as well.

Portfolio Manager
Manages non-trust accounts, such as the pension fund of a corporation or a university endowment. Decides what stocks should be bought and sold within the portfolio.

President
Plans, develops and establishes policies and objectives of the business organization in accordance with the Board of Directors and corporate charter.

Plans business objectives and develops policies to coordinate functions between departments. Reviews financial statements to determine progress and status in attaining objectives. Directs and coordinates formulation of financial programs to provide funding for new or continuing operations to maximize return on investments. May preside over board of directors. Evaluates performance of company executives.

President/Owner

Acts as president of a business and owns and operates it as well. *(See President)*

Press Coordinator

Arranges meetings and special events with the press. Contacts press either by phone or mail to detail upcoming events.

Private Secretary

As the executive's administrative partner, duties vary according to the size of the organization and the executive's responsibilities. May outline day's work for the office, schedule duties to be performed by all who work in the office, keeps everything on schedule, despite interruptions. Greets callers, handles mail, keeps track of financial records and processes data.

Product Manager

Oversees the research, development, and production of a particular product. Assess need for modifications on the product based on input from market research. Estimates timely and cost effective procedures for implementing periodic modifications. Ensures that quality of product is maintained.

Product Support Representative *(Computer Systems)*

Acts as the customer's liaison with the computer manufacturer. Assists with familiarizing the customer with the computer. Acts as part trainer, part salesperson and part advisor to the customer.

Production Coordinator

Coordinates flow of work within or between departments of manufacturer to expedite production. Reviews master production schedule and work orders, establishes priorities and availability or capability of workers, parts, or material. Confers with department supervisors to determine progress of work. Compiles reports on the progress of work.

Production Manager

Supervises and coordinates activities of those who expedite flow of materials, parts, and assemblies and processes within or between departments.

Production Planner

Assures that inventories of stock items are maintained at reasonable levels and that orders for non-stock items are processed in a timely, effective manner. Works with plant supervisor to establish manning levels which are appropriate based on current and projected levels of activity. Requisitions all raw materials and supplies required to manufacture products.

Production Technician

Assists engineer in preparing layouts of machinery and equipment, work-flow plans, time and motion studies and analyses of production costs to produce the most efficient use of personnel, materials and machines.

Program Coordinator

Oversees programs after the planning stage. Takes appropriate action to initiate planned programs, service them while in progress and arrange for program evaluation. May assist with recommending speakers, agendas, room set-up and promotional efforts.

Program Director

Plans and develops methods and procedures for implementing programs; directs and coordinates program activities, and exercises control over personnel according to knowledge and experience in area with which the program is concerned. Prepares program reports. Controls expenditures.

Programmer Analyst

Prepares detailed instruction for assigned programming systems or components enabling qualified personnel to proceed with implementation. Evaluates procedural and/or programming systems required to operate and support programs and systems.

Programmer Trainee

Writes the codes that make up a computer program, tests their programs, debugs them (eliminates errors), and sometimes writes the accompanying documentation that tells others why the program was written the way it was.

Project Director

Plans, directs and coordinates activities of designated project to ensure that aims, goals, or objectives specified for project are accomplished in accordance with set priorities, timetables, and funding. Develops staffing plan and establishes work schedules for each phase of the project. Prepares project status reports for management.

Proofreader

Reads typeset (original copy) or proof of type setup to detect and mark for corrections and grammatical, typographical, or compositional errors. Reads proof against copy, marking by standardized codes errors that appear in proof. Returns marked proof for correction and later checks corrected proof against copy.

Proofreader *(Paralegal)*

Reviews the content of law-related manuscripts to verify facts needed in case preparation. Also can act as person who checks for improper usage or spelling or grammar errors in legal copy.

Proofreader *(Word Processing)*

Checks the work of the correspondence secretary and word processor for accuracy of copy.

Public Relations Specialist
Writes news releases, directs advertising campaigns, or conducts public opinion polls. Tries to create favorable attitudes about a client or its products.

Purchasing Agent
Responsible for buying the raw materials, machinery, supplies and services necessary to run a business.

Purchasing Manager
Responsible for the management of the procurement functions of the company. Establishes practices and procedures to be followed by buyers and other department personnel. Negotiates price and delivery. Selects vendors, assesses vendor capabilities, develops alternate sources and evaluates vendor performance. Assures that department records are maintained.

Quality Assurance Manager
Develops and maintains a system to assure that all products manufactured by the organization meet customer specifications and achieve superior quality and reliability levels. Revises and updates quality control manual. Meets with vendors, customers and quality representatives to discuss and resolve quality problems as required.

Ramp Agent
Supervises baggage area to be sure baggage is sent to proper destinations.

Receptionist
Greets people who come into an office and directs them to the proper department. They may also do other tasks such as answering the phone and some typing. Learns the departments and key personnel in the company and what functions they perform.

Reception Manager
Supervises all activities of guest services including registration of incoming guests and check-out of departing guests; provides guests with information about functions at the hotel and about the general area where the hotel is located; takes messages for guests and provides wake-up calls; handles guest relations, problems with rooms, billing or any other routine difficulty.

Records Manager
Examines and evaluates records-management systems to develop new or improve existing methods for efficient handling, protecting and disposing of business records and information. Reviews records retention schedule to determine how long records should be kept.

Recreation Director *(Cruiselines)*
Develops safe recreation programs suitable for a cruiseline. Ensures adherence to established standards and policies. Ensures staff is properly certified for instruction when needed. Makes recommendations to activities coordinator for recreation schedules.

Regional Director
May oversee a group of regional managers. *(See Regional Manager)*

Regional Manager
Responsible for overseeing the activities of all operations in a particular geographical area of the country.

Regional Sales Manager
Recruits in-house personnel, recruits general agents and assists when needed with training new sales staff with "cold calling." Holds periodic sales meetings to strengthen competitive position and explain strategies for market penetration.

Registered Representative *(Account Executive or Broker)*
Buys or sells securities for customers. Relays the order to members of the firm who are stationed on the exchange floors; if the security is not traded on the exchange, sells it directly in the over-the-counter market. Advises customers on the timing of the purchase or sale of securities. Counsels customers about tax shelters, mutual funds and other investments.

Rental Sales Representative
Negotiates car rental rates with travel agents, corporate businesses and other commercial accounts and individual clients so as to remain competitive in the market.

Research Account Executive *(Advertising)*
Researches printed literature. Drafts reports from research. Gets competitive bids from suppliers. Sits in on planning sessions. Suggests new methods of data gathering. Helps design surveys.

Research Analyst
Evaluates research findings and determines their applicability to specific projects within the company. Recommends needed research projects. Compares research findings with similar studies, or surveys to determine reliability of results. Uses statistical data and measurement to examine and apply findings.

Research Analyst *(Financial)*
Researches and sells their research to institutional investors. Recommends portfolio managers on the stocks they believe should be bought and sold.

Research Assistant
Compiles and analyzes verbal or statistical data to prepare reports and studies for use by professional workers in a variety of areas. Searches sources, such as reference works, literature, documents, newspapers, and statistical records, to obtain data on assigned subjects. May interview individuals to obtain data or draft correspondence to answer inquiries.

Research Assistant *(Paralegal)*
Performs legal research by operating a computer-assisted legal research system.

Research Director
May supervise a group of research projects at a given time. *(See Project Director)*

Research Manager
(See Project Director)

Research Technician *(Electronics)*

Performs research to evaluate new methods for the electronics technician. Tests findings. May pass recommendations on to research and development. Upon request, works with other researchers and engineers to test findings.

Researcher and Evaluator *(Travel)*

Investigates and evaluates public relations efforts of the organization. Responsible for making recommendations on public relations programs based on goals and objectives and competition's position in the market place. Evaluates needs for expanding public relations efforts. Researches and recommends best strategy.

Reservationist

Sells reservations and other travel products such as tours, hotel accommodations, car rentals; operates computer reservations equipment; assists passengers in solving their travel needs.

Reservationist *(Cruiselines)*

Books cruises for individual clients and groups. Sells the cruise by telephone to inquirers. Explains details of the trip and accepts payment.

Reservationist *(Hotel)*

Responsible for confirming room reservations, either by mail or by telephone and for writing or typing out reservation forms. Works with computer to keep guest reservations current and for billing procedures. May assist guest with other reservations for local transportation, dining, or entertainment, depending on the staff size of the hotel.

Reservations Manager

Supervises and coordinates activities of personnel engaged in taking, recording, and cancelling reservations in front office of hotel. Trains front office staff. Reviews daily printouts listing guests' arrivals and individual guest folios received by room clerks. Approves correspondence going to groups and travel agents to answer special requests for rooms and rates. Evaluates computer system and manual record procedures for efficiency.

Revenue Officer

Investigates and collects delinquent Federal taxes and secures delinquent tax returns from individuals or business firms according to prescribed laws and regulations. Recommends civil penalties when necessary. Writes reports on all actions taken.

Robotics Technician

Performs the work of an electronics technician, specifically on various types of robotic devices. *(See Electronics Technician)*

Sales Assistant

Responsible for successful management of a selling area. Involves supervision of a selling area and customer service functions. In a large department store, may also direct inventory control and merchandise presentation and increasing the sales growth and profitability of an area.

Sales/Field Representative *(Electronics)*
Advises customers on installation and maintenance problems and serves as the link between the manufacturer and the customer.

Sales Manager
Coordinates sales distribution by establishing sales territories, quotas and goals, and advises dealers and distributors concerning sales and advertising techniques. Directs staffing, training, and performance evaluations to develop and control sales programs. Prepares periodic sales reports showing sales volume and potential sales. May recommend or approve budget, expenditures and appropriations for research and development work.

Sales Manager *(Retail)*
Oversees the various sales departments in wholesale and retail companies. Directs promotional sales campaigns for their merchandise or services.

Sales Representative
Secures orders from existing and potential customers by means of visiting the customer facility or calling by phone. Follows-up on quotations submitted to customers. Submits weekly activity/call reports concerning customer quotes, orders, or problems. Provides a territory sales forecast on a monthly basis.

Sales Representative *(Computer Systems)*
Calls on prospective clients to explain types of services provided by establishment, such as inventory control, payroll processing, data conversion, sales analysis, and financial reporting. Analyzes data processing requirements of prospective clients, and draws up prospectus of data processing plan designed specifically to serve client's needs. May also sell computers and related equipment directly.

Sales Secretary
Types drafts of newsletters, keeps track of company's dealings with outside printers, suppliers and creative people. Types, files, answers telephones and routes mail. Takes orders, books events, or handles whatever customer request comes in for the product or service being sold.

Sales/Service Manager *(Electronics)*
Oversees both the sales and service efforts of a branch or many branch operations of a company. Ensures that the quality and customer service levels are maintained in the field. Receives feedback from customers through the sales and service staff. Determines what action should be taken with repeated problems.

Sales Supervisor
(See Sales Manager)

Sales Trainee *(Insurance)*
Attends sales strategy sessions as an observer or "tails" an experienced agent on calls. Assists established agents to service accounts.

Schedule Planning Manager *(Travel)*
Approves and enforces scheduling recommendation for all air traffic coming and going into and out of the airport.

School Director

Plans, develops, and administers education programs. Confers with administrative personnel to decide scope of programs to be offered. Prepares schedules of classes and rough drafts of course content to determine number and background of instructors needed. Interviews, hires, trains, and evaluates work performance of education department staff. Assists instructors in preparation of course descriptions. Prepares budget for education programs and directs maintenance of records of expenditures, receipts and public and school participation in programs.

School Director/Administrator

(See School Director and See Administrator)

School Secretary

Handles secretarial duties in elementary and secondary schools; may take care of correspondence, prepare bulletins and reports, keep track of money for school supplies and student activities, and maintain a calendar of school events.

Script Writer

Provides the creative support in a telemarketing agency. Writes all material that is to be read by the telemarketing representative.

Secretary

Performs secretarial duties for a supervisor. Takes and transcribes dictation with speed and accuracy. Maintains correspondence and data files, arranges appointments, answers routine inquiries and handles general office duties. Often assists in performing administrative details using initiative and judgment. Requires thorough knowledge of company policies, the organization and how to operate in the channels of the organization. As part of the management team, must be ready to make decisions and provide relevant information to staff members on a daily basis.

Senior Accountant

(See Accountant)

Senior Account Executive

(See Account Executive)

Senior Analyst

Assists in developing the data processing procedures for solving business or mathematical problems. Assists in analyzing and evaluating proposed and existing systems.

Senior Analyst *(Marketing)*

(See Market Research Analyst)

Senior Claims Examiner

(See Claims Examiner)

Senior Consultant

(See Consultant)

Senior Copywriter

(See Copywriter)

Senior Drafter

Gives final approval to the plans drawn up by other drafters before presenting the plan to client. *(See Drafter)*

Senior Legal Assistant

Oversees the work of paralegals and legal assistants in the firm. *(See Paralegal and See Legal Assistant)*

Senior Programmer

Develops flow charts to establish logic of execution. Codes logic in programming language. Writes program language to initiate and control the program in the hardware. Reviews existing programs and effects changes as requested. Solves production hang-ups in existing system. Writes operating instructions for computer personnel. Reviews output for the user. Supervises other programmers and gives final approval on the programs they have written. Ensures senior management receives information as requested.

Senior Systems Consultant

(See Systems Consultant)

Senior Underwriter

(See Underwriter)

Service Representative

Goes out into the field upon customer's request to service problems with purchased equipment. May diagnose the problem, correct and test the equipment to see if it is working properly. Reports problem to research and development. Tells owners and dealers about new products, service techniques and developments in maintenance.

Service Technician *(Electronics)*

(See Service Representative)

Social Secretary

Arranges social functions, answers personal correspondence, and keeps the employer informed about all social activities.

Special Events Coordinator

Performs basic function of the meeting planner and also is directly responsible for the advertising and promotion of the event, the budget for the event, and for identifying the appropriate target market. Works with the press and media on promotion. Acts as the liaison between all participating parties.

Speaker

Person elected by an organization to present its views, policies, or decisions.

Staff Accountant

Oversees the general ledger of a firm. Reviews cost center and chart of accounts structure. Makes recommendation as to cost center/account structure which will identify the nature of expenses to their proper areas, assists in controlling annual expenditures. Reconciles daily cash flow statements and reconciles to monthly bank statements. Reconciles payroll and cash disbursement accounts. Reviews accounts payable ageing and vendor statements for problems.

State Travel Director

Promotes visitor traffic within the destination, whether for pleasure, business, or convention purposes, and from within or from without the state.

Station Manager

Supervises a car rental business.

Statistical Typist

Works in all types of businesses typing statistical data from source material such as: company production and sales records, test records, time sheets, and surveys and questionnaires.

Stenographer

Takes dictation in shorthand of correspondence, reports, and other matter, and operates typewriter to transcribe dictated materials.

Store Manager

An executive responsible for the profitable operation of the store. Has broad merchandising responsibilities, develops staff, contributes to the store's public relations effort and supervises the maintenance of the store. Spends significant amount of time on the selling floor and supplies other areas of management with detailed information on the operation of the store.

Supervisor *(Banking)*

Responsible for improving the overall productivity of a department or area, motivating staff and staying within budget. Oversees production, product development, marketing and systems functions in the bank.

Supervisor of Data Entry Services

Directs all data input activities serving the users of centralized data input facility. Directs the development of data input procedures, performance standards and controls. Directs the evaluation of new data entry equipment. Ensures accurate and timely completion of projects.

Supervisor of Gate Services

Observes staff to ensure that services to passengers are performed courteously and correctly. Supervises and coordinates the activities of staff engaged in admitting passengers to airplanes and assisting passengers disembark at terminal exist of commercial flights. Reviews flight schedules, passenger manifests, and information obtained from staff to determine staffing needs. Recommends alternate procedures if needed. Evaluates performance of staff.

Supervisor *(Telemarketing)*

Manages groups of telemarketing communicators and is directly responsible for their performance. May also be responsible for training and scheduling of staff.

Surveyor

Interviews people and compiles statistical information. Asks questions following a specified outline on questionnaire and records answers. Reviews, classifies, and sorts questionnaires. Compiles results in a format that is clear and concise and highlights findings relevant to the objective of the survey.

Systems Administrator *(Word Processing)*
Involves systems maintenance and management and systems analysis and design.

Systems Analyst
Solves the problems of adapting computer hardware and software to end-users' needs. Determines how the company can save money by adapting existing equipment. Coordinates and supervises the efforts of many computer professionals. Maintains quality control by assessing the system once it has been implemented.

Systems Consultant
Advises clients on developing, implementing, and maintaining automated programs for clients and for in-house use; on selecting hardware, writing software, and consulting with user-client when special programs must be developed.

Systems Operators Supervisor
Directs operations for optimum use of computer and peripheral equipment. Coordinates between users and other data processing functions in establishing and maintaining processing schedules. Recommends hardware changes and directs the installation of new equipment.

Systems Programmer
Prepares the computers to understand the language that the applications programmers will be using and tells the computer what peripheral equipment, such as printers and automatic teller machines, it will be controlling.

Systems Trainee *(Banking)*
Works in programming or part of a systems team project, refining the use of current equipment or developing systems for as yet unmet needs.

Tape Librarian
Documents and allots hardware space for all computer and peripheral equipment for schedules, produces debugging statistics and other statistical reports for the department management personnel.

Technical Secretary
Assists engineers or scientists. In addition to the usual secretarial duties, may prepare much of the correspondence, maintain the technical library, and gather and edit materials for scientific papers.

Telemarketing Center Manager
Responsible for executing the program once components have been assembled and the script written. This involves either making or receiving the calls in a way that achieves each client's objective.

Telemarketing Communicator
Delivers what everyone else sells. Coordinates or manages the allocation of the product to the proper sales and delivery channels.

Telemarketing Representative
Sells a product or "qualifies" customers for the field salesforce by telephone.

Telemarketing Trainee

Instructs communicators about the product or services and how to use the scripts. Trainers also teach telemarketing efficiency, listening skills and sales techniques.

Ticket Agent

Sells tickets to airline passengers at the airport and city ticket office; promotes and sells air travel; gives air travel and tour information; makes the flight and tour reservations; computes fares; prepares and issues tickets; routes baggage; and prepares cash reports.

Tour Director

Conducts the actual tour. Accompanies travelers as an escort throughout the trip. Solves problems and settles complaints. Has alternative plans set for the group so that tour will be successful even under adverse conditions. Coordinates the group to stay together and encourages questions about the area being visited.

Tour Escort

Assists passengers; generally assists with tours; accompanies the tour from start to finish; often handles large sums of money; makes necessary changes in group's accommodations or itinerary as needed.

Tour Guide

Does complete narration; has specialized knowledge of a particular region, or country; hired to accompany a tour only while it visits the area of special expertise.

Tour Operator

Puts together all the elements of a trip: transportation, accommodations, meals, sightseeing and the like; negotiates rates and block space; coordinates details of the itinerary; finally markets the product.

Tourist Information Assistant

Provides information and other services to tourists at state information centers. Greets tourists, in person or by telephone, and answers questions and gives information on resorts, historical sights, scenic areas, and other tourist attractions. Assists tourists in planning itineraries and advises them of traffic regulations. Sells hunting and fishing licenses and provides information on fishing, hunting, and camping regulations. Composes letters in response to inquiries. Maintains personnel, license-sales, and other records. Contacts motel, hotel, and resort operators by mail or telephone to obtain advertising literature.

Trader

Matches buyers and sellers of securities.

Traffic Manager

Negotiates price and service issues of all modes of transportation carrier contracts and determines the appropriate transportation mode to be utilized. Develops, maintains and disseminates logistical data.

Trainer (Word Processing)

Trains correspondence and word processing secretaries to make fewer errors by checking their work.

Training Manager

Develops on-going training programs for new and experienced personnel. Conducts training seminars. Writes and coordinates training manuals working with specialists for specified details. Prepares training videotapes and/or films; maintains library of video and film training aids. Notifies employees of training sessions. Introduces topic specialists at the beginning of the program and the program agenda. Develops means of measuring the effectiveness of programs through testing.

Training Specialist

Develops and conducts training programs for specialized functions within the company upon the approval of the training manager. *(See Training Manager)*

Training Supervisor

May supervise training manager(s) as well as the entire training function for the company. Responsibilities might include overseeing training programs at various divisions, and performing all budgetary responsibilities pertaining to the programs. Also may evaluate existing programs and make recommendations for modifications or new or additional programs. *(See Training Manager)*

Transportation Manager

Responsible for all aspects of transportation including inbound, between facilities, and outbound. Supervises various functions and personnel. Negotiates rates with warehouses and transportation companies. Plans, monitors, and implements the distribution department's fiscal budget. Establishes the most beneficial routing of company shipments for satisfactory customer service. Determines price levels. Plans for the department on a quarterly, yearly, and five-year basis.

Transportation Specialist

Advises industries, business firms and individuals concerning methods of preparation of shipments, rates to be applied, and mode of transportation to be used. Consults with clients regarding packing procedures and inspects packed goods for conformance to shipping specifications to prevent damage, delay or penalties. Files claims with insurance company for losses, damages and overcharges of shipments.

Travel Agency Manager

Supervises the day to day operations of the agency. Prepares sales reports and dictates office policies. Decides on promotion and pricing of packages. Supervises, hires, and trains employees. Attends trade shows to keep informed on latest computer systems, rates, and promotions being offered by the airlines, hotels and other related services. Initiates advertising for the agency and keeps budget.

Travel Agent

Plans itineraries, and arranges accommodations and other travel services for customers of the travel agency. Plans, describes and sells itinerary package tours. Converses with customers to determine destination, mode of transportation, travel dates, financial considerations and accommodations required. Books customer's mode of transportation and hotel reservations. Obtains travel tickets and collects payment. May specialize in foreign or domestic service, individual or group travel, or specific geographical areas.

Travel Counselor

Advises clients on best ways to travel; destinations, costs and safety issues. Offers advice to clients on packages available, preparation for a trip, or availability of transportation or accommodations. Researches information requested by the client.

Travel Director

Client-contact person who actually goes out with the incentive groups and on site, coordinating sightseeing trips and trouble-shooting.

Travel Editor

Buys articles submitted by freelance writers; selects unsolicited articles for publication; selects letters from readers to publish; replies to readers' letters of comment or criticism; works with layout and make-up of travel pages. May assign staff to stories almost anywhere in the world. Reviews manuscripts submitted by travel writers for content and readability. Chooses manuscripts for publication.

Travel Secretary

Coordinates all aspects of the travel function. Researches options to maintain an economical, efficient travel program. Schedules personnel for approved travel on corporate jets. Schedules personnel from approved travel authorizations on commercial flights. Makes hotel reservations. Performs clerical and secretarial duties pertaining to all travel arrangements.

Travel Specialist

Develops specialized expertise about a particular area of travel. May work for a travel agency, tour operator, publications department or other related areas using information mastered about a specialized area of travel. May specialize in a geographic area, type of destination or any other specific area in the travel industry.

Travel Writer

Provides practical guides and directories and language books and brochures. Contributes feature stories to travel sections of large newspapers.

Treasurer

Directs and coordinates organization's financial programs, transactions and security measures according to financial principles and government regulations. Evaluates operational methods and practices to determine efficiency of operations. Approves and signs documents effecting capital monetary transactions. Directs receipt, disbursement, and expenditures of money or other capital assets.

Treasurer/Controller

Has combined responsibilities of both the Treasurer and the Controller. *(See Treasurer and See Controller)*

Trust Officer
Manages money and securities as well as real estate and other property. Decides how assets will be managed.

Underwriter
Reviews applications, reports, and actuarial studies, to determine whether a particular risk should be insured. Specializations are usually in life, property, and liability, or health insurance.

Underwriter Specialist
Specializes as an underwriter in life, property, and liability, or health insurance. *(See Underwriter)*

Underwriter Trainee
Assists the underwriter. Usually spends much time on the telephone gathering information and verifying what has been reported before the underwriter makes final decisions. *(See Underwriter)*

Underwriting Supervisor
Oversees the underwriting department. Ensures staff is working within appropriate guidelines and regulations when reviewing submitted materials. Evaluates performance of the staff and hires new underwriters as needed.

Urban Planner
Works with city or state officials to produce plans for future building and construction projects. Must be able to project an area's future population and its needs and design facilities to meet those needs.

Vice President
Plans, formulates and recommends for approval of the President basic policies and programs which will further the objectives of the company. Executes decisions of the President and Board of Directors. Develops, in cooperation with the President and supervisors, an annual budget and operates within the annual budget upon approval. Recommends changes in the overall organizational structure to the President. Approves public relations programs.

Vice President of Account Services
Oversees the promotion, sales, and service of a product line to a variety of customers within a defined geographical area. Develops and seeks out business of a highly complex nature and of importance to the company. Ensures efficient servicing of all accounts, once obtained. Prepares programs for training and development of the field managers and other new and experienced personnel.

Vice President of Communications
Ensures the development and execution of advertising, public relations, public affairs, and members' relations' programs, together with effective internal and external communications to promote understanding, acceptance, and support of corporate activities and objectives by employees and the subscribing public.

Vice President of Finance
Acts under authority and responsibility delegated by corporate executive office. Conducts management studies, prepares workload and budget estimates for

specified or assigned operation, analyzes operational reports and submits activity reports. Develops and recommends plans for expansion of existing programs, operations, and financial activities.

Vice President of Human Resources

Develops Human Resource policies and programs for the entire company. The major areas covered are organizational planning, organizational development, employment, indoctrination and training, employee relations, compensation, benefits, safety and health, and employee services. Originates Human Resource practices and objectives which will provide a balanced program throughout all divisions. Coordinates implementation through Human Resource staff. Assists and advises senior management of Human Resource issues.

Vice President of Marketing/Sales

Represents the marketing function's needs in the development of corporate policy. Formulates sales goals, marketing plans, and strategy and directs the execution of these areas for the achievement of corporate marketing objectives. Manages the sales force to achieve marketing and sales goals for assigned products.

Vice President of Merchandising

Manages several divisions of merchandise. Responsible for planning and giving buyers both fashion and financial direction. Plans sales, inventory, and marketing by store, based on the turnover desires. Plans markups and ensures that inventory supports sales efforts.

Vice President of Operations

Directs the formulation of corporate policies, programs and procedures as they relate to distribution, operations, research, production, engineering, and purchasing. Maximizes group and divisional short- and long-range growth and profitability.

Vice President of Production

Plans, directs, and controls production and related support functions to provide timely manufacturing and delivery of output at lowest possible costs. Manages, controls and reviews all assigned resources: staff, technical, material and financial. Manages budgets and expense control to assure effective meeting of operating objectives.

Vice President of Sales

Responsible for the selling of the output of several different manufacturing facilities. Must develop effective sales policies which result in each plant's producing the optimum profit. Determines final prices and works closely with the salesmen, the production, scheduling and traffic staffs and research and development and production personnel. After the initial sale is made, the sales staff assumes continuing sales effort to such accounts.

Wage and Salary Administrator

Maintains files of updated job descriptions. Ensures that responsibilities are appropriately compensated according to established standards. Participates in and reviews local and national salary surveys to set current salary standards and pay rates for each position within the organization. Processes salary increases or other changes for personnel according to established policies.

Warehousing/Operations Manager

Determines and develops distribution strategies and practices that will support our corporate objective. Responsibilities include: identifying areas within the company that offer some opportunity for improvement; optimizing investments in all locations, in inventory, facilities and people, and matching the corporate distribution support capabilities to the outgoing marketing, business and operational needs. Makes use of financial and computer expertise in evaluating projects and allocation of resources.

Window Trimmer

Displays merchandise in windows or showcases or retail stores to attract attention of prospective customers. Originates display ideas or follows suggestions or schedule of manager. Arranges mannequins, furniture, merchandise and backdrop according to prearranged or own ideas. Constructs or assembles pre-fabricated displays.

Word Processing Center Manager

Responsible for word processing support given to a function or a number of departments. Trains and motivates personnel; maintains good working regulations with departments being serviced, and administers basic first-line management responsibilities. Develops new procedures, keeps records and orders supplies.

Word Processor

Uses computers and specialized word processing equipment to enter, edit, store, and revise correspondence, statistical tables, reports, forms, and other materials. Word processing systems include keyboard, a cathode ray tube (CRT) for display, and a printer. Some equipment also has telecommunications hookups and scanners to ready manuscripts.

Career Directions at
Johnson & Wales University

A MESSAGE FROM THE PRESIDENT

Career education is what *Johnson & Wales University* is all about. Graduates are looked upon favorably by the employment community because of their unique training and professional and realistic attitudes toward the world of work. **Career Directions** is a course *at* work. It is an important part of your career training because it teaches you how to relate your education and work experience to your career goal.

As a *Johnson & Wales* graduate you will have a competitive edge over the many other job candidates prospective employers will consider. To take advantage of that edge, you need to know the special skills you bring to an employer. You also need to confidently convince the employer that you are the right person for the job. **Career Directions** teaches you this. By working closely with the *Career Development Office* throughout your stay with us, you will be one of our successful graduates.

Your success is our success. Each year, many major corporations visit our campus to hire our graduates. Hundreds of job opportunities are received by the *Career Development Office* each year. We are pleased to help you make those important decisions about your future career and look forward to your success.

Sincerely,

Dr. John A. Yena
President

Table of Contents
Career Directions at Johnson & Wales University

THE JOHNSON & WALES UNIVERSITY CAREER DEVELOPMENT OFFICE

The Career Development Office makes every effort to assist *Johnson & Wales* students and graduates with their careers. Each year nearly 99% of all Food Service/Hospitality graduates and nearly 96% of all business graduates are employed within sixty days of graduation. *Johnson & Wales* students begin preparation for their success on day one at the university. Throughout your stay at *Johnson & Wales*, your career preparation continues. Your preparation may be accomplished through the many career services available to you.

Part-Time Job Opportunities
Career Counseling
Career Day
Professional Development Seminars
Industry Guest Speakers
Professional Development Course
Cooperative Education Program
Summer Job Opportunities
Summer Job Fair
Career Resource Library
Career Consultants' Program
On-Campus Recruiting Orientations
Company Open Houses
On-Campus Interviewing Program
Permanent Job Opportunities
Alumni Career Services

Career Development Services

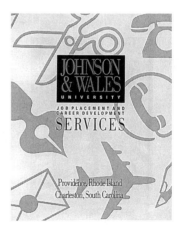

Part-Time Job Opportunities

Students seeking part-time employment during the academic year visit the *Career Development Office* to review the job listings available with local employers. The downtown area of Providence is a convenient location for work since you live and go to classes within the area. If you have a car, you can take advantage of the many job opportunities available throughout the rest of Rhode Island and nearby Massachusetts and Connecticut. Many *Johnson & Wales* students work afternoons and nights during the week, typically from twenty to twenty-five hours a week. Some Food Service/Hospitality students report working thirty-five to forty hours a week. A good number of students return to their home state on weekends to work at jobs available on Friday, Saturday and Sunday. This type of work schedule is possible because of the four-day school week.

Part-time jobs are major sources of financing tuition for *Johnson & Wales* students. Freshmen are encouraged to make individual decisions about the number of hours they work, if they choose to work at all. Some freshmen find it better to spend the first trimester or even the first year at college getting adjusted to the new routine and developing solid study habits. Annual part-time employment surveys conducted by the *Career Development Office* indicate that many more upperclassmen work while in school. Up to 80% of fourth year students are employed part-time versus 55% of the freshmen surveyed.

Part-time job experiences are valuable when you interview for a permanent position. Keep in mind that regardless of what kind of part-time job you have, school comes first. Keeping a proper balance between your school work and your commitment at work demonstrates your ability to manage yourself. You cannot lead other people if you haven't learned to manage yourself. Keeping a balance between your school work and your commitment at work is an important start to managing your career.

Career Counseling

Career counselors specializing in business, food service and hospitality career fields are available to assist you on an individual basis. You may stop in to the office at any time to speak to a career counselor. If you need a lot of time to spend with a counselor to work through a particular concern, you may schedule an appointment to do so . Career counselors address many different concerns. If you are considering changing your major, you should first speak to an academic counselor, but before making your final decision speak to someone in the *Career Development Office* about the impact that change may have on your career. Typically students wonder what kind of jobs will be available to them if they switch their major.

Placement reports from past graduates and career information provided by industry are used to advise you in this area. It is strongly recommended that you visit the *Career Development Office* before finally changing your academic major. You will find that you will be more comfortable with your decision knowing all the facts first.

If you are happy with your major, you may be having difficulty determining the jobs to which you are actually suited. The **Professional Development Course** will give you most of the information you need, but you may have specific questions about the decision you are making. A career counselor can help you clarify your career direction. Career counselors also help you with tips on interviewing, mock interviews, resumé preparation and choosing between job offers.

Career Day

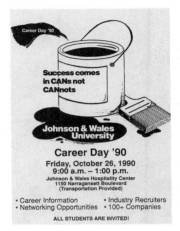

Career Day is a major event at *Johnson & Wales*. In addition to the advice you can obtain from the *Career Development Office*, Career Day provides you with the opportunity to talk directly to industry representatives about your career. Career Day is scheduled each fall to give you an opportunity to talk informally with prospective employers and learn more about your intended career.

Career Day is for all Business and Food Service/Hospitality majors. It is for all undergraduates as well as graduating students. Representatives of local, regional and national companies are invited to speak with you about their companies and educational requirements of their business or industry.

Part-time and permanent jobs are often obtained at Career Day, although the focus of the program is career counseling. By researching various companies, you can begin to think about the type of employer for whom you may want to work. You should ask company representatives about the kind of experience you need to qualify for the position you will want at graduation. Industry representatives can advise you on the benefits of furthering your education, gaining a particular type of work experience, developing particular personal skills that are important to their industry, the starting salaries available at their company, and on their training program and promotional opportunities.

Career Day provides you with the opportunity to speak informally to industry representatives. You can become familiar with the company's style through the people that represent it and do a better job at your actual interview with them at a later date. All students can benefit from learning more about particular job requirements in order to plan their academic programs accordingly.

How to Get the Most From Career Day

1. *Dress professionally*
2. *Bring questions*
3. *Record information for future reference*
4. *Arrange a company visit*
5. *Ask when the company will be recruiting on-campus*
6. *Send a thank-you letter*

Professional Development Seminars

These career seminars are offered throughout each academic year. After completing the **Professional Development Course** you will find these to be helpful just before your own personal job search actually begins. Freshmen students find that the seminars are a preview to the career planning and job search stage.

Seminars for all students focus on general topics such as resumé writing, interviewing techniques, letters to write during the job search, questions asked during an interview and "Success — *What Is It and How Do I Find It?*". *A schedule of the Professional Development Seminars that will be offered is distributed on-campus at the beginning of each school year.*

Professional Development Course

The **Professional Development Course** is designed to provide students with detailed information on:

> *Tomorrow's Jobs*
> *Lifelong Career Planning/Managing Your Career*
> *Personal Development*
> *Job Search Techniques*
> *Contemporary Issues in the Workplace*

Technical skills and work experience are often not enough to get the job you want. A third ingredient essential to your career education is Professional Development. Career planning and job search training are the "icing on the cake," which enables people to get the jobs they really want and for which they are qualified.

Understanding, early on, the career opportunities available upon graduation makes it easier to see how your classroom training and work experience as a student will prepare you for your first job and your entire career. By the time you graduate, you will be well aware of your career goals and how to achieve them.

The course teaches you how to manage your career by mastering specific career strategies. Upon completion of the course, *Johnson & Wales* students have commented:

> *"I think this is an excellent course. I have learned many things in this course that will help me get jobs and use my skills effectively."*

> *"I believe this class does present information pertinent to our majors. The class helps us present ourselves to possible employers on interviews."*

"I personally feel that this class has helped me greatly with a good perspective on the job world and it is an important part of this program."

"I felt this class was interesting and fundamental to student needs. I now know more about the working field."

"This course helped me a lot in understanding what I have to do to prepare for the job market."

Industry Guest Speakers

Throughout the academic year, Industry Guest Speakers address students in the **Professional Development Course** on career related topics. At "Professional Development Night," students are invited to hear industry representatives' presentations on current topics such as Executive Etiquette and Time & Stress Management. The advice that company representatives can provide through these programs is of tremendous value to students.

Cooperative Education

Selective ''Career Co-Ops'' can play an important part in your career education. Each trimester, selected students may participate in practical work experiences in place of classroom study. In order to qualify for this special program, you must demonstrate academic achievement, maturity and flexibility to work outside the college environment. Co-Op students work at college-approved sites under professional supervision for one trimester—either part-time or full-time. Students who qualify for Co-Op receive academic credit for the experience and most are also paid for their work by the cooperating employer. The student's grade is based on both the employer's evaluation, assigned projects and input from the *Johnson & Wales University* Co-Op Coordinator. In many cases, outstanding' Co-Op students have been offered permanent positions by their Co-Op employers after graduation.

You may consider applying to the Co-Op program for many reasons, but two of the most valuable purposes the program serves are: *1. Clarifying your career goal* and *2. Providing practical work experience in your field*. Second year culinary students and some business majors (ex: secretarial sciences and advertising & public relations) are eligible to apply to the program if they meet the criteria. Co-Op opportunities in all other business majors are for fourth-year students. you are selected for participation in the trimester before you actually go on Co-Op, thus you need to think about applying early.

If you are thinking of applying to the Co-Op program, visit the *Career Development Office* and speak to the appropriate Coordinator of Cooperative Education. Formal Co-Op agreements exist between the college and several

Johnson & Wales University

Partners in Careers

Student opportunities in cooperative education

major employers. Placement sites have included:

> *CDM—Carlo de Mercurio Hotels (Switzerland)*
> *WALT DISNEY WORLD Resort Complex*
> *John Hancock Financial Services*
> *Caesar's Tahoe*
> *LMS/Barrett Public Relations*
> *Rainbow Room*
> *NCR Corporation*
> *Hyatt Regency Grand Cypress*
> *Textron, Inc.*

For a complete list of participating employers, visit the *Carer Development Office*.

Summer Jobs

The value of selecting a worthwhile summer job cannot be overstated. Even if you cannot find a job in your field, the value of whatever work you perform will be clear when you look at the various skills you can transfer to future employment. Most important, working during the summer demonstrates initiative on your part.

Summer jobs are posted daily in the *Career Development Office* starting early in the spring. Major employers from across the country promote their opportunities to *Johnson & Wales* students. Whether you plan to stay in the Rhode Island area or return to your home state to work, employment resources are made available to you through the *Career Development Office*.

Summer Job Fairs are sometimes held on-campus in the spring. This is a day when employers with summer jobs visit the campus to interview *Johnson & Wales* students. Summer positions are another good way to test your career goals or gain practical work experience.

Career Resource Library

A large part of your career preparation will require research on companies and on other career related issues. A comprehensive library of information is located in the career resource library located in the *Career Development Office*. Information about companies that recruit *Johnson & Wales* students, including annual reports, employee handbooks, and corporate recruitment publications is available for your use. In addition, names and addresses of major corporations throughout the country are made available in the form of Employer Listings. Handouts, books and some trade journals are also available on various career and job search topics. The information contained in this area is of use to you no matter how far you've progressed in your career planning.

Career Consultants' Program

As part of your career counseling services, you have the opportunity to network with a select group of *Johnson & Wales* alumni and employers. Participating professionals are Career Consultants for *Johnson & Wales University* students.

For example, in 1982, Jack Kurilla graduated with a B.S. in Marketing, and went to work for Abraham & Straus in Queens, New York. As a department manager, Jack explained to *Johnson & Wales* students how he can assist them with their career planning by:

1. Providing information to students by mail or phone about:
   a. *the company*
   b. *his position*
   c. *relocation*
   d. *other companies in the area*
   e. *various aspects of the retail industry where employment may be found and the different types of positions that may be available*
2. Meeting individually with students at a mutually convenient location to discuss their careers
3. Being a guest speaker on-campus
4. Providing a student with an "informational interview" at the company
5. Posting job vacancies from his company in the *Career Development Office*

On-Campus Recruiting

Over 175 companies from throughout the U.S. and abroad visit the *University* each year to recruit future employees. They range from international corporations to local, family-owned businesses.

The On-Campus Recruiting Program is geared toward all graduating students. In January, printed interview schedules are distributed to all students. These schedules list the recruiters who will visit and also include interview guidelines and eligibility requirements that must be met. Over 3,000 interviews of *Johnson & Wales* students are conducted annually on-campus by prospective employers. In general, four-year program graduates averaged higher starting salaries than associate degree graduates with averages at both levels competitive with national averages.

Procedures For Securing On-Campus Interviews

1. *You must be a graduating student and meet the criteria stated by the company.*
2. *Attend one of the required On-Campus Interviewing Orientations.*
3. *Research each company with whom you wish to interview.*

4. *Bring professionally typed resumés to the Career Development Office.*
5. *Sign-up for your interviews at the times and locations designated by the Career Development Office.*
6. *Attend Open Houses hosted by companies with whom you have interviews.*
7. *Watch for additions/changes to the schedule throughout the spring.*
8. *If you are on a waiting list for an interview, contact the Career Development Office twenty-four hours before the company visit to see if there are any openings.*
9. *Review the policies on NO SHOWS and CANCELLATIONS before signing up for your interviews.*

Below is a partial listing of Companies that recruit Johnson & Wales Graduates.

Abraham & Straus
Adam's Mark Hotels
The Aetna Casualty & Surety Company
Alcar Restaurants
Allied Court Reporters
Alpha Court Reporting
A.L. Williams Company
Americana Great Gorge
Ames Department Stores
American Leisure Industries
ARA Services
AT&T Communications
The Balsam's Grand Resort Hotel
Bank of Boston
Bankers Life and Casualty Insurance Company
Bankers Trust Corporation
Bennigan's
Biltmore Plaza Hotel
Bishop's Restaurant
Blue Cross/Blue Shield of R.I.
Booz-Allen & Hamilton Inc.
Borel Restaurant Corporation
Boston Park Plaza
Bradlees
The Breakers
Bretton Woods Resorts
Buena Vista Palace
Burger King Corporation
Canteen Corporation
The Casual Male
Les Chefs de France
Cherry, Webb & Touraine Specialty Stores
Chess King
Children's Hospital
Citizens Bank
Collette Travel Services
Colonial Williamsburg Foundation

Commercial Union Insurance Company
Country Home Bakers
Creative Home Bakers
Creative Gourmets, Ltd.
Custom Management Corporation
CVS Pharmacy
Days Inn of America, Inc.
Dean, Witter, Reynolds, Inc.
Delb Restaurant Management
Diamond Foods
Denny's Restaurants
Dobb's International
Dun & Bradstreet
Edison Brothers
Entertaining Moments, Ltd.
Filene's Basement
First Investors Corporation
The Flatley Company
Footlocker
Foxmoor
Franklin Plaza Hotel
Friendly Ice Cream Corporation
Furrs Cafeterias
The Gap Stores
General Dynamics/Electric Boat
Gilbert/Robinson, Inc.
Gordon Jewelers
William Graulich & Associates
Grisanti, Inc.
Ground Round Restaurants
Guest Quarters
Hamilton Hotels
Harborside Inn
Harrah's Hotel & Casino
Harvard University
Harvey's Hotel & Casino
Hasbro Industries, Inc.

Hilton International Company
Hit or Miss
Holiday Corporation
Hotels of Distinction
Howard Johnson Company
Hyatt Corporation
Inn America Corporation
Interstate Hotels
In-Plant Catering
John Hancock Financial Services
John B. Polcari & Sons
Karten Jewelers
Kay Jewelers
Keebler Company
Kensington Investment Resources
Kinney Shoe Corporation
K-Mart Corporation
Lady Footlocker
Landfall Restaurant
The Lenox Hotel
Lerner Corporation
Liz Claiborne
The Limited
Magic Pan International, Inc.
Mardeck, Ltd.
Marriott Corporation
Marshalls
Meldisco
Mercantile Stores
Metro Hotels
Metropolitan Life Insurance Company
Mount Washington Hotel
New Orleans Hilton
Ninety Nine (99) Restaurants
New York Hilton
New York Athletic Club
Olive Garden
Omni/Dunfey Hotels
Opryland Hotel
The Paddock Restaurant
Papa Gino's of America, Inc.
Paragon Tours & Travel
Paramount Hotels
The Parker House

Park Suite Hotels
Pepperidge Farms
Pepsico
Petrie Stores Corporation
PFM-Professional Food Service
    Management
Red Lobster Inns of America
Resorts of Distinction
Restaurant Associates
The Restaurant Group
The Riese Organization
RIHGA Royal
The Ritz-Carlton, Boston
Rosenbluth Travel, Inc.
Rudi's Foods
S&A Restaurants
Sage-Allen & Company, Inc.
The Seiler Corporation
Service Direction
Sheraton Corporation
The 1661 Inn & the Manisses
Sky Chefs
Sonesta International Hotel
State Street Bank
Stouffer's Corporation
Susie's Casuals
THF—Eastern, Inc.
Thom McAn Shoe Stores
TJ McDermott
Tollgate Foods, Inc.
Trump Hotel Casino
Trusthouse Forte (London, England)
Tufts University
Vos & Vos Court Reporters
WALT DISNEY WORLD
    Resort Complex
Wang Laboratories, Inc.
Westbrook Inns
Westwood Restaurant Group
World Yacht Enterprises
Wyatt Cafeterias
Yale University
York Steak House Systems, Inc.

Company Open Houses

Many companies schedule "Open Houses" for students the evening before their day of interviewing. These "Open Houses" consist of the recruiter's presentation about the company followed by questions and answers from the students. If you have an interview scheduled with the company the next day, you are required to attend the Open House. All students, including undergraduates, having an interest in the company, are welcome to attend the "Open House."

On-Campus Recruiting Orientation

To prepare graduating students for participation in the On-Campus Recruiting program, the *Career Development Office* conducts orientation seminars. At the orientations, students learn how the On-Campus Recruiting Program works. Students are advised of the policies and procedures for the program at this time. Any graduating student wishing to participate in the On-Campus Recruiting program is required to attend one of the mandatory orientations offered.

Permanent Job Listings

In addition to the on-campus recruiting program, graduating students are encouraged to review the job opportunity books in their major regularly. Permanent jobs available throughout the country are posted daily in the *Career Development Office*.

Alumni Career Services

Career services are provided to *Johnson & Wales University* graduates on a lifelong basis. Many alumni seeking career changes forward their resumé to or call the *Career Development Office*. The office provides assistance to alumni as requested. In the fall, the annual Career Day date is publicized in *Visions Magazine* along with an invitation to alumni to participate. The number of alumni using the services of the office varies according to the ease or difficulty of the job market in their field.

POSITIONS OF RECENT GRADUATES

Business Graduates

An average of 3,000 student interviews are conducted on-campus each year.

Staff Accountant
Main-Hurdman
Boston, Massachusetts

Administrative Assistant
Booz-Allen & Hamilton, Inc.
New York, New York

Secretary
John Hancock Financial Services
Boston, Massachusetts

Staff Accountant
Providence, Rhode Island

Executive Trainee
Jordan Marsh Company
Boston, Massachusetts

Buyer Trainee
Abraham & Straus
Brooklyn, New York

Showroom Coordinator
Perry Ellis Sportswear
New York, New York

Sales Representative
St. Gillian Limited
New York, New York

Medical Secretary
Children's Hospital
Boston, Massachusetts

Groom
Hunters Rest Stables
Franklin, Tennessee

Assistant Manager
Saks Fifth Avenue
Balharbor, Florida

Systems Analyst
Department of Education
State of Maryland
Baltimore, Maryland

Assistant Barn Manager
Ablemarle Farms Inc.
Charlottesville, Virginia

Registered Representative
Fidelity Investments
Boston, Massachusetts

Financial Secretary
Fleet National Bank
Providence, Rhode Island

Staff Assistant
Harvard University
Cambridge, Massachusetts

Division Manager
Macy's of California
Los Angeles, California

Programmer
Liberty Mutual Insurance Company
Boston, Massachusetts

Account Controller
State Street Bank
North Quincy, Massachusetts

Business Teacher
Colby Sawyer Business School
Pawtucket, Rhode Island

Marketing Representative
NCR Corporation
East Providence, Rhode Island

Business Analyst
Dun & Bradstreet
East Providence, Rhode Islanbd

Administrative Assistant
Young & Rubican Advertising
New York, New York

Legal Secretary/Word Processor
Ricassi and Davis,
Attorneys at Law
Hartford, Connecticut

Johnson & Wales students stand out against others that I interview because of their eagerness, strong understanding of the job market as it relates to their field, and their acceptance of starting in our entry level position with the potential of growth in the future.
Elizabeth Gallogly
Personnel Specialist
Tufts University

Management Trainee
Hyatt Hotels
Tampa, Florida

Assistant Pastry Chef
New York Hilton
New York, New York

Rounds Cook
Sheraton Tara Hotel
Danvers, Massachusetts

Pastry Chef
Amelia Island Resort
Amelia Island, Florida

Assistant Baker
Harrah's Hotel & Casino
Stateline, Nevada

Assistant Food & Beverage Director
Holiday Corporation
Columbus, Ohio

Pastry Chef
Grand Mere Inn
Stevensville, Michigan

Culinary Trainee
Hyatt Corporation
Chicago, Illinois

Assistant Banquet Manager
Harvey's Hotel & Casino
Atlantic City, New Jersey

Food Service Graduates

*Ninety-nine percent of all food service/ hospitality graduates and **96%** of all business graduates are employed within sixty days of graduation.*

First Cook
Metro Hotels
South Padre, Texas

Management Trainee
Hilton International
New York, New York

Pastry Cook
Hotel Meridian
Boston, Massachusetts

Cook
The Woodstock Inn
Woodstock, Vermont

Assistant Restaurant Manager
Gilbert/Robinson
Garden City, New York

Pastry Shop Assistant
Balsam's Grand Resort
Dixville Notch, New Hampshire

Apprentice Chef
The Castle Restaurant
Leicester, Massachusetts

Hospitality Graduates

Management Trainee
Days Inns of America
Bridgeport, Connecticut

Supervisor
Stouffers Restaurants
New York, New York

Manager
Denny's
Spring Valley, New York

Assistant Manager
Boston Park Plaza Hotel & Towers
Boston, Massachusetts

Merchandising Assistant
THF — Eastern
Stamford, Connectiucut

Management Trainee
Mardeck, Ltd.
Washington, D.C.

Front Desk Clerk
Marriott Hotel
Newton, Massachusetts

Sales Director
Holiday Corporation
Manchester, New Hampshire

Management Trainee
Hyatt Hotels
Memphis, Tennessee

Management Trainee
Furrs Cafeterias
Kansas City, Missouri

Flight Attendant
Northwest Orient Airlines
Minneapolis, Minnesota

Operations Manager
JFK Airport
(For Sky Chefs Corporation)
New York, New York

Assistant Manager
Spirit of Boston Cruiselines
Boston, Massachusetts

Reservation/Sales Agent
U.S. Air
Syracuse, New York

Group Sales Assistant
Collette Travel
Pawtucket, Rhode Island

Rental Representative
Hertz Car Rental
Boston, Massachusetts

The staff at the *Career Development Office* is eager to work with you. Professionals with a unique combination of backgrounds in both industry and education are ready to share their expertise with you. Directors of Cooperative Education and Job Placement can assist you with the placement process. Decisions about your appropriateness for employment with different companies are made in conjunction with these staff members. They are in constant contact with industry and are aware of what companies need in their potential candidates.

The Career Development Staff

Student Development Counselors can assist you with defining your career goals and preparing your resumé. Student Development Counselors can explore with you the many career alternatives you have and help you decide which career direction to take. Student Development Counselors are great resource people for career information. They can also assist you with developing effective job search strategies.

Job opportunities are phoned in and mailed to the *Career Development Office* daily. The Coordinator of Job opportunities is responsible for maintaining good relations with employers wishing to hire *Johnson & Wales* students and graduates. The Coordinator obtains all pertinent information about available jobs from employers and posts those opportunities in the *Career Development Office*. Most important, Career Assistants are available to show you how to use the Career Resource Library and how to follow up on job opportunities posted in the office. Career Assistants spend much of their time providing students with preliminary help with their resumés and cover letters. If you have a question about any activity in the *Career Development Office*, a Career Assistant can help you.

Full-time secretaries and administrative assistants are also ready to answer your questions. The entire staff works as a team to assist you in the many areas of your career development.

Keeping informed about the activities of the *Career Development Office* on a regular basis is important. You can keep informed through:

- Classroom announcements from faculty
- *The Campus Herald*
- The C.D.O. *(Career Development Office)* Update
- Bulletin boards
- Flyers
- Regular visits to the office

A PERSONAL PLAN FOR CAREER DEVELOPMENT

Your *career development* is a process that will continue throughout your life. The key to successful career development is to put yourself in the driver's seat and follow your own course of action. Your definition of success will be very different from anyone else's and for that reason you must learn to use the many career planning techniques made available to you in your own unique way.

While a student (at *Johnson & Wales*), faculty, academic, personal and career counselors will be instrumental in your career planning. The key to your success is learning career planning skills that you can use independently throughout your life.

This course in **Professional Development** is designed to program you for success! It will teach you how to start your career and manage it through its different stages.

The following are some objectives you should set for your career planning while a student at *Johnson & Wales University.*

Career Planning For First-Year Students

- Know Student Development Counselors
- Visit *Career Development Office*
- Part-Time Job
- Career Day
- Professional Development Seminars

Student Objectives

- *Become familiar with your resources*
- *Preview career information*
- *Preview career planning and job search techniques*

Career Planning For Second-Year Students

- Part-Time Employment
- Career Day
- Company Open Houses
- Co-Op Informational Seminars

- Individual Counseling
- On-Campus Recruiting *(for graduating students only)* or Summer Employment *(for returning students)*
- Professional Development Seminars
- Completion of **Professional Development Course**

Student Objectives

- *Develop an awareness of the career planning process*
- *Develop an awareness of career options available*
- *Assess skills and abilities*
- *Learn job search techniques*
- *Obtain part-time and summer work experience useful to career goal*
- *Reserve electives if interested in Co-Op Program*
- *Assess alternative to receive a four-year degree*

Career Planning For Third-Year Students

- Career Day
- Company Open Houses
- Co-Op Informational Seminars
- Apply to Cooperative Education Program *(For Fourth Year Placement)*
- Individual Counseling
- Informational Interviewing Off-Campus
- Professional Development Seminars
- Summer Employment *(Experience in your field)*

Student Objectives

- *Define professional objectives*
- *Update resumé*
- *Develop list of potential employers*
- *Explore opportunities with potential employers*
- *Apply for Cooperative Education Program*
- *Obtain part-time or summer employment that will provide added skills in your field*

Career Planning For Fourth-Year Students

- Career Day
- Individual Counseling
- Participate in Cooperative Education Program
- Resumé — *Career Development Office*
- Sign-up for On-Campus Interviews **or** EXIT interviews

Student Objectives

- *Interview for prospective employment on and off-campus*
- *Conduct an EXIT Interview with the Career Development Office prior to graduation*

ARE YOU MOVING IN THE RIGHT DIRECTION?

Your Personal Plan for Career Development at Johnson and Wales

Your Career Goal _____

Freshman Year
- *Visit the Career Development Office*
- *Part-time job*
- *Career Day*
- *Get to know your student development counselors*
- *Professional Development Seminars*

Summer Vacation (Recommended pre-professional/part-time & summer work experience)

Sophomore Year
- *Career Counseling*
- *Co-Op Informational Seminars*
- *Company Open Houses*
- *Career Day*
- *Part-time employment*
- *Reserve electives for co-op*
- *Assess alternative 4-year degree*
- *Interview on campus (if graduating)*
- *Professional Development Course*

Summer Vacation (Recommended pre-professional/part-time & summer work experience)

Junior Year
- *Career Counseling*
- *Professional Development Seminar*
- *Co-Op Informational Seminar*
- *Company Open Houses*
- *Career Day*
- *Apply for Co-Op Program*
- *Informational Interviews*
- *Develop list of potential employers*
- *Update resumé*

Summer Vacation (Recommended pre-professional/part-time & summer work experience)

Senior Year
- *Job search*
- *Career information research*
- *Career Counseling*
- *Part-time job/co-op position*
- *Career Day*
- *Exit interview - Career Development Office*
- *Interview on/off campus*
- *Finalize resumé*
- *Refine professional objective*

Your Career/Job _____

THE PRODUCT IS YOU!

In this section, ''The Product is You,'' you will further identify your uniqueness as a job candidate. Your unique qualifications are a combination of: **1.** *your specialized career training* and **2.** *other experiences you have pursued,* i.e., work extracurricular activities, etc. The additional experiences that you have complement your formal training in school. The total package of experiences is YOU. As a graduate of *Johnson & Wales University,* your unique qualifications consist of:

1. *your specialized coursework*
2. *training on specialized equipment*
3. *work experience(s) that are part of your formal program of study (Internships, Externships, and/or Cooperative Education)*

Through each of these experiences, you gain professional skills that you can market to a potential employer. The benefit of what you have learned in the classroom and on the job is only as valuable as you make it. Experience does not have value unless you can clearly explain to an employer how you can apply it in your chosen career. In order for the unique features of your career education to work for you, you need to know what they are and how they benefit both you and your potential employer. When preparing to market yourself to a potential employer:

1. *be able to describe the specialized training you are getting at Johnson & Wales.*
2. *be able to identify the specialized courses that are part of your program.*
3. *be able to describe the type of equipment you have been trained on and how proficient you are with that equipment.*
4. *be able to identify any required work experience that you completed as part of a course requirement. This would include Internships, Externships, and/or Cooperative Education experiences.*

For example: if your program of study is Fashion & Retail Management at *Johnson & Wales University,* you would identify the following as unique features of your program.

Specialized Courses in Your Program of Study

A.S. - *Fashion Merchandising*		B.S. - *Fashion & Retail Management*	
Course	*Credits*	*Course*	*Credits*
Professional Development	1	Merchandising Mathematics	3
Retailing I	3	Comparative Merchandising	
Merchandise Buying	3	Techniques	3
Textiles	3	Advertising II	3
The Business of Fashion	3	Credit & Collections	3
Retail Internship Seminar	3	Personnel Practices	3
Advertising I	3		
Retail Internship	3		
Communication Skills	3		
Total	*25 credits*	*Total:*	*15 credits*

General courses that are common to other business courses at *Johnson & Wales* such as College English, College Reading & Study Skills, English Composition, Science Survey, Western Civilization I & II, can be discussed in an interview to demonstrate a well-rounded background. Initially it is the specialized courses in your program that you will highlight that will be of particular interest to an employer. They determine your qualifications for the job that is available.

Directions: Write in your program of study here.

Program of Study: _____

Specialized Courses

List the specialized courses that are part of your program of study.

Course	*Credits*	*Course*	*Credits*
_____	_____	_____	_____
_____	_____	_____	_____

_____ _____

_____ _____

_____ _____

Total credits _____

Specialized Equipment

List the specialized equipment you have been trained on:

_____ _____

_____ _____

_____ _____

_____ _____

_____ _____

(This may include cash registers, office equipment, typewriters, word processors, dictaphone machines, court reporting machines, computers, Telex equipment, switchboard training, etc. Where possible, list the type of equipment including the model.)

Work Experience

Program Example: Fashion & Retail Management

Twelve week internship at Gladdings. *Gladdings* is a retail store owned and operated by *Johnson & Wales University*. Founded in 1766 as *Gladding's Dry Goods,* it is one of the oldest retail stores in the country. It now serves as a training laboratory for retail students. *Gladdings* work experience develops competencies/skills in:

Mechandising Terminology _____

Sales Forecasting _____

Quantitative Skills _____

Profitability _____

Stock & Sales _____

Merchandising Techniques _____

Decision Making _____

Comments: Work rotations include: sales, clerical, shipping & receiving and display work.

By identifying the competencies/skills you developed through this experience, you **translate course work into skills** that can be applied on the job. When you can do this with your program of study, it will become easy to convince an employer that you have mastered skills important to your profession, as opposed to simply completing the coursework you need to graduate.

Directions: Describe any work requirements(s) for your own program of study.
(Internship, Externship, Cooperative Education experience)
Write in your program of study here.

Program of Study: _____

Work Experience

_____

_____

_____

_____

_____

_____

_____

Comments: _____

_____

_____

_____

List competencies acquired:

_____

_____

_____

_____

_____

_____

This exercise will help you apply your education to the job you are seeking. It will also help you identify specific qualifications that you can easily relate to an employer on an interview. *This exercise puts your courses to work!*

The second part of presenting your unique features to an employer is tying in individual experiences that have had relevance to your career. To complement the unique features of your career training you need to summarize related activities that you have pursued in preparation for your career. Such activities may include:

Part-Time Employment
Summer Employment
Industry Guest Speakers' Programs
Field Trips
Informational Interviews
Trade Shows Visited
Extracurricular Activities
Volunteer Work
Special Interests
Special Accomplishments

Briefly describe the value of your:

Part-Time Employment: _____

_____

Summer Employment: _____

_____

Industry Guest Speakers' Programs: _____

_____

Field Trips: _____

_____

Informational Interviews: _____

_____

Trade Show Visits: _____

_____

Extracurricular Activities: _____

_____

Volunteer Work: _____

_____

Special Interests: _____

_____

Special Accomplishments: _____

_____

Finally, before speaking to a prospective employer consider the information in "Career Paths" and the career choices you have made. Outline the progression of your career as you see it.

Your Career Path

Your Program of Study: _____

Your Graduation Date: _____

Your Career Goal: _____
(Professional Objective)

	Job Titles	**Estimated Salary**
Entry	_____	_____
	_____	_____
Mid-Management/ Specialist	_____	_____
	_____	_____
	_____	_____
	_____	_____
Management	_____	_____
	_____	_____
	_____	_____

Types of employers being considered:

(Manufacturers, restaurants, retail stores, banks, insurance companies, etc.)

_____

_____

_____

Names of companies being considered:

_____

_____

_____

_____

By identifying these unique features of your career training, the related activities you have pursued and the career path you wish to follow, you are ready to convince an employer that you know your career direction. Remember, **THE PRODUCT IS YOU,** and in order to really market your product well, you must know it and believe in it; then you will be able to market yourself convincingly and most important, be happy with the career you have chosen.

Specialized Career Paths

EQUINE

Level	Working With Horses	Scientific and Medical	Business and Industry	Education

1
Entry
($14,000-$18,000)
	Hot Walker
	Riding Instructor
	Groom
	Exercise Rider
		Veterinarian Assistant
		Blood Type Coordinator
		Lab Technician
			Secretary
			Breeding Farm
			  Accountant
			Feed Company
			  Representative
				Instructor

2
Mid-Management/
Specialists
($18,000-$26,000)
	Thoroughbred Trainer
	Foal Night Watchman
	Instructor
	Trainer
		Director of Registry
		  Services
			Insurance Broker
			Jockey's Agent
			Public Relations Mgr.
			Blood Stock Agent
			Equine Magazine
			  Publisher
			Marketing Director
				Department Head

3 Management *($26,000-$65,000+)*	Road Mgr. Barn Mgr. Breeding Farm Barn Mgr. Jockeys Professional Rider Horse Show Mgr.	Owner/Representative	Editor Auctioneer Vice President/ Marketing & Sales	Program Director School Director

Recommended Pre-Professional Part-time/Summer Work Experience
Any work within the industry would be recommended. Jobs are often available in teaching and training; stable work, especially at summer camps, is frequently available for students.

Working With Horses

Level	Job Title	Experience Needed
Entry	Hot Walker	Professional Training
Entry	Riding Instructor	Professional Training
Entry	Groom	Professional Training
Entry	Exercise Rider	Professional Training
2	Thoroughbred Trainer	2-4 years
2	Foal Night Watchman	2-4 years
2	Instructor	2-4 years
3	Road Manager	5-7 years
3	Barn Manager	4-6 years
3	Breeding Farm Manager	4-6 years
3	Jockeys	5-7 years
3	Professional Riders	5-7 years
3	Horse Show Manager	7-9 years

Salaries in Working with Horses

Level	Salary
Entry	$14,000 to $16,000
2	$16,000 to $22,000
3	$22,000 to $26,000
3	$26,000 to $40,000
3	$40,000 to $65,000+

Qualifications

Personal: Patience. Positive attitude. Excellent communication skills. Physical stamina. Willingness to work nights, weekends or holidays.

Professional: Knowledge of the horse industry. Basic business skills. Teamworker.

Where The Jobs Are
Race Tracks
Farms
Barns
Riding Academies
Riding Stables

Scientific and Medical

Level	Job Title	Experience Needed
Entry	Veterinarian Assistant	Professional Training
Entry	Blood Type Coordinator	Professional Training
Entry	Lab Technician	Professional Training
2	Director of Registry Services	2-4 years
3	Owner/Representative	4-8 years

Salaries in the Scientific and Medical Area

Entry	$16,000 to $18,000
2	$18,000 to $26,000
3	$26,000 to $65,000 +

Qualifications

Personal: Detail oriented. Patience. Aptitude for scientific work. Ability to work independently.

Professional: Knowledge of the horse industry. Resourcefulness. Basic business skills. Knowledge of scientific and medical developments related to the horse industry.

Where The Jobs Are
Breed Registries
Racing Organizations
Rodeo Organizations
Laboratories
Veterinary Clinics
Race Tracks

Business and Industry

Level	Job Title	Experience Needed
Entry	Secretary	Professional Training
Entry	Breeding Farm Accountant	Professional Training
Entry	Feed Company Representative	Professional Training
2	Insurance Broker	2-4 years
2	Jockey's Agent	2-4 years
2	Public Relations Manager	4-6 years
2	Blood Stock Agent	2-4 years
2	Equine Magazine Publisher	4-6 years
2	Marketing Director	6-8 years
3	Editor	8-10 years
3	Auctioneer	8-10 years
3	Vice President/Marketing and Sales	8-10 years

Salaries in Business and Industry

Entry	$16,000 to $18,000
2	$18,000 to $24,000
3	$24,000 to $65,000 +

Qualifications

Personal: Positive attitude. Enthusiasm. High energy level. Excellent communication skills.

Professional: Strong marketing and sales skills. Teamworker. Perception of customer needs. Resourcefulness. Product knowledge.

Where The Jobs Are
Insurance Companies
Feed Companies
Equine Publications
State Organizations
Trade Associations
Show Organizations
Sports Organizations
Racing Organizations
Show Barns

Education

Level	Job Title	Experience Needed
Entry	Instructor	Professional Training and/or College Degree
2	Department Head	4-6 years
3	Program Director	6-8 years
3	School Director	8-10 years

Salaries in Education

(See Salaries in Teacher Education)

Qualifications

Personal: Patience. Positive attitude. Enthusiasm. High energy level. Excellent communication skills.

Professional: Teamworker. Organizational skills. Knowledge of both the business and "hands-on" aspects of the equine industry. Basic business skills. Some work experience in the equine industry helpful.

Where The Jobs Are

Riding Academies
Education
Race Tracks

Trade Publications

The Horseman's Journal, 6000 Executive Boulevard, Suite 317, Rockville, MD 20852

Equus, 656 Quince Orchard Road, Gaithersburg, MD 20878
Horse & Rider, Rich Publishing Inc., Box 555, Temecula, CA 92390

Modern Horse Breeding, 656 Quince Orchard Road, Gaithersburg, MD 2087

Professional Associations

American Horse Council
1700 K Street, NW
Washington, DC 20006

American Association of Equine Practitioners
Route 5
22363 Hillcrest Circle
Golden, CO 80401

Thoroughbred Racing Association of North America
Suite 2W4
3000 Marcus Avenue
Lake Success, NY 11042

United Thoroughbred Trainers of America
19363 James Couzens Highway
Detroit, MI 48235

United States Harness Writers' Association
Box Ten
Batavia, NY 14020

FOOD SERVICE

Level	Production	Support	Control	Service
1 Entry *($19,000-$24,000)*	Sauce Cook Roasting Cook Soup Cook Vegetable Cook Seafood Cook Pastry Cook Baker Garde Manger Rounds Cook/ Swing Cook Butcher Commis Line Cook Prep Cook Sous Chef Pantry Person	Foodservice Salesperson Sanitation Supervisor	Purchasing Assistant Manager Trainee	Bartender Assistant Steward Waiter

2
Mid-Management/
Specialists
($24,000-$38,000)
	Chef
	Pastry Chef
	Assistant Chef
	Assistant Pastry Chef
	Kitchen Mgr.
	Catering Mgr.
	Cafeteria Mgr.
	Food Production Mgr.
	Banquet Mgr.
		Product Development
		  Technologist
		Menu Planner
		Chef Instructor
		Director of Recipe
		  Development
		Nutritionist
		Administrative
		  Dietitian
		Quality Assurance
		  Specialist
		Research & Develop-
		  ment Specialist
		Sales & Marketing
		  Specialist
		Packaging Specialist
		Home Economics
		  Teacher
		Foodservice Engineer
		Account Executive
		Training Mgr.
		Personnel Director
		Sales Mgr.
		Director of Marketing
		  & Advertising
		Marketing & Promo-
		  tion Mgr.
		Facilities Designer
		Real Estate Mgr.
			Assistant Manager
			Merchandising
			  Supervisor
			Storeroom Supervisor
			Purchasing Agent
			Accountant
			Computer Specialist
			Assistant Food &
			  Beverage Mgr.
			Production Mgr.
			Foodservice Mgr.
			Unit Mgr.
			Vending Mgr.
			Purchasing Mgr.
			Quality Control Mgr.
			Restaurant Mgr.
				Wine Steward
				Head Bartender
				Dining Room Mgr.
				Hostperson
				Head Waiter
				Dining Room Captain
				Banquet Captain

3
Management
($38,000-$60,000 +)
	Executive Chef
	Chef de Cuisine
		Educator/
		  Administrator
		Foodservice
		  Consultant
			Food & Beverage Mgr.
			Controller
			Regional Vice President
			District Mgr.
			Owner/Operator
			General Mgr.
				Beverage Mgr.
				Foodservice Director
				Maitre d'Hotel

Recommended Pre-Professional Part-time/Summer Experience
Cook, Grill Person, Prep Cook, Baker, Dishwasher, Checker & Cashier, Receiver, Storeroom Clerk, Barback, Waitperson, Counterworker, Hostperson, Busperson, Dining Room Attendant.

Production

Level	Job Title	Experience Needed
Entry	Sauce Cook	Professional Training
Entry	Roasting Cook	Professional Training
Entry	Soup Cook	Professional Training
Entry	Vegetable Cook	Professional Training
Entry	Seafood Cook	Professional Training
Entry	Pastry Cook	Professional Training
Entry	Baker	Professional Training
Entry	Garde Manger	Professional Training
Entry	Rounds Cook/Swing Cook	Professional Training
Entry	Butcher	Professional Training
Entry	Commis	Professional Training
Entry	Line Cook	Professional Training
Entry	Prep Cook	Professional Training
Entry	Sous Chef	Professional Training
Entry	Pantry Person	Professional Training
2	Assistant Chef	2-4 years
2	Assistant Pastry Chef	2-4 years
2	Chef	4-6 years
2	Pastry Chef	4-6 years
2	Kitchen Manager	5-7 years
2	Catering Manager	5-7 years
2	Cafeteria Manager	5-7 years
2	Banquet Manager	5-7 years
2	Food Production Manager	6-8 years
3	Chef de Cuisine	8 + years
3	Executive Chef	8 + years

(In all career areas in the Foodservice Industry it is important to note that the experience needed to progress to different positions varies widely according to the size, type and volume of the operation.)

*Salaries in Production

Entry	$19,000 to $22,000
2	$22,000 to $27,000
2	$27,000 to $38,000
3	$38,000 to $45,000
3	$45,000 to $60,000 +

*Some positions including Kitchen Managers, Banquet Chefs, Banquet Managers & Sales Personnel, earn bonuses and/or commissions based on sales volume. Chefs' salaries are frequently based on food cost percentages and labor cost percentages.

Salaries vary widely according to the size, type, and location of the foodservice operation. In many large, or fine dining establishments, and luxury hotels, top management positions are salaried over $100,000.

Special combinations of bonus, housing, meals, clothing allowance, company car, etc. are often in addition to salary.

Qualifications

Personal: Positive attitude. Enthusiasm. High energy level. Confidence. Diplomacy. Accuracy and attention to detail. Reliability. Excellent communication skills. Ability to work under pressure. Ability to handle stress. Good grooming and hygiene habits. Professional appearance.

Professional: Knowledge of and commitment to professional standards. Teamworker. Perception of customer needs. Creative talent. Ability to conceptualize. Aptitude for finances, figures, inventories and budgets.

Where The Jobs Are

Restaurants

Hotels

Motels

Resorts

Private Businesses

Institutional Foodservice Operations
(schools, universities, in-plant, hospitals, health-care facilities, etc.)

Clubs

Transportation

Education

Catering Firms

Fast Food Operations

*Franchises

Contract Food Operations

Government

*Franchising is a form of licensing by which the owner *(the franchisor)* obtains distribution through affiliated dealers *(the franchisee)*. Franchise agreements call for the parent company to give an independent business person rights to a successful restaurant concept and trademark, plus assistance in organizing, training, merchandising and management.

Level	Job Title	Experience Needed
Entry	Foodservice Salesperson	Professional Training
Entry	Sanitation Supervisor	Professional Training
2	Menu Planner	1-3 years
2	Chef Instructor	1-3 years
2	Nutritionist	1-3 years
2	Home Economics Teacher	1-3 years
2	Administrative Dietitian	1-3 years
2	Quality Assurance Specialist	3-5 years
2	Product Development Technologist	3-5 years
2	Research & Development Specialist	3-5 years
2	Sales & Marketing Specialist	3-5 years
2	Packaging Specialist	3-5 years
2	Foodservice Engineer	3-5 years
2	Quality Assurance Specialist	3-5 years
2	Account Executive	3-5 years
2	Facilities Designer	3-5 years
2	Training Manager	5-7 years
2	Sales Manager	5-7 years
2	Marketing Manager	5-7 years
2	Marketing & Promotion Manager	5-7 years
2	Real Estate Manager	5-7 years
2	Director of Recipe Development	6-8 years
2	Personnel Director	6-8 years
2	Director of Marketing & Advertising	6-8 years
3	Educator/Administrator	8-10 + years
3	Foodservice Consultant	8-10 + years

Salaries in Support Services

Level	Salary
Entry	$19,000 to $24,000
2	$24,000 to $28,000
2	$28,000 to $35,000
2	$35,000 to $40,000
3	$40,000 to $50,000
3	$50,000 to $60,000 +

Qualifications

Personal: Positive attitude. Enthusiasm. Excellent verbal and written communications skills. Ability to judge and make decisions. Accuracy and attention to detail. Well-groomed. Ability to work independently.

Professional: Knowledge of and commitment to professional standards. Technical knowledge. Product knowledge. Strong marketing and sales skills. Perception of customer needs. Creative talent. Ability to conceptualize. Teamworker.

Where The Jobs Are

Restaurants
Hotels
Motels
Resorts
Private Businesses
Institutional Foodservice Operations
(schools, universities, in-plant, hospitals, health-care facilities, etc.)
Clubs
Transportation
Education
Catering Firms
Fast Food Operations
*Franchises
Contract Food Operations
Consulting
Wholesalers
Restaurant Equipment Suppliers
Manufacturers of Food Products
Government

Control

Level	Job Title	Experience Needed
Entry	Purchasing Assistant	Professional Training
Entry	Manager Trainee	Professional Training
2	Assistant Manager	2-4 years
2	Accountant	2-4 years
2	Purchasing Agent	2-4 years
2	Computer Specialist	2-4 years
2	Merchandising Supervisor	3-5 years
2	Storeroom Supervisor	3-5 years
2	Assistant Food & Beverage Manager	3-5 years
2	Production Manager	4-6 years
2	Foodservice Manager	4-6 years
2	Unit Manager	4-6 years
2	Vending Manager	4-6 years
2	Purchasing Manager	5-7 years
2	Quality Control Manager	5-7 years
2	Restaurant Manager	5-7 years
3	Food & Beverage Manager	6-8 years
3	Controller	8-10 years
3	District Manager	8-10 years
3	Regional Vice President	8-10 years
3	Owner/Operator	8-10 years
3	General Manager	8-10 years

Salaries in Control

Level	Salary
Entry	$19,000 to $23,000
2	$23,000 to $26,000
2	$26,000 to $32,000
2	$32,000 to $38,000
3	$38,000 to $45,000
3	$45,000 to $60,000 +

Qualifications

Personal: Positive attitude. Enthusiasm. Ability to make quick and accurate decisions. Attention to detail. Excellent written and verbal communication skills. Confidence. Ability to handle pressure.

Professional: Demonstrated leadership ability. Aptitude for dealing with figures, finances, inventories and quotas. Teamworker. Product knowledge. Perception of customers' needs. Planning and organizational skills. Ability to work with budgets.

Where The Jobs Are
Restaurants
Hotels
Motels
Resorts
Institutional Foodservice Operations
(schools, universities, in-plant, hospitals, health-care facilities, etc.)
Clubs
Catering Firms
Fast Food Operations
Franchises
Contract Food Operations
Lounges
Drinking Establishments
Government

Service

Level	Job Title	Experience Needed
Entry	Bartender	Professional Training
Entry	Assistant Steward	Professional Training
Entry	Professional Waiter	Professional Training
2	Hostperson	1-3 years
2	Wine Steward	1-3 years
2	Head Bartender	1-3 years
2	Dining Room Manager	2-5 years
2	Head Waiter	2-5 years
2	Dining Room Captain	2-5 years
2	Banquet Captain	2-5 years
3	Beverage Manager	4-6 years
3	Foodservice Director	5-7 years
3	Maitre d'Hotel	7-10 years

*Salaries in Service

Entry	$19,000 to $22,000
2	$20,000 to $25,000
2	$25,000 to $30,000
3	$30,000 to $35,000
3	$35,000 to $45,000 +

In many service positions, especially at the entry level, tips and gratuities constitute a portion of the salary. Salaries involving tips and gratuities vary according to the volume and type of operation.

Qualifications

Personal: Positive attitude. Enthusiasm. High energy level. Good communication skills. Ability to work under pressure. Well-groomed. Professional appearance. Flexibility.

Professional: Product knowledge. Perception of customer needs. Teamworker. Demonstrated leadership ability. Commitment to professional standards. Ability to supervise others. Good organizational and planning skills.

Where The Jobs Are

Restaurants
Hotels
Motels
Resorts
Lounges
Drinking Establishments
Transportation
Clubs
Franchises
Institutional Foodservice Operations
(In-plant)
Contract Food Operations
Government

Trade Publications

Nations Restaurant News, Lebhar-Friedman, 425 Park Avenue, New York, NY 10022

Restaurants and Institutions, Cahners Publishing Co., Cahners Plaza, 1350 East Touhy Avenue, P.O. Box 5080, Des Plaines, IL 60018

Restaurant Business, 633 Third Avenue, New York, NY 10017

Restaurant Management, Harcourt, Brace, Jovanovich, 7500 Old Oak, Blvd., Cleveland, OH 44130

Professional Associations

American Culinary Federation *(ACF)*
Box 3466
St. Augustine, FL 32084

National Restaurant Association *(NRA)*
311 First Street, N.W.
Washington, DC 20001

Council on Hotel, Restaurant and Institutional Education *(CHRIE)*
Henderson Blvd., S-208
University Park, PA 16802

International Food Service Executives Association
111 East Wacker Dr.
Chicago, IL 60601

HOSPITALITY

Level	Rooms Division	Food & Beverage Services	Support
1 Entry *($19,000-$25,000)*	Guest Services Agent Reservationist Information Specialist Head Cashier Concierge Front Desk Supervisor Inspector/ress Assistant Manager *(Front Office)* Assistant Housekeeper Housekeeper Team Leader *(Floor Supervisor)*	*See Foodservice Careers —* *Production, Control & Service*	*See Foodservice Careers —* *Support* Accountant Night Auditor Sales Trainee Sales Representative
2 Mid-Management/ Specialists *($25,000-$42,000)*	Front Office Manager Rooms Attendant Executive Housekeeper Superintendent of Service Rooms Division Supervisor	*See Foodservice Careers —* *Production, Control & Service*	*See Foodservice Careers —* *Support* *See Travel Tourism Careers —* *Hotels, Motels, Resorts* Sales Director Group Sales Manager Area Sales Manager Auditor Corporate Account Executive Association Account Executive International Account Executive Tour & Travel Account Executive
3 Management *($38,000-$65,000+)*	Resident Manager Assistant Hotel Manager Vice President/Operations General Manager	*See Foodservice Careers —* *Production, Control & Service*	*See Foodservice Careers —* *Support* *See Travel Tourism Careers —* *Hotels, Motels, Resorts* Chief Accountant Vice President/Finance Vice President/Marketing

Recommended Pre-Professional Part-time/Summer Work Experience
Room Clerk, Starter, Telephone Operator, Messenger, Bell Hop, Lobby Porter, Maid, Linen Room Attendant, Cashier, Seamstress, Doorperson, Cook, Waitpersons, Buspersons, Pantry Worker

Rooms Division

Level	Job Title	Experience Needed
Entry	Guest Services Agent	Professional Training
Entry	Reservationist	Professional Training
Entry	Information Specialist	Professional Training
Entry	Head Cashier	Professional Training
Entry	Concierge	Professional Training
Entry	Front Desk Supervisor	Professional Training
Entry	Inspector/ress	Professional Training
Entry	Assistant Manager (*Front Office*)	Professional Training
Entry	Assistant Housekeeper	Professional Training
Entry	Housekeeper	Professional Training
Entry	Team Leader (*Floor Supervisor*)	Professional Training
2	Front Office Manager	1-2 years
2	Rooms Attendant	1-2 years
2	Executive Housekeeper	2-4 years
2	Superintendent of Service	4-6 years
2	Rooms Division Supervisor	4-6 years
3	Resident Manager	6-8 years
3	Assistant Hotel Manager	6-8 years
3	Vice President/Operations	8-10 years
3	General Manager	8-10 years

*Salaries in Rooms Division

Level	Salary
Entry	$19,000 to $24,000
2	$24,000 to $28,000
3	$28,000 to $38,000
3	$38,000 to $43,000
3	$43,000 to $46,000
3	$46,000 to $65,000 +

Salaries in Rooms Divisions vary widely according to the type of hotel. In many large, or luxury hotels, top management positions are salaried over $100,000. Special combinations of bonus, housing, meals, clothing allowance, company car, etc. are often in addition to salary. For details on salaries in the Hospitality Industry, consult the Roth Young Hospitality Industry Wage and Salary Review.

Qualifications

Personal: Positive attitude. Enthusiasm. High energy level. Diplomacy. Courtesy. Confidence. Ability to make quick decisions and work independently. Good grooming and professional appearance. Ability to handle pressure. Excellent communication skills.

Professional: Computer knowledge helpful. Aptitude for figures, finances, inventories, and quotas. Knowledge of and commitment to professional standards. Teamworker. Ability to plan, organize and forecast.

Where The Jobs Are

Hotels

Motels

Resorts

Inns

Bed & Breakfast Operations

Food and Beverage Service

Level	Job Title	Experience Needed
Entry	*See Foodservice Careers —*	
	Control & Services	Professional Training
2	*See Foodservice Careers —*	
	Control & Services	Professional Training
3	*See Foodservice Careers —*	
	Control & Services	Professional Training

Salaries in Food and Beverage Services
(See Salaries in Food Service Careers — Production, Control & Service)

Qualifications

(See Qualifications in Food Service Careers — Production, Control and Service)

Where The Jobs Are
Hotels
Motels
Resorts
Inns
Bed & Breakfast Operations

Support

Level	Job Title	Experience Needed
Entry	*See Foodservice Careers —*	
	Support	Professional Training
Entry	Accountant	Professional Training
Entry	Night Auditor	Professional Training
Entry	Sales Trainee	Professional Training
Entry	Sales Representative	Professional Training
2	*See Foodservice Careers —*	
	Support	
	See Travel & Tourism Careers	
	— Hotels, Motels & Resorts	
2	Auditor	2-4 years
2	Group Sales Manager	2-4 years
2	Area Sales Manager	3-5 years
2	Corporate Account Executive	2-4 years
2	International Account	
	Executive	3-5 years
2	Tour & Travel Account	
	Executive	3-5 years
3	*See Foodservice Careers —*	
	Support	
	See Travel Tourism Careers —	
	Hotels, Motels & Resorts	
3	Chief Accountant	
3	Vice President/Finance	
3	Vice President/Marketing	

Qualifications
(See Qualifications in Foodservice Careers — Support and Qualifications in Travel Tourism Careers — Hotels, Motels, and Resorts)

Where The Jobs Are
Hotels
Motels
Resorts
Inns
Bed & Breakfast Operations

Salaries in Support
(See Salaries in Foodservice Careers — Support and Salaries in Travel Tourism Careers — Hotels, Motels & Resorts)

Trade Publications

Hotel & Motel Management, 545 Fifth Ave., New York, NY 10017

Lodging Hospitality, 1100 Superior Ave., Cleveland, OH 44114

Hotel & Motel Red Book, American Hotel Association Directory Corporation, 888 Seventh Ave., New York, NY 10019

Cornell Hotel & Restaurant Administration Quarterly, School of Hotel Administration, Cornell University, Ithaca, NY 14853

Nation's Restaurant News, Lebhar-Friedman, Inc., 425 Park Ave., New York, NY 10022

Restaurant and Institutions, Cahners Publishing Co., Cahners Plaza, 1350 East Touhy Ave., P.O. Box 5080, Des Plaines, IL 60018

Professional Associations

American Hotel and Motel Association
888 Seventh Avenue
New York, NY 10019

Council on Hotel, Restaurant, and Institutional Education *(CHRIE)*
Henderson Bldg., S-208
University Park, PA 16802

Hotel Sales and Marketing Association International
1400 K St., NW, Suite 810
Washington, DC 20005

National Executive Housekeepers Association
1001 Eastwind Dr., Suite 301
Westerville, OH 43081

Foodservice and Lodging Institute
1919 Pennsylvania Ave., NW
Washington, DC 20006

American Bed and Breakfast Association
6811 Kingwood Drive
Falls Church, VA 20042

Club Managers Association of America
7615 Winterberry Place
Bethesda, MD 20817

National Restaurant Association
311 First St., NW
Washington, DC 20001

International Food Service Executives' Association
111 East Wacker Drive
Chicago, IL 60601

RECREATION/LEISURE MANAGEMENT

Level	Amusement and Theme Parks	Club Management	Parks and Natural Resources	Special Programs

1
Entry
($14,000-$18,000)
	Operations
	  Assistant
	Ticket Agent
	Guest Services Agent
		Assistant Mgr.
		  Trainee
			Grounds & Facilities
			  Maintenance
				Camp Counselor

2
Mid-Management/
Specialists
($18,000-$25,000)
	Operations Mgr.
	Games Mgr.
	Arcade Mgr.
	Manager of Public
	  Relations
	Purchasing Agent
		Assistant Club Mgr.	Park Ranger
			Outdoor Recreation
			  Specialist
			Forester
			Park Manager
			Landscape Architect
			Conservationist
				Senior Citizens Program
				  Director
				Program Specialist
				Outdoor Recreationist
				Wilderness Leader
				Camp Manager
				Therapeutic Recreation
				  Specialist

3 Management *($25,000-$60,000)*	Director of Group Sales Promotion Director Entertainment Director Food Director Maintenance Director Ride Superintendent V.P./Marketing & Sales V.P./Operations	Club Mgr.		Program Director Manager of Recreation Services

Recommended Pre-Professional Part-time/Summer Work Experience
Ride Operator, Game Attendant, Foodservice Employee, Souvenir & Gift Shop Clerk, Guide, Volunteer at Local Park & Recreation Departments, YMCA's, Churches, Nursing Homes, Recreation Programs

Amusement and Theme Parks

Level	Job Title	Experience Needed
Entry	Operations Assistant	Professional Training
Entry	Ticket Agent	Professional Training
Entry	Guest Services Agent	Professional Training
2	Operations Manager	1-3 years
2	Games Manager	1-3 years
2	Arcade Manager	1-3 years
2	Purchasing Agent	2-4 years
2	Manager of Public Relations	2-4 years
3	Director of Group Sales	3-5 years
3	Promotion Director	3-5 years
3	Entertainment Director	3-5 years
3	Food Director	3-5 years
3	Maintenance Director	3-5
3	Ride Superintendent	3-5
3	Vice President/Marketing & Sales	6-8 years
3	Vice President/ Operations	6-8 years

Qualifications

Personal: Positive attitude. Enthusiasm. Flexibility. Excellent communication skills. High energy level.

Professional: Knowledge of standard regulations and safety procedures. Ability to plan and organize. Ability to work with budgets. Strong marketing and sales skills. Teamworker. Demonstrated leadership ability.

Where The Jobs Are
Amusement Parks
Theme Parks
State Agencies

Salaries in Amusement & Theme Parks

Entry	$14,000 to $16,000
2	$16,000 to $18,000
2	$18,000 to $23,000
3	$23,000 to $28,000
3	$28,000 to $35,000

Club Management

Level	Job Title	Experience Needed
Entry	Assistant Manager Trainee	Professional Training
2	Assistant Club Manager	2-4 years
3	Club Manager	4-8 years

Qualifications

Personal: Positive attitude. High energy level. Enthusiasm. Excellent communication skills. Flexibility.

Professional: Good decision-making skills. Aptitude for figures, finances and inventories. Strong marketing and sales skills. Ability to supervise, plan, and organize. Ability to work with budgets.

*Salaries in Club Management

Entry	$17,000 to $23,000
2	$23,000 to $26,000
3	$26,000 to $38,000 +

Salaries vary widely depending on the type, size, and location of the club as well as the volume of business conducted

Where The Jobs Are

Government	Travel Clubs
Private Clubs	Resorts
Association Clubs	

Park and Natural Resources

Level	Job Title	Experience Needed
Entry	Grounds Facilities Maintenance	Professional Training
2	Park Ranger	2-4 years
2	Outdoor Recreation Specialist	2-4 years
2	Forester	4-6 years
2	Park Manager	4-6 years
2	Landscape Architect	6-8 years
2	Conservationist	6-8 years
3	Park Supervisor/ Administrator	8-10 years

Salaries in Parks and Natural Resources

Entry	$15,000 to $18,000
2	$18,000 to $28,000
2	$28,000 to $34,000
3	$34,000 to $45,000 +

Qualifications

Personal: Positive attitude. High energy level. Enthusiasm. Flexibility. Ability to work under pressure. Ability to handle stress. Responsible. Dependable.

Professional: Licensing by state. Successful completion of state entrance examination. Knowledge of standard regulations and safety procedures. Ability to make accurate and quick decisions. Ability to enforce policies and procedures. Ability to plan and organize. Ability to conceptualize. Creative talent. Demonstrated leadership ability.

Where The Jobs Are

Towns	State & Local Government
Cities	Federal Government

Special Programs

Level	Job Title	Experience Needed
Entry	Camp Counselor	Professional Training
2	Senior Citizens Program Director	1-3 years
2	Program Specialist *(drama, sports, fine arts)*	1-3 years
2	Outdoor Recreationist	1-3 years
2	Wilderness Leader	2-4 years
2	Camp Manager	3-5 years
2	Therapeutic Recreation Specialist	3-5 years
3	Program Director	5-7 years
3	Manager of Recreation Services	6-8 years

Salaries in Special Programs

Entry	$14,000 to $16,000
2	$16,000 to $18,000
2	$18,000 to $23,000
2	$23,000 to $27,000
2	$27,000 to $33,000
3	$33,000 to $38,000
3	$38,000 to $43,000

Qualifications

Personal: Positive attitude. Enthusiasm. High energy level. Flexibility. Enjoyment of the outdoors. Excellent communication skills. Patience.

Professional: Knowledge of standard regulations and safety procedures. Ability to enforce policies and procedures. Creative talent. Ability to work with budgets. Ability to plan and organize. Demonstrated leadership ability. Teamworker.

Where The Jobs Are

Camps	Schools
Parks	Federal Programs
Associations	State Programs
Clubs	Athletic Organizations
Health Care Facilities	Community Centers

Trade Publications

Employ
National Job Bulletin
Parks & Recreation
Recreation and Parks Law Reporter
Therapeutic Recreation Journal
Journal of Leisure Research

All publications of:
National Recreation and Park Association, 3101
Park Center Drive, Alexandria, VA 22302

Professional Associations

American Association for Leisure and Recreation
1900 Association Drive
Reston, VA 20091

National Recreation and Park Association
3101 Park Center Drive
Alexandria, VA 22302

National Forest Recreation Association
Route 3, Box 210
Flagstaff, AZ 86001

Council for Therapeutic Recreation Certification
P.O. Box 16126
Alexandria, VA 22302

International Association of Amusement Parks and Attractions
4230 King Street
Alexandria, VA 22302

TEACHER EDUCATION

Level	Secondary	Post-Secondary	College/Universities	Business & Education
1 Entry *($17,000-$25,000)*	Teacher	Instructor	Instructor	Seminar Facilitator Sales Representative

2
Mid-Management/
Specialists
($25,000-$36,000)
	Academic Dept. Head	Academic Dept. Head
		Curriculum Developer
			Assistant Professor
			Associate Professor
			Academic Dept. Head
			Department
			  Chairperson
				Training Specialist
				Training Manager
				Corporate Training
				  Manager
				Sales Manager

3
Management
($34,000-$45,000 +)
	Principal
	Administration
	Superintendent
		Program Director
		School Director
		Administrator
			Dean
			School Director
			Vice President
			President
				Director of Training &
				  Development
				Director of Marketing &
				  Sales
				Consultant
				See Marketing Careers —
				Sales & See Management
				Careers — Personnel

Recommended Pre-Professional Part-time/Summer Work Experience
Teacher's Aide, Camp Counselor, Tutor, Peer Tutor, Volunteer, Sales, Telemarketing; *(Any work recommended for the specialized area you may want to teach such as: Secretarial Sciences, Culinary Arts, Computer Systems)*

Secondary Education

Level	Job Title	Experience Needed
Entry	Teacher	College Degree
2	Academic Dept. Head	5-7 years
3	Principal	8-10 years
3	Administrator	8-10 years
3	Superintendent	8-10 years

*Salaries in Secondary Education

Entry	$17,000 to $25,000
2	$25,000 to $36,000
3	$36,000 to $45,000 +

*SALARIES vary widely from school systems state to state. The highest average reported for teachers with some experience is approximately $38,000 in Alaska, while the lowest average is approximately $17,000 in Mississippi.

Qualifications

Personal: Positive attitude. Enthusiasm. High energy level. Flexibility. Excellent interpersonal skills. Listening skills.

Professional: Knowledge of and commitment to professional standards. Proper certification. Subject knowledge. Effective teaching techniques. Ability to plan, organize and supervise. Creative talent. Ability to work with budgets. Ability to conceptualize.

Where The Jobs Are
Private & Public Schools
Tutoring

Post-Secondary Education

Level	Job Title	Experience Needed
Entry	Instructor	College Degree
2	Academic Deptment Head	5-7 years
2	Curriculum Developer	5-7 years
3	Program Director	6-8 years
3	School Director	8-10 years
3	Administrator	8-10 years

Salaries in Post-Secondary Education

Entry	$20,000 to $25,000
2	$25,000 to $36,000
3	$36,000 to $42,000
3	$42,000 to $45,000
3	$45,000 to $55,000 +

Qualifications
(See Qualifications in Secondary Education)

Where The Jobs Are
Junior Colleges
Private Colleges
Public Colleges
Trade Schools
Private Career Schools

Colleges/Universities

Level	Job Title	*Experience Needed
Entry	Instructor	College Degree (*often Advanced Degrees required*)
2	Assistant Professor	2-4 years
2	Associate Professor	2-4 years
2	Department Chairperson	4-6 years
2	Academic Department Head	4-6 years
2	Professor	6-8 years
3	Dean	7-10 years
3	School Director	8-10 years
3	Vice President	8-10 years
3	President	10 + years

*EXPERIENCE needed to move through various positions in higher education varies greatly depending on the size of the college or university, the type of training it provides and whether it is privately or publicly run.

Salaries in Colleges/Universities
(See Salaries in Post-Secondary Education)

Qualifications
(See Qualifications in Secondary Education)

Where The Jobs Are
Colleges
Universities

Business and Industry

Level	Job Title	*Experience Needed
Entry	Seminar Facilitator	College Degree (*often Advanced Degrees required*)
Entry	Sales Representative	
2	Training Specialist	2-4 years
2	Training Manager	4-6 years
2	Corporate Training Manager	4-6 years
2	Sales Manager	5-7 years
3	Director of Training & Development	6-8 years
3	Director of Marketing & Sales	6-8 years
3	Consultant	7-10 years

See Marketing Careers — Sales & See Management Careers — Personnel

Salaries in Business & Industry
(See Salaries in Marketing Careers — Sales & See Salaries in Management Careers — Personnel

Qualifications
(See Qualifications in Marketing Careers — Sales & See Qualifications in Management Careers — Personnel)

Where The Jobs Are
Private Corporations
Government
Consulting

J&W Specialized Index
of Job Descriptions

J&W SPECIALIZED INDEX OF JOB DESCRIPTIONS

Academic Department Head
(Refer to General Index of Job Descriptions)

Accountant *(Food Service)*
Prepares and analyzes financial reports that furnish up-to-date financial information. Accountants employed by large restaurant firms may travel extensively to audit or work for clients or branches of the firm.

Accountant *(Hospitality)*
Sets up the financial recordkeeping for the hotel or other lodging facility. Estimates future revenues and expenditures to prepare the operation's budget for each year.

Account Executive *(Food Service)*
Initiates and signs new customers which includes scouting new business, helping survey clients' needs, writing formal request letters, and making formal presentations, usually accompanied by management representative(s). Representative of the foodservice contractor who deals directly with the liaison designate of the client.

Administrative Dietitian
Responsible for training and supervision of foodservice supervisor and assistants in food preparation and formulating policies, enforcing sanitary and safety regulations. Buys food, equipment and other supplies, so must understand purchasing and budgeting.

Administrator *(Education)*
Involved with curriculum and program development and directing teaching personnel of the school system. Confers with teaching and administrative staff to plan and develop curriculum designed to meet needs of the students. Visits classrooms to observe effectiveness of instructional methods and materials. Evaluates teaching techniques and recommends changes for improving them. Conducts workshops and conferences for teachers to study new classroom procedures, new instructional materials, and other aids to teaching.

Arcade Manager
Oversees the complete operation of arcade amusement facility. Supervises staff who assist patrons and maintains game machines. Enforces safety policies. Develops promotions and works with specified budgets to keep the operation profitable. Involved with customer complaints. Keeps informed on local ordinances that may affect the property.

Area Sales Manager *(Hospitality)*
Responsible for sales promotion for a group of hotel properties in a specified geographic area.

Assistant Chef
(See Chef)

Assistant Club Manager
(See Club Manager)

Assistant Food and Beverage Manager
(See Food and Beverage Manager)

Assistant Hotel Manager
Assists with supervising the operations of the different departments of a hotel: food service, housekeeping, front office, and maintenance. Ensures the smooth functioning and profitability of the hotel by maintaining the property and quality guest service.

Assistant Housekeeper
(See Housekeeper)

Assistant Manager *(Food Service)*
Performs supervisory duties under the manager's direction. Must be capable of filling in when the manager is absent, thus needs good management skills and knowledge of the operation.

Assistant Manager *(Front Office)*
(See Front Office Manager)

Assistant Manager Trainee *(Recreation)*
(See Assistant Club Manager)

Assistant Pastry Chef *(See Pastry Chef)*

Assistant Professor
A designation of faculty rank used to refer to faculty members with some, but not extensive, teaching experience in their area of expertise. *(See Professor)*

Assistant Wine Steward
(See Wine Steward)

Associate Professor
A higher designation of faculty rank used to refer to faculty members with more extensive teaching experience in their area of expertise. Often, this ranking is also marked by research work, publications, or industry experience. *(See Professor)*

Association Account Executive *(Hospitality)*
Responsible for the development of and service of professional or trade association business coming into the hotel or other related facility.

Auctioneer *(Equine)*
Officiates at horse auctions. Acts as an intermediary between buyers and sellers of horses.

Auditor *(Hospitality)*

Examines and analyzes accounting records of hotel or foodservice operation and prepares reports concerning its financial status and operating procedures. Analyzes data to check for duplication of effort, extravagance, fraud, or lack of compliance with management's established policies.

Baker

Prepares all the baked items that are not desserts; such as breads, rolls, muffins, danish and croissants for use in dining rooms of hotels and restaurants and related facilities. Depending on the size of the staff and the operation, may also make pies, cakes, and some pastry items.

Banquet Captain

May greet the host, hostess and guests. Ensures that everything is as ordered. Ensures that all party rooms are in order at all times and checks before and after a function to make sure that the patrons are satisfied. Presents the bill for signature or payment when the function is over. Pays employees at the end of the function.

Banquet Manager

Arranges banquet and foodservice functions. Arranges banquet details after they have been agreed upon by the catering manager and the customer. Prepares and updates banquet menus. Reports inventory needs to purchasing agent and storeroom and may supervise the scheduling of staff to work the functions.

Barn Manager

Supervises and coordinates activities of workers engaged in maintenance of stables and care of horses. Establishes amount and type of rations to feed animals according to past food consumption, health, activity, and size of the animals. Inspects animals for evidence of disease or injury and treats animals according to experience or following instructions of the veterinarian. Inspects barns and stables for cleanliness. Supervises the upkeep of stalls, feed and water troughs, and equipment, and in the care and feeding of animals.

Bartender

Mixes and serves alcoholic and nonalcoholic drinks for patrons of a bar following standard recipes. Mixes ingredients, such as liquor, soda, water, sugar, and bitters to prepare cocktails and other drinks. Serves wine and draught or bottled beer. Collects money for drinks served. Orders or requisitions liquors and supplies. Places bottled goods and glasses to make an attractive display. May slice and pit fruit for the garnishing of drinks. May prepare appetizers, such as pickles, cheese and cold meat.

Beverage Manager

Responsible for compiling statistics of liquor costs, sales, profits, and losses. Inventories the bar as needed, sometimes daily, and prepares the daily consumption report that is forwarded to the auditing office. Issues merchandise to all bar areas but usually does not buy liquor. Instead, forwards purchase orders to a central purchasing agent, who may order for several hotels in a chain.

Blood Stock Agent

Maintains reports and records of different blood types of pedigree horses and issues them to breeders at their request. Makes recommendations to breeders about horses available for breeding based on their past medical records and genealogy.

Blood Type Coordinator

Tests blood of horses to ascertain blood type and presence of any diseases. Provides reports to breeders so that proper breeding can occur.

Breeding Farm Accountant

Maintains accounts pertaining to the management of the breed farm. This would include payments and purchases to feed companies, service people, veterinarians; as well as payroll of employees engaged in working at the farm. Keeps records of all sales of horses that have been bred on the farm.

Breeding Farm Barn Manager

Supervises activities of workers who breed and raise horses. Selects and breeds horses according to knowledge of horses, genealogy traits, and offspring desired. Examines animals to detect symptoms of illness or injury. Treats minor illness or injury or ailment. Supervises the building and maintenance of the barn. Arranges for sale of horses. May exhibit horses at shows.

Butcher

Responsible for cutting, boning, and otherwise caring for and preparing meats for cooking.

Cafeteria Manager

In charge of a unit with as few as one employee to as many as seventy or more. Oversees all employees, sometimes giving limited on-the-job training. Hiring and firing responsibilities. Purchases what is needed for unit, usually from a central purchasing office and keeps records of the same.

Camp Counselor

Leads and instructs campers in nature-oriented forms of recreation such as swimming, hiking, and horseback riding as well as outdoor education. Provides campers with specialized instruction in a particular area such as music, drama, gymnastics, tennis, or computers. Must ensure that the campers have adequate living conditions and understand the rules of the camp.

Catering Manager

Works with the Executive Chef on menus, food quality or service problems. Responsible for arranging any catered functions held at the establishment from weddings to conventions, from banquets to dances. Draws up necessary contracts. Helps customers select menu, decorations, and room arrangement and transmits these requirements to various departments for execution.

Camp Manager

Supervises camp counselors and their related activities. Ensures that campers remain with the group throughout their stay. Oversees food production, first aid, campsite, and other areas pertaining to the day-to-day operation of the camp. May organize promotional efforts to generate more business to the campsite. Responsible for all campers during their stay with the camp. Evaluates success of programs and staff. Makes recommendations for improvements.

Chef

Supervises, coordinates, and participates in activities of cooks and other kitchen personnel engaged in preparing foods for a hotel, restaurant, cafeteria, or other establishment. Estimates food consumption, and requisitions or purchases foodstuffs. Receives and checks recipes. Supervises personnel engaged in preparing, cooking, and serving meats, sauces, vegetables, soups and other foods. May employ, train and discharge workers. In small establishments, may maintain time and payroll records.

Chef de Cuisine *(Maitre de Cuisine)*

In complete charge of food services. Reporting to the Food and Beverage Director in large operations or to the owner or manager in smaller operations; may assume duties of the Food and Beverage Director as well when needed.

Chef Instructor

Brings a chef's perspective to the "lab" classroom and teaches hands-on cooking techniques. *(See Instructor)*

Chief Accountant *(Hospitality)*

Responsible for the supervision and control of the general accounting functions of the hotel. This includes night audit functions, general ledger, payables, payroll, property, budget reporting, and statistical accumulation. Responsible for financial statement and report preparation and budget reviews. Supervises and trains hotel employees in accounting, payroll, and accounts payable.

Club Manager

Estimates and orders food products and coordinates activity of workers engaged in selling alcoholic and non-alcoholic beverages for consumption on the premises. May manage staff involved in operating club with recreational facilities for private groups or the general public. Responsible for grounds and buildings, payroll, and promotion.

Cold Cook *(Garde Manger)*

Responsible for cold hors d'oeuvres, cold plates, salads, buffets, ice and vegetable carvings, tallow and butter sculpturing, etc.

Commis

A professional assistant in the kitchen or dining room.

Computer Specialist *(Food Service)*

Coordinates inventory control, restaurant accounting activities, employee statistics, accounting data and advertising lists for large foodservice establishments.

Concierge

(Refer to General Index of Job Descriptions)

Conservationist

Protects, develops, and manages forests, rangelands, wildlife, and soil and water resources to ensure that future ecological needs will be met.

Consultant
(Refer to General Index of Job Descriptions)

Controller *(Food Service)*
(Refer to General Index of Job Descriptions)

Cook
Prepares, seasons, and cooks soups, meats, vegetables, desserts, and other foodstuffs for consumption in hotels and restaurants. Reads menu to estimate food requirements and orders food from supplier or procures it from storage. Adjusts thermostat controls to regulate temperature of ovens, broilers, grills and roasters. Measures and mixes ingredients according to recipe, using a variety of kitchen utensils and equipment, such as blenders, mixers, grinders, slicers, and tenderizes to prepare soups, salads, gravies, desserts, sauces and casseroles. Bakes, roasts, broils, and steams meat, fish, vegetables, and other foods. Observes and tests foods being cooked by tasting, smelling, and piercing with fork to determine that it is cooked. Carves meats, portions food on serving plates, adds gravies, sauces and garnishes servings to fill orders.

Corporate Account Executive *(Hospitality)*
Responsible for the development of and service of corporate *(business and industry)* business coming into the hotel.

Corporate Training Manager
Develops on-going training programs for the corporate staff in a company. Conducts training seminars. Writes and coordinates corporate training manuals. Brings in other seminar facilitators who are experts on the various aspects of corporate training to be covered by the program. Writes curriculum for in-house corporate education programs.

Curriculum Developer
Works individually or with a committee or team to evaluate existing curriculum in school systems and make recommendations for additions, deletions or changes according to knowledge of required standards. May write curriculum outlines for schools. May act as consultants to school administrators evaluating their own curriculum. Requires constant updating on state and federal laws pertaining to course requirements and specialized knowledge in critical subject areas.

Dean
(Refer to General Index of Job Descriptions)

Department Chairperson
(See Academic Department Head)

Dining Room Captain
Under the general supervision of the dining room manager, dining room captains are in charge of one section of the dining room. They instruct, supervise, and give help to the staff working their area when needed. Dining room captains watch all the tables under their jurisdiction to detect any dissatisfaction and may make adjustments in response to complaints.

Department Head *(Equine)*
(See Academic Department Head)
(Refer to General Index of Job Descriptions)

Dining Room Manager
Supervises all dining room staff and activities, including staff training, scheduling of staff working hours, keeping time records and assigning work stations. Should be capable of working in a formal public atmosphere.

Director of Groups Sales *(Recreation)*
Develops client base of small or large groups to use recreational facilities. May arrange for group discounts for large group business. Writes promotional pieces and coordinates advertising aimed at securing group business. May direct mass mailings to organizations, schools, associations or other special groups as part of promotional program.

Director of Marketing and Advertising *(Food Service)*
Plans and carries out advertising and promotional programs. Works with company's top level management to prepare an overall marketing plan. Arranges with various suppliers regarding schedule and cost of brochures, menus, advertisements, etc. being promoted. Responsible for the advertising budget.

Director of Marketing and Sales *(Education)*
(Refer to General Index of Job Descriptions)

Director of Recipe Development
These people create new recipes for the menus of larger restaurants or restaurant chains. Requires thorough knowledge of food preparation and the ability to apply this knowledge creatively.

Director of Registry Services
Maintains official directory containing information relating to the identification of special breeds of horses. The registry is used to verify identification of horses such as show horses and thoroughbreds.

Director of Training and Development *(Education)*
(See Director of Training)

District Manager *(Food Service)*
Supervises smaller facilities in certain areas. Purchasing, negotiation and supervision of area personnel are main responsibilities.

Editor
(Refer to General Index of Job Descriptions)

Educator/Administrator *(Food Service)*
Designs and teaches courses tailored to students of food service, such as sanitation, foodservice management and nutrition. Develops curriculum and hires staff. Works with designated budget to purchase equipment and materials needed to operate the school. Seeks support from industry with instruction and funding.

Entertainment Director

Responsible for planning and booking the entertainment for the season. Calls on performers to arrange appearances at individual locations. Confirms booking and develops public relations effort to advertise upcoming events to the public.

Equine Magazine Publisher

Works for publishing house that caters to articles and trade publications pertaining to the equine industry. Publishes stories and articles in a variety of media submitted by both assigned writers and freelancers.

Executive Chef

Coordinates activities of and directs indoctrination and training of chefs, cooks, and other kitchen personnel engaged in preparing and cooking food. Plans menus and utilization of food surpluses and leftovers, taking into account probable number of guests, marketing conditions, population, and purchases or requisitions foodstuffs and kitchen supplies. Reviews menus, analyzes recipes, determines food, labor, and overhead costs, and assigns prices to the menu items. Observes methods of food preparation and cooking, sizes of portions, and garnishing of foods to ensure food is prepared in prescribed manner. Develops exclusive recipes and varied menus.

Executive Housekeeper

Supervises housekeeping staff. May hire and train new employees. Orders supplies, takes inventories and keeps records, prepares budgets, sees to needed repairs, draws up work schedules, inspects rooms. May be in charge of interior decoration.

Exercise Rider

Rides horses to exercise and condition them. Rides racehorse during workout and training races, following specific instructions of training personnel. Informs training personnel of horse's temperament, peculiarities, and physical condition as demonstrated during exercise so that training plans can be modified to prepare horse for racing.

Facilities Designer

Plans and designs utilization of space and facilities for hotels, foodservice operations and other related properties. Draws design layout, showing location of equipment, furniture, work spaces, doorways, electrical outlets, and other related facilities. May review real estate contracts for compliance with regulations and suitability for occupancy. Suggests decor that is both practical and attractive to suit the purpose of the facility as well as maximize client business.

Feed Company Representative

Performs the sales and marketing functions required to secure customer accounts for a feed company. Calls on owners and caretakers of horses to sell feed company's product line. Services the account once it has been established.

Foal Night Watchman

Responsible for supervising the care of young horses up to the age of twelve months throughout the night. Reports any unusual occurrences or reactions that may indicate illness or other potential problem with the young horses. Maintains horses quarters.

Food and Beverage Manager

Responsible for compiling statistics of food and liquor costs, sales, and profits and losses. May also develop the procedures of portion control and item usage. May inventory bars as needed and prepare daily consumption reports that are forwarded to the auditing office. Takes inventory of food stuffs with the chef and works closely with the chef on matters of buying and producing.

Food Director *(Recreation)*

Responsible for all foodservice areas at a particular theme park, amusement park arcade, or other type of recreational facilities. Supervises the procurement and preparation of food and drinks for concession stands, snack bars and dining halls, and rooms. Hires and trains staff. Maintains control on food costs and inventories. Deals directly with suppliers in ordering and paying for all food products. Enforces sanitation policies and health department codes throughout all foodservice facilities.

Food Production Manager

Responsible for all food preparation and supervision of kitchen staff. Workers must possess leadership skills and have knowledge of food preparation techniques, quality, and sanitation standards and cost control methods.

Foodservice Consultant

Advises clients on site selection for foodservice operation, menu design and selection, interior decor, equipment, and overall design and layout of dining facility. Advises owner/operator of expected food and beverage costs, and helps to develop effective pricing strategy for all menu items.

Foodservice Director

Exercises general supervision over all production areas in one or more kitchens. Also responsible for all the service that may be needed on counters and in the dining rooms. Responsible for the buying of food, its storage, its preparation, and the service necessary to handle large groups.

Foodservice Engineer

Analyzes and creates efficient and cost-effective production processes, designs manufacturing equipment or operates a plant's physical systems.

Foodservice Manager

Responsible for the operation's accounts and records; compliance with all laws and regulations, especially those concerning licensing, health and sanitation.

Foodservice Salesperson

Tells customers how a given item performs against the competition, how it will benefit the buyer, and ultimately, how it can increase profits and encourage repeat business. Demonstrates new products, gives customers actual product samplings, advises on menu ideas and serving suggestions and even helps them work out portion costs.

Forester

Manages and develops forest lands and their resources for economic and recreational purposes. Plans and directs projects in forestation and reforestation. Maps forest areas, estimates standing timber and future growth, and manages timber sales. Directs suppression of forest fires and conducts fire prevention programs. Plans campsites and recreation centers. Assists in planning and carrying out projects for control of floods, soil erosion, tree diseases, and insect pests in forests.

Front Desk Supervisor *(Hospitality)*

Directs the front desk operations in the hotel. Oversees those reponsible for guests' reservations, special needs, check in and check out. Reviews status reports on available rooms. Ensures that guests' complaints are handled promptly and properly.

Front Office Manager *(Hospitality)*
(Refer to General Index of Job Descriptions)

Games Manager

Develops promotions and policies pertaining to games available to customers at concession booths in parks, carnivals, stadiums, or similar amusement places. Hires and trains staff.

Garde Manger *(Cold Cook)*

Prepares and works with all cold meat, fish and poultry dishes. Prepares appetizers or hors d'oeuvres such as canapes. Makes all salad dressings and mayonnaise according to recipe. Works with leftover foods to make appetizing dishes. Prepares and serves pate maison. Makes ice and vegetable carvings.

General Manager *(Food Service)*

Acts as overseer to all phases of a particular group, working with the management team to plan future accounts and solve day-to-day problems.

General Manager *(Hospitality)*

Establishes standards for personnel administration and performance, service to patrons, room rates, advertising, publicity, credit, food selection and service, and type of patronage to be solicited. Plans dining-room, bar and banquet operations. Allocates funds, authorizes expenditures, and assists in planning budgets for departments.

Groom

Any person responsible for looking after a horse. Cleans the coat and feet of the horse.

Grounds and Facilities Maintenance–Assistant

Responsible for the upkeep of all park grounds and facilities. Oversees workers tending to the property and ensures that grounds and facilities are kept safe and clean for patrons under the guidelines prescribed by both the city and state.

Group Sales Manager *(Hospitality)*
(Refer to General Index of Job Descriptions)

Guest Services Agent *(Hospitality)*
Works as a liaison between hotel guests and party providing desired services. Informs guests on services available to them in the hotel facility and assists them with making the proper connections. Concerned with any requests the guest may have and with providing answers to questions that concern guests.

Guest Services Agent *(Recreation)*
Ensures that guests or participants in recreational activities are fully informed about the activities available at a recreational facility. Assists guest with getting to and from activities or with determining locations of certain events. Answers all concerns of the guest regarding the rules and regulations and safety procedures for certain activities.

Head Bartender
In charge of the entire bar. Responsible for stocking and dispensing. Responsible for hiring and firing. Must know how to mix all drinks served in the bar. Establishes drink formulas and sets up portion controls concerning each drink. Coordinates inventory, requisitioning and stocking needed items, proper accounting and receipt of proper payment for bar items.

Head Cashier *(Hospitality)*
Oversees the duties of the hotel's cashiers which include receiving guests' payments when checking out of the hotel. Approves the cashing of guests' checks and the processing of certain loans. Responsible for security of the safe deposit box.

Head Waiter/ress
Supervises and coordinates the activities of dining room employees engaged in providing courteous and rapid service to the diners. Greets the guests and escorts them to tables. Schedules dining reservations. Arranges parties for patrons. Adjusts any complaints regarding the food or service. Hires and trains the dining room employees. Notifies the payroll department regarding work schedules and time records. May assist in preparing menus. May plan and execute the details of a banquet.

Home Economics Teacher
Teaches everything from balancing menus to hygiene to food journalism.

Horse Show Manager
Oversees competitions that are held to test or display the qualities and capabilities of horses and their riders.

Hostperson
Supervises and coordinates the activities of the dining room personnel to provide fast and courteous service to the patrons. Schedules dining reservations and arranges parties or special services for the diners. Greets the guests, escorts them to tables, and provides their menus. Adjusts complaints of the patrons.

Hot Walker *(Equine)*
One employed to cool out horses.

Housekeeper

Ensures clean, orderly, attractive rooms in the hotel or related facility. Inventories stock to ensure adequate supplies. Issues supplies and equipment to workers. May record data and prepare reports concerning room occupancy, payroll expenses, and department expenses.

Information Specialist (Hospitality)

Provides specific information on area attractions and services to guests staying at the hotel. May work in conjunction with the Concierge in providing guests with information on restaurants, shopping areas, museums, historical sites, theatre and local entertainment. Is well informed on the history of the area and information available at the area's Chamber of Commerce and Visitor and Convention Bureau.

Inspector/ress

Supervises cleaning staff and inspects hotel guest rooms, corridors and lobbies. Assigns work to cleaning staff and trains personnel in housekeeping duties. Posts room occupancy records. Adjusts guests' complaints regarding housekeeping service or equipment. Writes requisitions for room supplies and furniture, renovation or replacements.

Instructor (Education)

Entry level designation of faculty ranking in a college or university. In a career school, teaches career training subjects in specific trades to students. Organizes programs of practical and technical instruction, involving demonstration of skills required in trade and lectures on theory, practices, methods, processes and terminology. Instructs students in subject areas. Plans and supervises work of students in shop or laboratory. Tests and evaluates achievement of students in technical knowledge and trade skills.

Instructor (Equine)

Instructs equine students in all areas of the field, including the hands-on experience gained through field experiences and working directly with horses. Teaches the business-related course that will enable the equine student to pursue a business career in the industry as well as a career as a practitioner. Keeps students notified of all current policies and regulations pertaining to the industry.

Insurance Broker (Equine)

Sells and processes insurance to horse owners for protection of their investment.

International Account Executive (Hospitality)

Responsible for the development of and service of international client business coming into the hotel. May also be responsible for referring clientele to international properties in other countries. May assist with providing information to client on the foreign country, its currency, passport and customs regulations and overall familiarization with the area.

Jockey

Rides racehorse at racetrack. Confers with the training personnel to plan strategy for race based on ability and peculiarities of own and other horses in the competition. Mounts horse in paddock after weighing-in and rides horse to specified numbered stall of starting gate. Races from starting gate to finish line. Talks to training personnel after race to analyze horse's performance.

Jockey's Agent

Represents the jockey and arranges for the jockey to ride different horses in various shows and races. Convinces owners of the expertise of the jockey and keeps informed about the condition of horses in which the jockey is interested.

Kitchen Manager

Supervises all the production personnel in the kitchen area. Oversees the buying, storing, and preparation of all food. Takes inventory and reorders when necessary. Usually employed in operations where chefs are not employed.

Lab Technician (Equine)

Prepares samples for analysis or examination and performs routine laboratory tests. Gives injections, takes samples of various body fluids or tissues, observes reactions of horses to different tests, makes chemical analyses, and takes physiological recordings. Works under the direction of a veterinarian.

Landscape Architect

Gives professional advice on land-planning problems; selects suitable sites; makes preliminary studies, sketches, models and reports; prepares working drawings, cost estimates, and specifications for the taking of contractors' bids; supervises construction; and approves the quality of materials and work.

Line Cook

Responsible for any duties necessary in order to prepare and produce menu items efficiently. Duties may include cutting and portioning items, cooking items, and serving items.

Maintenance Director (Recreation)

Supervises and coordinates activities of workers engaged in keeping buildings and grounds in clean and orderly condition and in maintaining and repairing utility systems and physical structures of buildings. Compiles report of costs of completed work. May supervise workers engaged in installing, servicing, and repairing mechanical equipment.

Maitre de Hotel

In charge of the dining room in a hotel or restaurant. Supervises a team of captains, waitpersons, and junior waitpersons.

Manager Trainee (Food Service)

Assists with all functions of the area assigned. Learns the overview of the entire operation before specializing. If in a large operation may rotate within one area of the facility such as the production or purchasing area to learn all of its functions if that is the area of specialty. Usually trains by rotating among various stations in the kitchen itself and among related areas such as purchasing, the storeroom, front of the house, etc.

Manager of Public Relations (Recreation)

Plans, directs, and conducts public relations programs designed to create and maintain public awareness of new and existing programs and services.

Manager of Recreation Services

Manages a program or group of programs or a facility or group of facilities providing recreational programs. Hires, supervises and trains staff according to required regulations and standards. Assigns staff to specific programs. Makes program modifications and recommendations and evaluates them periodically with staff and through clientele. Responsible for the recreational facility as well as the staff.

Marketing Manager (Food Service)

Responsible for compiling information on the age, sex and income level of restaurants' potential clientele and their dining habits and preferences. Marketing managers consider customer preferences in order to suggest appropriate sales advertising techniques. This information provides the basis for success/failure projections in certain demographic areas.

Marketing Director (Equine)

Organizes promotions for equine-related products. Identifies customer needs through surveys, interviews and by studying the competition. Recommends new product lines of clothing for riders, food for horses, grooming accessories, etc. based on results of market surveys. Implements advertising and public relations activity for new and existing products.

Marketing and Promotion Manager (Food Service)

Supervises any advertising or sales promotion for the operation. Works with food production staff to create menus and promotions with customer appeal. Often coordinates these activities with an advertising agency.

Menu Planner

Works with the Executive Chef to select all items offered on menus. Must know foodservice costs, preparation techniques and equipment, customer trends and preferences.

Merchandising Supervisor (Food Service)

Plans and carries out promotional programs to increase sales. Works with printers, artists, writers, and other suppliers. Must know employer's foodservice operations thoroughly and be able to apply market research techniques as well as budgeting and planning skills.

Night Auditor (Hospitality)
(Refer to General Index of Job Descriptions)

Nutritionist

Identifies the kinds and amounts of nutrients in food, translates this knowledge for schools and health care menus and restaurants and hotels; develops new foods and ingredients.

Operations Assistant (Recreation)

Responsible for assisting with overseeing the general operation of a recreational facility. Solves problems that arise concerning facilities and grounds. Contacts vendors, contractors, equipment repair technicians as needed. Obtains and renews necessary licenses and permits.

Operations Manager *(Recreation)*
Supervises the entire recreational facility. Makes policy and pricing decisions. Hires and trains staff. Oversees budget and promotional efforts.

Outdoor Recreation Specialist
Conducts recreation activities with groups in outdoor facilities. Organizes, promotes and develops interest in arts and crafts, sports, games, music, dramatics, social recreation and camping.

Owner/Operator *(Food Service)*
Coordinates all employees; may be responsible for buying food and supplies; may help with menu planning; keeps the restaurant within health and sanitation guidelines; oversees payroll function. In small restaurants, may oversee marketing and promotion effort.

Owner/Representative *(Equine)*
Represents the interests of the horse owner in the owner's absence. Notifies the owner of all activities pertaining to the horse and makes decisions about opportunities for the horse's involvement in various activities with or without the owner.

Packaging Specialist
Develops packaging to fit specific products for industry needs.

Pantry Person
Draws from the storeroom all the raw materials needed to prepare all the fruit or vegetable salads, seafood cocktails, canapes, and other cold dishes. Serves these items to waiters and waitresses. May slice and portion cold meats and cheeses. Serves desserts and side dishes such as bread and butter. Makes sandwiches and prepares garnishes for other departments.

Park Manager
Coordinates the activities of park rangers and others engaged in development, protection, and utilization of national, state or regional parks. Prepares estimates of costs to plan, provide, or improve fish and wildlife protection, recreation, and visitor safety.

Park Ranger
Enforces laws, regulations and policies in state or national parks. Provides information pertaining to park use, safety requirements, and points of interest. Directs traffic, investigates accidents, and patrols area to prevent fires, vandalism, and theft. Directs or participates in first aid and rescue activities. May supervise workers engaged in construction and maintenance of park facilities.

Park Superintendent/Supervisor
Coordinates efforts of many parks in the area *(county or state)* to maintain consistency with policies and regulations for a given area. Oversees budgets and promotional programs for the designated area.

Pastry Cook
Prepares desserts, both hot and cold, ices, and cakes for both daily use and for special occasions.

Pastry Chef
Oversees the bread and pastry needs of all kitchens and departments in a large hotel, club, or restaurant. Supervises pastry cooks and bakers. Requires ability to coordinate the activity of others. Supervises the preparation of desserts, pastries, frozen desserts, fondants, fillings and fancy sugar decorations. Creates new recipes and produces delicate items that require mastery of fine techniques.

Personnel Director
Hires, trains, and directs foodservice personnel; draws up working schedules; sets personnel policies, and may administer employee benefit, safety and communications programs. Usually employed in large restaurants, foodservice chains or as a specialist in hotel or institutional foodservice operations.

Prep Cook
Responsible for any duties necessary in order to prepare food items for production.

President *(Education)*
Formulates plans and programs for and directs administration of college or university within the authority delegated by governing boards. Confers with board of control to plan and initiate programs concerning organizational, operational, and academic functions of the campus and oversees their execution. Administers fiscal and physical planning activities, such as development of budget and building expansion programs, and recommends their adoption. Establishes rules, procedures, and standards relating to faculty, staff, financial disbursements and accounting requirements.

Principal *(Education)*
Directs and coordinates educational, administrative, and counseling activities of primary or secondary school. Evaluates educational programs to ensure conformance to state and school board standards. Coordinates educational programs through meetings with staff, review of teaching department's activities, and issuance of directives. Confers with teaching personnel, pupils and parents on matters pertaining to educational and behavioral problems in school. Requisitions and allocates supplies, equipment, and instructional material as needed. Supervises assignment of teachers and pupils to classes.

Product Development Technologist
Technologist working in the foodservice industry conducting experiments to improve flavor, texture, shelf life or other product characteristics; develops new products or packaging materials; compares competitive products; assures that every item meets quality standards, and interprets and solves the problems of the foodservice operator.

Production Manager *(Food Service)*
Takes leadership position in such production operation areas as engineering,

scheduling, purchasing, quality control, inventory control, distribution and human relations.

Professional Rider *(Equine)*

Rider who has been trained to ride horses to be demonstrated in shows or major events. Masters the body movements required to solicit the desired response from the horse to induce a smoothly paced ride with the horse maintaining a sleek and proper staunch.

Professional Waiter/ress

Serves meals to the patrons according to the established rules of etiquette. Presents a menu to the diner, suggesting dinner courses, appropriate wines, and answering questions regarding the food preparation. Writes the order on a check or memorizes it. Relays the order to the kitchen and serves the courses from the kitchen and service bars. Garnishes and decorates the dishes preparatory to serving them. Serves the patrons from a chafing dish at the table, observes the diners to fulfill any additional requests and to perceive when the meal has been completed. Totals the bill and accepts payments. May carve the meats, bone the fish and fowl, and prepare flaming dishes and desserts at the patron's table.

Professor

Conducts college or university courses for undergraduates or graduate students. Teaches one or more subjects within a prescribed curriculum. Prepares and delivers lectures to students. Compiles, administers and grades examinations, or assigns this work to others. Serves on faculty committees as requested.

Promotion Director *(Recreation)*

Seeks out and decides on major promotions that will bring increased business to the recreational facility. Works with advertising agencies and the media to alert clients of the promotion. Responsible for adding to the overall profitability of the operation.

Program Director *(Education)*

Supervises the development of a variety of academic programs or other programs related to an educational institution. Such programs might involve parents, student organizations, industry , or other special interest groups. *(See Program Director)*

Program Specialist *(Recreation)*

Leads and directs one or more specialized recreational programs. May specialize in outdoor recreational programs, programs for the handicapped or for senior citizens or any other area requiring specialized expertise, knowledge or certification. May develop program independently or may follow set guidelines given by the state or city or agency.

Public Relations Manager *(Equine)*

Acts as an agent representing the owner of a horse in the promotion of show or race participation and recognition of accomplishments. May also work for a business in which special programs for the industry are developed such as an organization or association pertaining to the equine field which promotes programs, events, special memberships, etc. Can be involved in public relations efforts pertaining to almost any aspect of the equine business.

Purchasing Agent *(Food Service)*
Purchases foodstuffs, kitchen supplies and equipment. Makes large contracts for several products. Purchases all supplies with the exception of capital goods such as furniture and fixed equipment.

Purchasing Assistant
(See Purchasing Agent)

Purchasing Manager *(Food Service)*
Responsible for the actual purchase of all supplies and equipment, usually coordinated through the Executive Chef or cook. Required to monitor and control costs and to maintain accurate inventories. Supervises purchasing agents responsible for a particular product line.

Quality Assurance Specialist *(Food Service)*
Analyzes ingredients and finished products and checks standards of production, packaging and sanitation. May be assigned to a particular type of product or food item.

Quality Control Manager *(Food Service)*
Travels to various units to inspect those units and make sure they adhere to company and state standards. Usually responsible for more than one operation.

Real Estate Manager *(Food Service)*
Supervises the negotiations for the acquisition and disposition of properties. Supervises staff engaged in preparing lease agreements, recording rental receipts, and performing other activities necessary to efficient management of company properties, or in performing routine research on zoning ordinances and condemnation considerations. Directs appraiser to inspect properties and land under consideration for acquisition and recommends acquisitions, lease, disposition, improvement, or other action consistent with best interests of the company. Negotiates contracts with sellers of land and renters of property.

Regional Vice President *(Food Service)*
Deals with new business development, senior management contact, both internal and external, pricing analysis; proposal development and presentation, and contract negotiations. Works with planning and achieving marketing objectives within the responsible geographic territory.

Research and Development Specialist *(Food Service)*
Conducts research on new product lines and equipment for the foodservice industry. May work with food products in test kitchens or with new equipment in operating foodsevice establishments. Reports findings to manufacturers of food products and equipment and publicizes results in trade publications to inform the industry about the possible alternatives the findings may provide for foodservice professionals.

Resident Manager *(Hospitality)*
Administrator living on the premise to manage the day-to-day operations of the

hotel or other lodging facility.

Restaurant Manager

Responsible for efficiency, quality and courtesy in all phases of a foodservice operation. In large organizations, the manager may direct supervisory personnel at the next lower level. In smaller operations they might supervise kitchen and dining room staffs directly. Knowledge of the responsibilities of all restaurant staff is essential to this position.

Reservationist *(Hospitality)*
(Refer to General Index of Job Descriptions)

Ride Superintendent

Supervises the safety, cleanliness and service of riding devices. Trains and supervises ride operators and ride attendants who direct patrons on and off rides, collect tickets, clean and maintain the riding devices.

Riding Instructor

Teaches riders to adopt the correct posture on the horse to obtain desired movement by the horse. May also train horses to have the controlled, free forward movement, correct bend, and even rhythm required for being ridden.

Road Manager *(Equine)*

Directs and coordinates road travel or horses and riders or jockeys en route to horse shows and other competitions.

Roasting Cook

Responsible for all meat preparation that is made to order. Also responsible for all items that are deep fried, shallow fried, sauteed, or broiled.

Rooms Attendant

Coordinates service for a block of rooms in a hotel. Ensures room service operations are running smoothly. Arranges for any special requests concerning accommodations from guests. Checks the room rack and key rack frequently. Oversees the operation of switchboard and messages going to guests.

Rooms Division Supervisor

Directs all activities involved with the rooms division of the hotel. This includes staffing, housekeeping, occupancy, service and promotion.

Rounds Cook

Replaces every member of the kitchen brigade who may be absent from each station. Must be efficient and versatile in cooking techniques.

Sales Director *(Hospitality)*

Responsible for research and analysis, short-term and long-range planning, determination of marketing strategies and tactics, setting of goals and objectives, budgeting, the booking of individual as well as group business and for the securing of business for the food and beverage department as well as for the rooms division.

Sales Manager *(Education)*
(Refer to General Index of Job Descriptions)

Sales Manager *(Food Service)*

Responsible for the development of and operation of the sales department. Maintains files on past group business. Works with the social director and promotion office on contacts and may do some traveling to other areas to bring new business into the establishment. Also trains and supervises sales representatives and some account executives.

Sales and Marketing Specialist *(Food Service)*

Plans, researches, promotes, and sells products to the foodservice industry.

Sales Representative *(Education)*
(Refer to General Index of Job Descriptions)

Sales Representative *(Hospitality)*

Follows initial lead on a prospective client. Responsible for explaining hotel's services to government, business and social groups to generate interest in the facility as a site for a major function. Sales representative conducts "cold calls" as well as calls to a selected prospect list. The sales representative may pass the interested client on to an account executive, who will actually set up, service and maintain the account.

Sales Trainee *(Hospitality)*

Usually begins with front office experience to learn client relations and total product line offered by the hotel. May go on sales calls with sales representatives or assist an account executive with servicing an account.

Sanitation Supervisor *(Food Service)*

Supervises porters, dishwashers, kitchen persons and pot washers. Ensures that dishes, cooking utensils, equipment and floors are kept clean. Ensures that kitchen always meets health department regulations and standards.

Sauce Cook

Responsible for all preparation of sauces to be used on main items on the menu. In a middle-sized operation, the sauce cook is also the sous chef.

School Director *(Vocational)*

Directs and coordinates schools with vocational training programs. Confers with members of industrial and business community to determine manpower training needs. Reviews and interprets vocational educational codes to ensure that programs conform to policies. Prepares budgets and funding allocation for vocational programs. Reviews and approves new programs. Coordinates on-the-job training programs with employers and evaluates progress of students in conjunction with program contract goals.

Seafood Cook

Prepares all seafood dishes, mousses, souffles, etc. Also prepares the fish for cold display or for hors d'oeuvres and then sends to the garde manger for final decoration.

Secretary *(Equine)*

Works for an association, an organization, an independent owner, a breed farm, a racetrack, or a feed company performing general office work and handling situations and transactions that occur daily requiring in-depth knowledge of the horse industry and business policies and procedures. Assists managers and owners with overall duties pertaining to the operation.

Secretary *(Food Service)*
In large foodservice operations, performs a variety of administrative duties; works with customers on group business and with vendors on orders and supplies. Frees the employer to work on other areas outside the property.

Seminar Facilitator *(Education)*
Prepares and delivers seminars at the request of a business or organization. May instruct, inform, or update the audience on a topic or issue. During the delivery, it is the job of the facilitator to create interaction with the group. Initiates participation with questions or by exercises that exemplify a concept. Measures results of the seminar by follow-up evaluations and studies.

Senior Citizens Program Director
Plans, develops, and implements various programs for senior citizens based on knowledge of an area, the group, and health and safety issues pertaining to the elderly. Involves the group in community activities, trips, or other programs that allow senior citizens to actively participate. May follow prescribed programs arranged by agency. Makes recommendations for new and existing programs.

Soup Cook
Responsible for all soups, both cold and hot, plus garnishes, stocks, etc.

Sous Chef
Principal assistant of the Chef de Cuisine. In a large operation, the sous chef will assist the Chef de Cuisine in general administrative and supervisory duties and will implement every order given. The sous chef must have the same professional background as the chef but not necessarily the same number of years of experience.

Steward/ess *(Food Service)*
Supervises and coordinates activities of the pantry, storeroom and noncooking kitchen workers and purchases or requisitions the foodstuffs, kitchen supplies, and equipment. Inspects the kitchens and storerooms to ensure that the premises and equipment are clean and in order and that sufficient foodstuffs and supplies are on hand to ensure efficient service. Establishes controls to guard against theft and waste.

Storeroom Supervisor *(Food Service)*
Responsible for supervising, receiving, inspecting, counting, and storing of all food and other articles delivered to the storeroom. Responsible for filling out all requisitions and, under the instructions of the house auditor, for keeping a journal in ledger of all goods received and delivered. Names of purveyors, the costs and descriptions of articles, and other required information are recorded. Supervises monthly inventories with the auditor.

Superintendent *(Education)*

Directs and coordinates activities concerned with administration of city, county, or other school system in accordance with the board of education. Formulates plans and policies for educational program and submits them to school board for approval. Administers program for selection of school sites, construction of buildings, and provisions of equipment and supplies. Directs the preparation and presentation of school budgets and determines amount of school bond issues required to finance educational programs. Addresses community and civic groups to enlist their support.

Superintendent of Service *(Hospitality)*

Responsible for overseeing all functions providing guest services in the hotel. This may include the front office and housekeeping as well as foodservice operations. Ensures quality service while keeping informed about any client-centered problems that may affect new or repeat business. Solves problems related to guest services.

Swing Cook
(See Rounds Cook)

Team Leader *(Floor Supervisor)*

Responsible for supervision of a floor in a hotel. Oversees the maintenance and upkeep, the repair and security of all rooms on an assigned floor. Supervises housekeeping staff assigned to that floor and coordinates the group to work efficiently. Submits work reports to Executive Housekeeper if requested.

Teacher *(Secondary School)*

Teaches one or more subjects to students in public or private secondary school. Instructs students in subject matter, utilizing various teaching methods, such as lectures and demonstrations, and uses audiovisual aids and other materials to supplement presentations. Prepares teaching outline, assigns lessons and corrects homework. Administers tests to evaluate students' progress, records results and issues reports. Keeps attendance records. Maintains discipline in the classroom. Participates in faculty and professional meetings, educational conferences, and teacher training workshops. Assists with sponsoring activities or student organizations, and with counseling students.

Therapeutic Recreation Specialist

Professionally trained in the techniques of exercise for persons with chronic injuries, handicaps, or other serious afflictions that require special attention. Usually deals with people whose conditions are alleviated by systematic and properly executed exercise and/or activity. May require special training and licensing.

Thoroughbred Trainer

Trains horses of selective breeding. The thoroughbred horse is predominantly bred for speed or perfect conformation. *(See Trainer-Equine)*

Ticket Agent *(Recreation)*

Dispenses tickets for admittance to amusement parks and related entertainment. Oversees the processing and sales of tickets for special events at recreational facilities. May also purchase entertainment tickets at box-office prices, usually before an attraction opens. Processes tickets for profitable resale and sells tickets to the public in accordance with legal regulations.

Tour and Travel Account Executive

Responsible for the development of and service of group tour business coming into the hotel. Brings travel and tour groups to the hotel. Consults with the tour operators and travel agents and collaborates with the hotel staff to find best strategy for servicing the group.

Trainer *(Equine)*

Trains (race)horses for racing. Studies past performance record, observes horse during workout and utilizes knowledge of training, based on peculiarities of each horse. Conditions horse for competitive racing with exercise and workouts to bring it to top physical condition. Enters horse in training races to familiarize it with starting gate and racing procedures. Clocks horse during workout to determine when it is ready for official race. Instructs jockey on how to handle specific horse during race. Directs workers in exercising, grooming and feeding horse. May train horses as independent operator and advise owners on purchase of horses.

Training Manager *(Education)*
(Refer to General Index of Job Descriptions)

Training Manager *(Food Service)*
(Refer to General Index of Job Descriptions)

Training Specialist *(Education)*
(Refer to General Index of Job Descriptions)

Unit Manager

Representative of a foodservice contractor who is permanently assigned to one particular client installation.

Vegetable Cook

Prepares all garnishes such as potatoes, vegetables, egg dishes, etc.

Vending Manager

Independent business person who places own machines in various installations in a community or facility. Responsible for locating new machine sites, developing good public relations for the firm by handling complaints, maintaining quality control of the product and proper functioning of the machines. Handles cash funds and keeps required records.

Veterinarian Assistant

Assists doctors specializing in the diagnoses and treatment of horses. Coordinates laboratory tests and reports pertaining to the investigation, prevention, and control of horse diseases. Advises on care and breeding of horses. May assist with research and development, consultation, administration, teaching, technical writing, sale or rendering of technical services for commercial firms.

Vice President *(Education)*

In a small institution, oversees the entire operation on a day-to-day basis. In a larger institution, oversees the policy-making and execution of those policies on a regular basis, but depends more on administrative department heads to care for the actual day-to-day operations of the institution. May represent the institution at community or industry events and is actively involved in fund raising.

Vice President of Finance *(Hospitality)*
(Refer to General Index of Job Descriptions)

Vice President of Marketing *(Hospitality)*

In addition to overseeing the sales function, also coordinates the advertising, public relations, publicity, and community relations for the hotel. *(See Vice President of Marketing)*

Vice President of Marketing and Sales *(Recreation)*
(Refer to General Index of Job Descriptions)

Vice President of Marketing and Sales *(Equine)*
(Refer to General Index of Job Descriptions)

Vice President of Operations *(Recreation)*
(Refer to General Index of Job Descriptions)

Vice President of Operations *(Hospitality)*
(Refer to General Index of Job Descriptions)

Wilderness Leader

Directs groups exploring wildlife areas and wilderness trails as to course to follow, safety procedures, and special features of the given area being explored. Leads hike through the trail to view wooded areas characterized by historical or natural landmarks. Informs hikers of significant findings in the area and of the natural wildlife special to that area. Advises hikers on difficulty of the trail ahead of time and assists those having difficulties. Keeps informed about the area through regular contact with preservation society and other local associations whose job it is to explore the area for new findings.

Wine Steward

Administers scheduling of all bar personnel both on regular shifts and for catering work and keeping records of their hours. Responsible for hiring, firing, and training all bar personnel, keeping customer account files, maintaining liquor and wine storage; setting standards and ensuring that they are maintained.

NOTES

NOTES

NOTES

NOTES

NOTES

NOTES

NOTES

NOTES

NOTES

NOTES

NOTES

NOTES